PRAISE FOR
# WHEN WILL THE HEAVEN BEGIN?

"I was captivated by the YouTube video that Ben Breedlove produced just before his return to heaven. And now I have been captivated by his complete story, as shared in *When Will the Heaven Begin?* Reading these pages, you'll discover how one precious young man treated life as a gift from God and thus became a gift from God. Just as his many videos and devotion to family and friends touched many hearts, I pray that this book will, too."

—Don Piper, *New York Times* bestselling author of
*90 Minutes in Heaven*

How Ben Breedlove Changed My Life

I was introduced to Ben Breedlove by my fans on Twitter through a series of retweets of his video links. I was touched by his story in the same way many of you were, but more so because I was mentioned and acknowledged as one of his favorite artists as well as being included in his vision. I didn't know how to consume it. Why me? Out of all the people in the world to look up to, to admire, he chose me. I did not feel worthy and to be honest I still don't. I was having this moment in my life where I didn't feel like anything special, I wasn't happy with myself. Ben's message snapped me out of it. He made me see how truly important I really am as an artist and I needed that at the time. Ever since Ben came into my life I have been on a new journey. He saved me. Not drugs, not liquor, Ben. I think it's safe to say that he single-handedly reignited the spark in me to keep going and to keep creating. I do believe that he was sent here on a mission from God. As human beings we need to know there is a greater power. That there is more than what we can see and there are angels watching over us. It really hurts I never got the pleasure of meeting Ben, but I am truly honored to have connected with him through music and in spirit. I'll create till the day I die in his honor and for all my fans new and old across the world.

We love you, Ben.

Your Big Brother,

—Scott Mescudi (aka Kid Cudi)

*continued . . .*

"Ben Breedlove's story affected me deeply from the moment I first heard it. We are all lucky that Ally Breedlove shared Ben's incredible experiences and discovery with the world in *When Will the Heaven Begin?* Ben's life was filled with struggles that no person or family would ever wish for, but what he ultimately came to realize was that every life, and *everything in your life,* truly matters and has a purpose. His unshakable belief in God and the perfect peace that is waiting for all of us in heaven will provide hope and inspiration to millions."

—Glenn Beck

*"When Will the Heaven Begin?* shares Ben Breedlove's profound message of hope and peace with the world. Ally Breedlove has done a remarkable job in this beautifully simplistic, heartfelt narrative that will endear every reader to Ben, while reminding us to live every day with joy. "

—Elizabeth Bryan, author of *Chicken Soup for the Soul: Count Your Blessings*

"Breedlove pays tribute to her irrepressible, fun-loving younger brother Ben Breedlove . . . [and] wins readers over with the genuine, heartfelt tone. . . . Both heartbreaking and uplifting, the book resonates on basic human and spiritual levels."

—*Kirkus Reviews*

# WHEN WILL THE HEAVEN BEGIN?

## ALLY BREEDLOVE

WITH **KEN ABRAHAM**

 NEW AMERICAN LIBRARY

New American Library
Published by the Penguin Group
Penguin Group (USA) LLC, 375 Hudson Street,
New York, New York 10014

USA | Canada | UK | Ireland | Australia | New Zealand | India | South Africa | China
penguin.com
A Penguin Random House Company

Published by New American Library, a division of Penguin Group (USA) LLC. Published
simultaneously in a New American Library hardcover edition.

First New American Library Trade Paperback Printing, November 2013

All photos are courtesy of the Breedlove family unless stated here: Kirk Miller, page 5 middle; Grant
Hamill, page 6 bottom, page 7 top; Debbie Hamill, page 8 bottom right, page 9 bottom, page 12 top;
Jake H. Breedlove, page 10 top; Jamie Buchsbaum, page 11 bottom; Clay Davis, page 15 bottom.

NEW AMERICAN LIBRARY TRADE PAPERBACK ISBN: 978-0-451-46815-4

THE LIBRARY OF CONGRESS HAS CATALOGED THE HARDCOVER EDITION OF THIS TITLE AS FOLLOWS:
Breedlove, Ally.
When will the heaven begin?: this is Ben Breedlove's story/Ally Breedlove with Ken
Abraham.
    p. cm.
ISBN 978-0-451-23964-8 (hardback)
1. Breedlove, Ben, 1993–2011. 2. Breedlove, Ben, 1993–2011—Philosophy. 3. Heart—
Hypertrophy—Patients—United States—Biography. 4. Near-death experiences. 5. Heaven.
6. Teenage boys—United States—Biography. 7. Celebrities—United States—Biography.
8. YouTube (Firm)—Biography. 9. Austin (Tex.)—Biography. I. Abraham, Ken. II. Title.
RC685.H9B69 2013
616.1'20092—dc23    2013025605
[B]

Printed in the United States of America
10  9  8  7  6  5  4  3  2  1

Set in Granjon
Designed by Sabrina Bowers

*On Christmas Day, December 25, 2011,*
*my brother left his life as a gift to the world.*

*Ben's story is dedicated to you who seek peace.*
—ALLY BREEDLOVE

*Ben's story is also dedicated to the loved ones*
*of the following children, who recently left us:*

Alexander John
Andris Reinis
FEBRUARY 12, 1991–
NOVEMBER 23, 2011

Carson Ross Cummings
JULY 7, 1987–
JANUARY 13, 2012

Jordan Gibbs Nash
JANUARY 15, 1988–
FEBRUARY 5, 2012

Riley Jane Clark
DECEMBER 7, 2001–
MARCH 7, 2012

Eric Michael
Dramberger Jr.
JANUARY 9, 1991–
MARCH 17, 2012

Daniel Gerard Barden
SEPTEMBER 27, 2005–
DECEMBER 14, 2012

Chase Michael Anthony
Kowalski
OCTOBER 31, 2005–
DECEMBER 14, 2012

Grace Audrey
McDonnell
NOVEMBER 4, 2005–
DECEMBER 14, 2012

Josephine Grace Gay
DECEMBER 11, 2005–
DECEMBER 14, 2012

Charlotte Helen Bacon
FEBRUARY 22, 2006–
DECEMBER 14, 2012

Dylan Christopher
Jack Hockley
MARCH 8, 2006–
DECEMBER 14, 2012

James Radley Mattioli
MARCH 22, 2006–
DECEMBER 14, 2012

Ana Grace
Marquez-Greene
APRIL 4, 2006–
DECEMBER 14, 2012

Jack Armistead Pinto
MAY 6, 2006–
DECEMBER 14, 2012

Jessica Adrienne Rekos
MAY 10, 2006–
DECEMBER 14, 2012

Emilie Alice Parker
MAY 12, 2006–
DECEMBER 14, 2012

Catherine Violet
Hubbard
JUNE 8, 2006–
DECEMBER 14, 2012

Jesse McCord Lewis
JUNE 30, 2006–
DECEMBER 14, 2012

Allison Noelle Wyatt
JULY 3, 2006–
DECEMBER 14, 2012

Madeleine F. Hsu
JULY 10, 2006–
DECEMBER 14, 2012

Olivia Rose Engel
JULY 18, 2006–
DECEMBER 14, 2012

Caroline Phoebe Previdi
SEPTEMBER 9, 2006–
DECEMBER 14, 2012

Benjamin Andrew
Wheeler
SEPTEMBER 12, 2006–
DECEMBER 14, 2012

Avielle Rose Richman
OCTOBER 17, 2006–
DECEMBER 14, 2012

Noah Samuel Pozner
NOVEMBER 20, 2006–
DECEMBER 14, 2012

Thomas "Ty"
Boone Pickens IV
SEPTEMBER 13, 1991–
JANUARY 29, 2013

Ann Elise McGuffey
JUNE 1, 1994–
FEBRUARY 8, 2013

# CONTENTS

## PART 2
# THE PASSION

## PART 3
# THE PURPOSE

# PREFACE

White. Pure white. Ben could see no walls, but only white, a brighter white than he could ever describe that seemed to engulf his surroundings in every direction. In the whiteness, Ben listened to the most quiet he had ever heard in his life.

Wait.

He suddenly realized the space was not completely empty. A full-length mirror stood before him. Ben stared into it intently. He was looking not only at his reflection, but his entire life. In that moment, viewing his image perfected in the mirror, Ben felt proud of himself, of his entire life, of everything he had done. It was the *best* feeling. Ben couldn't stop smiling. He knew he was ready for something more important.

# WHEN
# WILL THE
# HEAVEN
# BEGIN?

## PART 1

# THE GIFT

## CHAPTER 1

# YOUNG FOREVER

Forever young,
I wanna be forever young

—"YOUNG FOREVER" (JAY-Z AND MR. HUDSON)

The doctor returned to the examination room with a broad smile. "What would you say if I told you that you are three months pregnant?"

Deanne Breedlove was elated! *I can't believe we are going to have another baby!* she thought to herself. She knew *exactly* how to tell her husband, Shawn. Despite her own baby joy, she knew that her left-brained, real estate–developing husband had probably already calculated the best time to have another child—and it was not now. Nevertheless, Deanne devised a plan to surprise Shawn in such a way that he would have no option but to respond positively.

The news had arrived with perfect timing, two days before Valentine's Day. On the way home from her appointment, Deanne stopped to purchase a Valentine's Day card to present the big message to Shawn. At home, Deanne was rummaging through her kitchen junk drawer for a pen when she found her old abandoned journal, open to her last entry. Awed to read her own forgotten words, she leafed through the pages.

Deanne had treasured her first year with their daughter, Ally, so much she decided she was ready to have another baby. She had not failed to remember Shawn's response to the news of her first pregnancy. With blanched face and a voice trembling with nerves, he'd said, "Well, we will sell the house, or whatever we have to do."

So when Deanne contemplated having another baby, rather than worrying Shawn with the financial burden of a second child within a couple of years, she opted to talk to God about her request. Making careful note to mark the date, November 10, 1992, she had written in her journal, "I would love to have a second baby!"

Deanne had totally forgotten about the journal she had neglected in her kitchen junk drawer; but now, as she read those words after returning home from her doctor's appointment, she remembered with absolute clarity the prayer she had written exactly three months earlier. Placing her hands on her belly and looking up toward the ceiling, Deanne exclaimed, "Thank you, God!"

As she sat at the coffee table in the living room of their condo, writing her Valentine to Shawn, Deanne reminisced about how they had fallen in love.

A little more than ten years earlier, Deanne had attended the University of Texas as a freshman in 1980. Shawn, who was a junior at the time, had somehow convinced the all-girls Scottish Rite Dormitory—the same dorm where Deanne lived—to hire him as the lone male lifeguard. The only other males allowed be-yond the main lobby were the dining waitstaff, which Shawn had also joined, eventually becoming headwaiter. Deanne and her friends often joked that waiters applied for jobs there only to find their future wives. One night at dinner, Deanne eyed Shawn for the first time, and, giggling, said to her friends, "I'll take *him*!"

They kept in contact following graduation and, seven years later, they had fallen in love. Around Christmastime, after dating for six months, Shawn asked Deanne to an intimate dinner at the historic Adolphus Hotel in Dallas. Elegant harp music drifted through the room as restaurant patrons received their dessert plates, with the word *Noël* beautifully handwritten in chocolate sauce. When Deanne received her plate, however, she was pre-sented with the word *Congratulations!*

Assuming their French-speaking waiter had mistranslated her holiday word, she took her first bite of dessert without ques-tion. Inside her delicious pastry, tucked in among the raspberries, sparkled a beautiful diamond ring!

"Oh, Shawn!" Deanne said, beaming. Even though Shawn didn't officially pop the question, they both understood that the answer was, "Yes!"

Averse to long engagements, Shawn gave Deanne a three-month expiration on the proposal, and they were married the fol-lowing spring. The couple set up housekeeping in Austin, where Shawn pursued a career in corporate real estate, and Deanne began writing a column for a local newspaper until she could ful-fill her dream of becoming a mom. Baby Ally was born four years later, on January 16, 1992, and on August 8, 1993, Benjamin Dan-iel Breedlove became the newest addition to their family.

Already considerate, Ben didn't keep the family waiting long, demanding only four hours of labor before making his debut at four o'clock in the afternoon, weighing in at a whopping eight pounds, nine ounces. But he didn't throw his weight around. Ben was a wonderfully contented baby, seemingly healthy and happy, and he seldom fussed. He opted to smile or gaze into everyone's eyes instead.

"You can touch him," Deanne told Ally in a tender, loving voice. Seventeen-month-old Ally crawled closer on the hospital bed, reluctantly extending her index finger. Staring at newborn Ben with wide-eyed wonder, she quickly touched the tip of his nose, then immediately recoiled in tears. Never having encountered a real, live baby before, she was afraid that Ben would bite her. The excitement of his arrival must have been overwhelming, because she promptly left the room and threw up in the hallway. Despite their dramatic introduction, Ben and Ally soon became steadfast friends.

As Deanne held Ben in her arms his first night in the hospital, he maintained eye contact *forever*! Throughout the night, his gaze never left hers. Ben bonded with Deanne instantly and deeply, as he would with many other people during his life. Gently kissing him on the forehead, Deanne told Ben, "You are an important and permanent part of this family. Nothing will *ever* tear us apart."

# CHAPTER 2

# WASHED BY THE WATER

Even when the storm comes
I am washed by the water

—"WASHED BY THE WATER" (NEEDTOBREATHE)

That *smile*! People's hearts melted from the moment that big, toothless grin stretched across Ben's face. Smiles and laughter followed the little entertainer everywhere he went. Whenever he and Deanne went on an outing, women gushed over his irresistible smile. He would laugh and "talk" all day long, oftentimes even "dancing," by kicking his legs to keep his company occupied. Ben was a constant source of joy. Not everything, however, was perfect.

During Ben's routine three-month-old checkup, his pediatrician, Dr. Ellis Gill, remained uncharacteristically stoic as he moved the stethoscope across Ben's chest.

"Hmm . . ." Dr. Gill said as he positioned the stethoscope back around his neck.

"What is it?" Deanne inquired apprehensively.

"Oh, I don't think it's anything to worry about," Dr. Gill assured her, "but Ben has a slight heart murmur. We'll just keep an eye on it."

By the time Ben was twelve months old, the heart murmur had not gone away. Dr. Gill was concerned, and urged Deanne to schedule an appointment with a cardiologist. The murmur could mean nothing at all, but Dr. Gill recommended Dr. Robert Castle, just to be safe.

The following month, Ben underwent an examination with Dr. Castle, and was scheduled for an ultrasound echocardiogram to see whether he had an atrial septal defect, meaning a hole in the heart.

"Hmm . . ." The medical technician grimaced, as she stared at the echocardiogram screen.

"What is it?" Deanne asked. "What do you see?"

"Umm, I'm sorry," the technician replied, still staring at the screen. "I'm not permitted to tell you anything. The doctor will give you a call as soon as we have the results."

For the remainder of the day, Deanne's stomach was in knots. With rudimentary knowledge of heart complications, she was overwhelmed by thoughts of serious imminent surgeries and hospitalizations. She recalled how close friends had recently gone through a similar situation. Their son, who had been born with a series of health issues, also had a heart condition diagnosed by Dr. Castle. Immediate surgery was necessary, but tragically their precious child lived only a few more months.

Deanne's mind would not rest until she knew the truth about Ben. Late the next morning, the phone rang. Deanne answered the call, and was greeted by Dr. Castle. "We have the results of the echocardiogram," he told her. "Ben has a condition known as hypertrophic cardiomyopathy, making it difficult for his heart to pump blood throughout his body. There is no cure. He will have this disease for the rest of his life. HCM, for short, is a condition that sometimes causes sudden death. You may have heard about athletes dying as a result of it, such as a basketball player who has had no previous health issues, but who suddenly collapses. A lot of times, people don't know they have the condition, so it is good that we found out that Ben has it. When he gets older, we don't want him to play competitive sports. When you come into the office next week, we'll talk more about it."

Deanne remained silent for a moment, stunned. As a tear trickled down her cheek, she whispered into the phone, "I'm so thankful Ben doesn't have to go into surgery right now." Rather than being overcome with the fear and anxiety that had riddled her mind the day before, Deanne was relieved to know that Ben did not have to rush into surgery, to know that he did not have to suffer right then. Today, Ben was okay.

"So this is just something we'll live with?" Deanne confirmed. "We don't have to fix it right now?"

"You can't fix it," Dr. Castle replied.

• • •

"Um, excuse me; where are the card catalogs?"

Deanne had just walked into the public library, carrying little Ben on her hip. The librarian, a young man in his twenties, stared back at her blankly.

"Well, ma'am," he said, a bit condescendingly, "the *computers* are over there." He pointed to the back wall.

"Oh . . ." Deanne replied, feeling embarrassed and somewhat confused. "Thanks." Deanne had not visited the public library since the prehistoric days of the card catalog, but she had some research to do. After searching *hypertrophic cardiomyopathy* at one of the computers, Deanne made her way up to the third floor, where she pulled a giant medical journal off a shelf. Taking a seat at a library table with Ben nestled in her lap, Deanne leafed through the enormous book, eventually discovering the two pages dedicated to HCM.

Deanne was overwhelmed. Desperately, she searched the pages for any layman's terms or phrasing that she might understand, but obviously this journal had been written by doctors, for doctors. She perused vocabulary including *ejection fractions, ventricular outflow tract gradient, systolic anterior motion, diastolic dysfunction, syncope, dyspnea, outflow obstruction, myocardial disarray*, and one phrase she understood all too well—*proclivity to sudden death*. Sifting through this medical jargon, Deanne gleaned nothing but exasperation. Despite the thorough explanations Dr. Castle had given her when she met with him, and the journal in front of her, she could not seem to find any information that told her what would happen to *her* child as a result of HCM.

Finally, Deanne had read enough. She shut the cumbersome book and dragged it back over to its place on the shelf. After a few hours of research, she had gathered, basically, that Ben's heart wasn't pumping blood properly. The symptoms ranged anywhere from light-headedness to sudden death.

As she walked away, the bookshelves towering over her, Deanne looked down at Ben on her hip. He smiled sweetly up at her with contentment in his big brown eyes. Deanne smiled back.

Although leaving without the information she had hoped to find, she exited through the library doors still holding her sweet, precious baby tightly in her arms. She wasn't going to let the medical books steal their joy.

• • •

What proved even more difficult for Deanne than researching and understanding HCM was helping Ben through the condition's daily challenges. The doctor prescribed the drug Atenolol, with strict instructions that Ben should never skip a dose. Every morning and evening, Deanne cut a tiny white pill in half, then schemed ways to trick little Ben into eating the medicine.

"*Benjamin* . . ." Deanne smiled at Ben with a knowing, motherly expression in her eyes. "Did you take your medicine?" She had noticed the missing chunk in his breakfast waffle where she had hidden the Atenolol, and instinctively knew that if Ben had found it, he probably had not eaten it. More likely, Ben had detected the hard, bitter pill in his food, and had spit it out.

Ben looked up at Deanne with big, guilty eyes, twisting his mouth and trying not to smile. "No, Mama," he replied. "I didn't."

"Okay, Ben, then where *is* the medicine?" Deanne asked him.

Now smiling, Ben shamelessly piped up, "I spit it out!"

"Oh, Ben!"

Deanne sighed as she got down on her hands and knees to look under the kitchen table. She spotted the tiny pill, dusted it off, hid it in another piece of waffle, and handed it to Ben. "Here, Ben! Here's another yummy bit of waffle!"

No matter how well Deanne hid the Atenolol, or how many

gumballs she bribed him with, Ben resisted swallowing. By now, he was well aware that he had a heart condition. But Ben wasn't able to grasp how vital it was for him to take his medication. To Ben, every day was just a normal, happy day.

Eventually, Deanne found a trick that worked. She hid the pill in a spoonful of grape jelly with rainbow sprinkles on top. Ben crunched the tiny pill without detecting it among the sprinkles, and then swallowed the sweet spoonful with a smile. The sugary disguise eventually became one of Ben's favorite childhood treats.

Unfortunately, he was not permitted to consume *anything* containing caffeine, so his sweet options were limited. He was not allowed to eat chocolate cake at birthday parties, or to drink a soda with a kid's meal, or to have even a small handful of M&M's. This rule, however, was one of the first that brought out Ben's mischievous side.

During the summer of 1998, the Breedloves took a camping trip to the mountains in Colorado with Aunt Kim, Uncle Dave, and cousins Amber and Zach. When the adults decided to go mountain biking one evening, they left Amber, a teenager, in charge of the younger children while the adults were gone. Not long after the parents had departed, the cousins were snuggled under blankets in the tent, taking turns telling scary stories, when they realized that five-year-old Ben was missing.

They all emerged from the tent, prepared to search for Ben. They didn't have to look far, as they immediately spotted his mischievous smile beaming from the front seat of Uncle Dave's Jeep. As Amber approached the driver's-side door, Ben slowly, deliberately raised Uncle Dave's keys in his little fist, waved them tauntingly at Amber through the window, and then, *click*. The Jeep was locked. As Amber, Zach, and Ally peered through the window, they beheld Ben holding the giant family coffee can full of trail mix, picking out all of the M&M's and eating them one by one!

Ben compensated for the sweets he missed out on by developing a love of all things salty. Oftentimes, after dinner, he enjoyed chips and salsa as his favorite "dessert."

Once, as a toddler, he asked whether he could have some "shot." Deanne was confused. "Ben, what is shot?" she asked. Ben tried to explain it to her, but Deanne still did not understand. She asked for hints. "Where did you see it? What color is it? Do we have it in the house?" After some guesswork, she finally realized that Ben was asking for permission to eat a handful of salt!

• • •

Throughout Ben's childhood, even on his best days, the arrhythmia—the irregular heartbeat—occasionally flared. At first, Ben didn't know how to express what was happening, but Shawn and Deanne could tell that his heart was doing something odd, because Ben became tired, listless, and weak, and his breathing pattern changed.

Since no cure existed for HCM, Ben would often have to perform seemingly ridiculous exercises to alleviate his symptoms. The doctor prescribed the Valsalva maneuver, in which Ben covered his mouth and nose, and then blew out of his nose as forcefully as he could, hopefully causing the arrhythmia to cease by changing the pressure in his heart. Another technique the doctor suggested was for Shawn or Deanne to hold Ben upside down and press ice against his cheeks to stop the irregular heartbeat. Shawn and Deanne soon realized these exercises proved more entertaining for Ben than effective for his heart.

• • •

"Mama, my heart is bumping!" little Ben called out from the backseat. Deanne pulled over to the side of the road, ran around to the backseat, and pressed her ear to Ben's chest. His heart was beating erratically. Looking up, Deanne recognized that they were parked only a block away from Ben's cardiologist's office, and decided to drive straight there. Ben had never mentioned his "heart bumping" before, but Deanne understood that it was his way of explaining that his heart was beating irregularly, and he could feel it.

"You really should have gone to the emergency room, Deanne," the receptionist told her once they arrived. "Our office isn't set up to receive patients without an appointment."

But because Ben had been able to express that his heart was in arrhythmia, and because they were so close to the doctor's office, Ben's cardiologist was able to capture an electrocardiogram (EKG) reading of the irregular heartbeat for the first time. The reading served as an immensely vital supplement to Ben's diagnosis, since people suffer from so many different types of arrhythmias. After the incident, Ben continued to use the phrase, "My heart is bumping," to express that he was experiencing an abnormal rhythm.

Ben's cardiologist later suggested that he be fitted with a Holter monitor to wear at home, which would emulate the EKG conducted in the office. The portable, battery-operated device continuously monitors activity in the heart for an extended period of time, typically twenty-four to forty-eight hours, recording electrical signals from the heart, which are later analyzed by a cardiologist. Ben's first Holter monitor was contained in a black box about eight inches long, six inches wide, and two inches thick. Ben carried it around in a small black pouch attached to his waist, from which wire EKG leads attached to his chest.

Ben was thrilled the first time he was fitted with his "police box," as he called the monitor. He rode his bike around the driveway, speaking into the monitor and pretending to arrest runaway criminals. He soon grew averse to the box, however, when he realized how cumbersome it proved to be. It would twist around his waist, become tangled in his clothing, and prevent him from participating in ordinary, fun activities such as swimming.

The worst part of wearing the Holter monitor proved to be detaching the sticky leads once the recording was complete, since the electrodes were designed *not* to easily fall off an active little boy. Removing the adhesives was a major undertaking, sometimes taking hours to get all the sticky stuff off him. It hurt Ben to have each electrode lead pulled off his skin, and he sometimes had as many as ten of them at a time attached to his little body, each one with adhesive stronger than the toughest Band-Aid. Getting those things off was *not* fun. Deanne tried everything to make removal easier, using baby oil, adhesive remover, even Goo Gone, but nothing worked well. Over the years, with improvements in technology, the Holter boxes became smaller and the adhesive would become less irritating, but they were still a painful inconvenience Ben was forced to endure.

• • •

*Clang!* An enormous, decorative glass platter crashed to the kitchen floor. Deanne was startled by the noise when the kids accidentally knocked the platter off the counter, but Ben seemed more troubled by the sound. His face turned white, his lips blue. Deanne immediately knelt down beside Ben and pressed her ear to his chest. His heart was bumping. Slowly, the rhythm returned to normal as Ben sat still for a while. This event was an early indicator that even common situations could trigger the arrhythmia.

When Ben turned four years old, his new cardiologist, Dr. Stuart Rowe, had given him an additional diagnosis of Long QT syndrome. Like HCM, this condition consisted of a type of heartbeat that could lead to fainting, seizures, and sudden death. With Long QT syndrome, however, patients could just as easily experience sudden death during sleep, when being startled by a loud noise, or when physically exerting themselves.

Deanne and Shawn had plenty of reasons to worry about their son's well-being, now even when he was sleeping. Dejected, they were left at a loss as to how to protect him and keep him safe, as they longed to do.

• • •

A few months later, Ben's heart was bumping again, so the doctor admitted him to the hospital, where they could administer various medicines for several days to see whether the medication alone would control his arrhythmia. For more than forty-eight hours, the doctors could not get Ben's heart to regulate. They gave him higher dosages of medication, causing him to be zonked out most of the time. But when Ben was awake, he was constantly smiling at the nurses and playing tricks on them.

As much as Ben loved to pull pranks, he also loved to give.

Akin to the joy of entertaining others, the joy of giving always delighted him.

• • •

Ben loved to give from his heart. A few examples drawn from Ben's early childhood became part of the Breedlove family lore.

When Ben was about three years old, he developed a penchant for pecans. Ben must have noticed all the squirrels scurrying about, gathering up the pecans that had fallen to the ground, because one day, he marched outside to the driveway in his red cowboy boots and diaper, clutching a hammer in his tight little fist. Like the squirrels, he began cracking pecans into halves and eating them. Once in a while, when Ben missed a pecan with his hammer, he'd exclaim, "D*mn it!"

Although profanity was discouraged in the Breedlove home, Shawn and Deanne couldn't help but stifle a laugh every time they heard this earnest expression. At the end of a long morning at the hammer, Ben's favorite part of the endeavor was getting to share all of his pecan halves with the squirrels.

• • •

"Come on, Ben! We're going to be late!" Deanne grabbed her purse and knocked on Ben's bedroom door. She peeked her head inside to see little Ben holding a football, packaging it in some wrapping paper he had found, using tape—lots of tape. Ben had actually applied more Scotch tape to the present than wrapping paper, and he remained intently focused on his work.

"What are you doing, honey?" Deanne wondered.

Ben looked up at her, beaming. "I can't go on a playdate without bringing a gift for my friends!" he told her.

When Ben arrived at Austin's Zilker Park, he ran up to his friends, twins Benjamin and Brendon, and thrust the gift into one of their hands. He then stepped back, folded his arms behind his back, and relished the sight of his friends' eyes lighting up with surprise. Ben repeated this ceremony with other friends on playdates, with some of the gifts including a baby turtle he had found, a huge, heavy orange toy tractor, and a five-dollar bill.

• • •

Ben not only enjoyed giving tangible gifts, but he also found opportunities to share his compassion. When Deanne's mom, known as "Gee Gee" to her grandchildren, was hospitalized in St. David's physical rehabilitation center, Deanne and the kids visited her as often as possible.

One day, as Deanne and Ally talked with Deanne's mom in the large visiting room, which also served as the cafeteria for the patients, Ben noticed someone else who might appreciate some company. Before long, he meandered to the other side of the room and began conversing with an elderly man, engaging in a long, animated discussion about things only they were privy to. As Deanne and Gee Gee watched, they saw Ben smiling big as ever, and obviously enjoying talking with and relating to this man. The other man was smiling in his own way, though his smile didn't come easily. He was a paraplegic in a wheelchair and was unable to speak. He moved his wheelchair only by manipulating a knob with his mouth. Nevertheless, his eyes revealed that he was thoroughly enjoying their conversation. Ben was a little boy at the time, but his empathy proved to be that of a more mature person who understood adversity on a much deeper level. This compassion for people continued to manifest itself throughout Ben's life.

• • •

"Mama, how do we know if we get to go to heaven?"

Deanne was driving when the question came out of the blue from four-year-old Ben, sitting in the passenger seat. Deanne smiled; she loved getting to answer these questions from her children.

"Well, you just invite Jesus to come into your life," she said with a smile. "Then you will live forever with him in heaven."

"How do I *invite* him?" Ben wanted to know.

"You pray," Deanne replied.

"Well, how do I pray?" Ben wondered.

"Well, Ben," Deanne told him, "this is what I prayed: 'God, if you're real, then come into my life.' Praying is just talking to God and letting him know what's in your heart."

"Will you ask him for me?" Ben asked.

"When you're ready, I'm sure that God would really enjoy hearing directly from you!" Deanne encouraged.

Ben decided he would talk to God right there in the car. With some trepidation, he tipped his head forward, cast a last glance sideways at his mom, and began speaking quietly, but aloud. He spoke in a normal tone of voice, honestly and naturally talking to God about how he wanted to get to live in heaven someday. He asked

God whether he would be his friend for the rest of his life. Satisfied with his conversation, he looked up with tears in his big brown eyes. He let out a sigh of relief and seemed content and happy.

It was a simple transaction, really, devoid of religion and formality, but it was a genuine and important moment in Ben's life, one on which he depended forever.

# CHAPTER 3

# EVERY FEAR HAS NO PLACE

Every fear has no place at the sound of your great name

—"YOUR GREAT NAME" (JIMMY MCNEAL)

T he first time Ben cheated death, he was four years old.

Ally uncurled her body from beneath the down comforter and stretched her arms above her head. From her open doorway, she could see into her parents' bedroom across the hall. Atop the king-size bed, Deanne and little Ben were nestled under the covers. Shawn had just left for work, and Ally wondered why Ben was awake so early. Curious, Ally took sleepy steps into her parents' bedroom. "Mama, why is Ben up already?" she asked.

"He doesn't feel good, sweetie," Deanne replied in a tender, hushed voice. She leaned over her sick little boy, stroking his forehead. With a running head start, Ally hopped onto the bed and crawled up between them.

Ben didn't look himself; his lips were paling and his skin was clammy. The most telltale symptom of his illness, however, was his exceptional lack of animation. Ben lay motionless on the bed, eyes closed and palms up, subconsciously absorbing the conversation between his mom and his sister. He expended what little energy he had on breathing. He didn't want to move or speak, but only to lie there and wait for sleep to take him.

Deanne hoped he wasn't coming down with a virus, which could cause complications with his heart. She pressed her ear to Ben's chest and listened to his heart, a habit she had developed during the past few years, always checking to make sure Ben's heart was beating "normally." His heart's behavior was far from normal this morning.

Deanne listened again, this time carefully counting the heartbeats. She reached over to pick up the phone from her nightstand and dialed the number for Dr. Rowe, Ben's cardiologist. "Hi, I need to speak to Dr. Rowe's nurse immediately," Deanne said kindly but firmly to the receptionist. A moment later, the nurse came on the line, and Deanne gave her a rapid-fire report. "Hello, this is Deanne Breedlove. My son, Ben, is a patient of Dr. Rowe's and he doesn't look right. His skin is clammy; he's sweaty, pale, and very tired-looking. I think I need to take him to the emergency room, but what can I do to help him right now?"

After quizzing Deanne with a series of routine questions, the nurse calmly informed her that Ben was not experiencing an emergency, but he might be coming down with a virus. The nurse knew that Ben's medications caused his heart rate to slow, and as long as it was beating regularly, he was safe. Deanne clicked the phone back onto its cradle, and checked on Ben again. Although his eyes were closed and his body seemed at rest, Deanne couldn't help but doubt the nurse's assessment. *Should I go on to the ER, which is what I think I should do, or would that be overreacting?*

"Ally, could you keep an eye on Ben for me?" Deanne asked, after making a decision to take him to the pediatrician. "I'm going to hop in the shower for a minute, and then we'll take Ben to the doctor."

"Okay, Mama." Ally complied.

Ally peered over a lump of covers at her brother. She could feel him shivering beneath the sheet. "Ben, why are you shivering? It's not even cold." There was no reply. What seemed like a slight shiver began to intensify into a violent tremor throughout Ben's body. In a panicked frenzy, Ally hopped off the bed and flung open the bathroom door, shrieking to Deanne in the shower, "Mom! Ben's not answering me, and he won't stop shaking!"

Deanne bounded out of the shower, threw on a towel, and ran to Ben. She saw that he was now perspiring heavily, his pupils were dilated, and his eyes were staring straight ahead instead of merely looking sleepy. "Ben. Ben!" She shook him gently but he did not respond. After dressing in a matter of seconds, Deanne scooped up her little boy, hollered to Ally to follow her, then sprinted barefoot out the back door to the driveway.

Grabbing a pair of tennis shoes for her mom, Ally scurried behind. Deanne knew that ambulances often had difficulty finding their neighborhood on the outskirts of the city limits, and refused to risk the wait. Ben would have to be driven to help.

Winding down the road with hazard blinkers on, Deanne tested the speed limit as much as she dared with her two passengers. Ben's rigid body reclined in the passenger seat, his pale complexion now tinged with blue. Beneath the strap of the seat belt,

Ben's chest heaved with short, belabored breaths. His eyes were open wide, yet remained fixed in an unresponsive gaze. For a moment, Deanne feared she had made a terrible mistake by driving to the hospital herself. She silently responded to her own second-guessing: *The ambulance would not have even been close to our neighborhood yet, but at least we are nearing help.* Deanne pressed down harder on the gas pedal.

After driving ten gut-wrenching minutes toward the main road, Deanne refused to wager another half hour to the hospital. Clutching the steering wheel tightly, her eyes darting between Ben and the winding road in front of her, she recalled the actions of her neighbor Sheri Miller in a similar emergency. Sheri had taken her son, Justin, to the fire station about ten minutes away from their neighborhood when he was having trouble breathing because of croup late one night. The firemen had been able to give Justin oxygen and help him until it was safe for them to continue on to the hospital. Deanne passed that same fire station every day while running errands. She knew exactly where it was located. She decided she would stop and seek help instead of driving to the hospital.

A minute later, she was pulling into the familiar fire station. Still unbuckling her seat belt, Ally watched her mom scramble around to the passenger seat to get Ben out. Deanne failed to noticed that his foot had gotten stuck in the seat belt, so at first she could not lift Ben out of the car.

Deanne yelled out for help, and several firemen ran outside to assist her. They freed Ben from the seat belt and carried him inside the firehouse, where they laid him on a mat on the concrete floor and began taking his vital signs while asking Deanne questions about Ben's health.

Ally's view of Ben on the concrete floor was obscured by a wall of crouching firefighters. Everything seemed to happen in a matter of seconds. Firefighters were replaced by paramedics as Ally blended into the background, observing the scene unfolding before her eyes.

Swiftly, the paramedics hooked up wires to beeping monitors and administered oxygen. With a stethoscope pressed to Ben's chest, one paramedic determined that his heart was beating slowly, but regularly. The oximeter clamped onto Ben's finger detected his oxygen levels at an adequate ninety-eight percent. Perplexed by their findings, the team continued to check Ben's vitals, searching for the culprit causing his condition. Finally, a reading of Ben's blood detected that his blood sugar had plummeted to fourteen. Immediately, a paramedic attempted to inject a dose of glucose into the crook of Ben's arm, only to find that his veins had collapsed. As the paramedics continued to work on Ben, Deanne held on to Ben's foot, the only part of him she could reach.

Ally still stood in the background. She was too young and naive to understand the severity of the situation. She knew only her own fear, a fear of *what*, she did not know. If Ben could only get to the hospital, Ally thought, he would be fine.

Ally watched one of the paramedics attempt to insert a needle into Ben's thin arm, to no avail, and then one last horrific needle into Ben's ankle. As Ally began to swoon from the sight, a firefighter approached her and placed something soft and fuzzy into her arms. Ally dropped her gaze to see her arms wrapped around a miniature stuffed Dalmatian. She lifted her eyes to the firefighter with a faint smile. He smiled sympathetically back at her. Before she could formulate the words to thank him, she felt a firm hand grasp her arm, spinning her around to face one of the paramedics.

"Do you want to ride up front with me?" a woman asked with a smile.

At once, Ally was led out to the parking lot and hoisted up onto the passenger seat of a gigantic ambulance. The woman ran around the back of the vehicle and climbed up into the driver's seat. She shoved an oversize pair of headphones over Ally's ears, flipped on the radio, and switched on the sirens. Ally heard the ambulance back doors slam shut, and assumed that her mom was riding in the back with Ben. Eased by the cheerful reassurance of the paramedic, Ally clicked on her seat belt and zoned out to the music of a Mexican mariachi band playing through her headphones.

• • •

Sitting on the side bench in the back corner of the ambulance, watching intently as the paramedics continued to work on her son, Deanne was not sure that he would make it. She momentarily closed her eyes and prayed a desperate, aching plea for Ben's life to be saved. Then, just as fervently, she asked that if Ben was being taken home to heaven, God would prepare his heart and protect him from pain and fear. In that intimate moment, known only to Deanne and the one to whom she prayed, something changed. She was forced to let Ben go. As his mother, she had brought Ben into the world and devoted her life to caring for him and his sister. But Ben needed more than his mother. He needed someone who could save him.

Although to some people, this transformation might seem insignificant, it was a pivotal moment for Deanne. This was the first of her many prayers in which she would pray initially for Ben's spiritual heart, even before asking God to protect his physical heart. Then and there, Deanne decided that she would savor every minute of Ben's life. Nevertheless, nothing within her wanted him to be taken to heaven yet, and her new commitment didn't keep Deanne from fervently asking God to comfort and heal Ben, and to bring him back to consciousness.

Lost in her prayers, Deanne was suddenly jolted out of her reverie by the two EMS paramedics in the back of the ambulance, both of whom were perspiring profusely in their efforts to save Ben's life. Trying to get glucose into his bloodstream, they were about to put an IV in his shin. For this sort of procedure, the needle is injected all the way to the bone, through the bone's hard cortex, and into the soft marrow interior. Just before they were to administer the shot, however, the attendant closest to Ben's head shouted, "Yes! I have a response!"

Apparently, he had rubbed some glucose gel directly onto Ben's gums, and it was enough to evoke a small response, which the attendant said he confirmed by a slight movement in Ben's eyes. Although the paramedic seemed certain he had seen something, Ben still looked comatose, stiff and rigid, pale and perspiring, with labored breathing. Despite the attendant's confident assertion, Ben did not look as though he was going to make it to the ER.

A few moments earlier, Deanne had been to the deepest, most desperate place in a mother's heart, pleading with God to save her child's life. Then, at the paramedic's hopeful report, she believed that she was witnessing God's immediate answer.

But Ben was not yet out of the woods. In fact, Deanne soon fretted that she might have been premature in thinking Ben would be okay.

Out in the field, Shawn was working on a land development

project. Just as he and his colleague trudged back to their mud-bathed cars to get on the road, Shawn received a call from his assistant.

Almost as soon as he had answered, he ended the call and bolted to his car. Alarmed and concerned, he sped to the Brackenridge ER. Shawn had a company-provided mobile telephone, but like many people in 1997, Deanne did not yet have a cellular phone, so there was no way he could contact her to find out what was happening. He knew that Deanne would not have called him at work unless something was seriously wrong. He simply prayed and pressed the gas pedal toward the floor, weaving in and out of traffic as fast as he could go.

The ambulance jolted to a halt just outside of the emergency wing. As Deanne dashed through the hospital doors following the stretcher, she was intercepted by a nurse. The stretcher vanished beneath a white curtain, leaving Deanne stranded on the other side. Even with the loud whirring and beeping of medical equipment, she could hear the urgent voices of ER doctors and nurses. She lingered there for a moment, hesitant to let Ben out of her sight. Reluctantly, she resigned herself to the waiting room on that side of the curtain.

There, Ally waited with Deanne, longing to see Ben safe and sound. She resented the sterile, astringent smell of hospitals. She also resented the deceitful white curtain that always obscured the truth about her brother. In fact, she disliked everything inside the hospital's cold, austere walls.

After what seemed like an eternity, Shawn arrived at the ER. Heading directly into the emergency room, he walked onto a scene of emergency medical personnel still attempting to resuscitate his son. The doctor leaned over Ben's face. He began patting his cheeks, speaking to him emphatically and hoping for a response. Shawn was surprised to see the doctors attempting to physically stimulate Ben back to consciousness, a sign that neither advanced technology nor medicine was working. He was even more disheartened to see that Ben remained unresponsive. Ben had just endured a forty-five-minute-long seizure, leaving the slightest hope for his brain function and, more critically, his life. Had Deanne not stopped at the fire station along the way, their son could be dead. Now Shawn stood at the foot of the bed, praying that either the doctors were sufficiently skilled to bring Ben back, or that God would intervene.

Shawn was then ushered to the other side of the curtain, where Deanne and Ally awaited his arrival. Deanne fell tearfully into his embrace, relating that morning's events, releasing pent-up stress and anguish with every word. As Deanne concluded her suspenseful saga, a boisterous cheer erupted from the other side of the curtain.

# CHAPTER 4

# CALLING ALL ANGELS

I need a sign to let me know you're here...

—"CALLING ALL ANGELS" (TRAIN)

"**W**elcome back, Ben!" someone exclaimed.

The Breedloves were relieved to see a smiling nurse appear and beckon them over to Ben. Deanne, Shawn, and Ally entered the room to find Ben sitting up, grinning ear to ear, and asking for an orange soda, as if nothing had happened. Atop a wheeled table on the right, however, lay a chilling reminder of the event: a grotesque, giant syringe that had been used to inject glucose into Ben's jugular vein. The thought of the needle piercing Ben's neck made Deanne sick, but at the same time, she was grateful for it. The glucose had saved Ben's life.

Deanne grabbed Ben's face in her hands, overjoyed to see him sitting up and smiling, but Shawn remained more pensive. Although he was thrilled that Ben pulled through, it seemed that

Ben was working hard to gather his thoughts. Concerns about any brain damage sustained during the time of Ben's seizure still plagued Shawn. But as time passed, Ben's speech and cognitive abilities improved. A few days later, Shawn and Deanne talked with a pediatric neurosurgeon, who eased their anxiety, predicting that Ben would make a full recovery and return to "normal." However, the effects of this trauma were felt throughout the rest of Ben's life, as he would sometimes forget the meaning of simple words, asking, "Now, what is a hot dog again?" or, "What is that vegetable called? Esophagus?" (referring to asparagus).

That morning, Ben was released from the ER and the nerve-racking memories that lingered there, and moved to the ICU, where he could continue to be monitored. Shawn and Ally headed home to get overnight clothes for Ben and Deanne. As Deanne accompanied the nurses wheeling Ben to a room in the ICU, they passed through a hall lit only by windows along one side. The hospital was apparently undergoing some type of renovation, and the electricity had been turned off in certain areas of the building. Deanne looked out into the gloomy, overcast day that seemed to mirror her mood.

Ben's vital signs were being analyzed closely, and his telemetry had already been hooked up to the ICU unit to be monitored by their nursing staff. While they were walking down the hallway to his new room, the nurse pushing Ben's stretcher received a radio call from the nurses' station. A voice rang through the radio's muffled static.

*Cshh*. "How is the patient doing?" *Cshh*.

The nurse who had received the signal picked up the radio to respond, casting a quick glance at her patient. *Cshh*. "Fine. He is alert and talking with us. Why?" *Cshh*.

For a few seconds, the radio was filled with static silence. *Cshh.* "Because his heart rate is in the low thirties," rang in the reply.

As they continued to wheel Ben down the dim, unlit hallway, Ben's eyes fixed on something right above him. "Look at the bright light! Do you see that, Mama?" Above him hovered what he described as a "pitch white" light.

"Ben, I don't see a light . . ." Deanne replied, glancing curiously at the ceiling to see what he was talking about. "All the lights in the hall are turned off."

But in that moment, Ben felt as if nothing else in the world mattered. He could see nothing but the bright light above him. All he felt was calm. He couldn't take his eyes off it, and he couldn't help but smile. As he was wheeled down the remainder of the hall, the light never left him.

Walking with Ben through the corridor, Deanne focused her thoughts completely on the fact that Ben had just survived an extremely difficult situation. More than anything else, she was grateful that he had made it through. During the previous hour she had been frantic, worried that Ben was going to die. Now she was thrilled to simply be holding his precious warm hand as they moved down the hallway.

She didn't think much about it when Ben asked her about the light above him. She believed him—that he saw something, for sure—but in that instant, Ben didn't describe what he saw in any great detail.

Later that night, after Shawn and Ally left the hospital, Deanne stayed behind in Ben's room. She was snuggling in his hospital bed with him, where she intended to remain all night long. Ben wanted her to hold him and not let go. It was while

Deanne was holding Ben close that he told her about seeing the light in the hallway, which he felt sure was the light of an angel, and how he had felt so good while it was with him.

Because Ben was only four years old, Deanne didn't really know what to say, how to react, or, for that matter, what she truly thought about his experience at the moment. She was, however, awed that Ben had been comforted by God, which was what she believed he had experienced. She had prayed in the ambulance that God would save Ben's life, and that Ben would not be in pain or afraid. These prayers had been answered. Throughout that sleepless night, Deanne marveled again and again at how God had spared Ben. Not only had Ben not been in pain, he couldn't remember any of the events of the traumatic day after crawling into his parents' bed that morning, then waking up wanting some orange soda in the ER.

Deanne chose not to tell Shawn about the "angel" just yet. She knew her husband was much more skeptical about such things. She felt sure that if Ben wanted to tell his dad, he would—which he eventually did. In fact, Ben would talk about this event several times throughout his life.

Almost fourteen years later, in a rough draft of an essay he wrote for college applications, Ben described what he experienced in the hospital hallway that day:

> When I was four years old, I had a seizure. . . . The only part that I remember is when they were wheeling me down a long dark hall on a stretcher. No lights were on and my mom was walking alongside me at a quick speed. I was lying there, staring up at the ceiling, and there was this huge bright white light right above me, about as long and wide as the stretcher. I said to my mom, "Look

*at the bright light!" As I was saying this, everything was slow and muffled, just like in the movies when a soldier is on the battlefield and a bomb has just exploded right by him, and all sound is tuned out of his head. I was so focused on this light hovering over me, I don't even recall my mom answering me saying, "There is no light; all the lights in the hall are turned off." [The light] continued to stay right over me all the way down the hall.*

*I got a feeling that I didn't have to care about anything that was happening in the world at that moment. I couldn't see anything else around me, not even in my peripheral vision, just this bright white light above me. Nothing could be heard; everything was calm. I have always prayed to God about my heart, that I would stay healthy, and whenever I'm scared about something having to do with my heart, that I will just be calm.*

*When I was in that hall, I was definitely not thinking it was an angel, but I know that a part of me knew that it was. I know God wanted me to be calm during the situation and have a sense of peace, and not worry about anything that was going on during those moments. Now that I look back at it, I get chills just thinking about it, because I know an angel was looking over me, literally. After experiences like these, you view life in a different way.*

Even on that stretcher, in one of the lowest moments of his life, Ben was at peace. From that day on, Ben would attribute that experience to shaping his perspective on life. To Ben, every day was a gift. Even the days that brought him closer to his last.

CHAPTER 5

# DON'T WORRY

Don't worry about a thing,
'Cause every little thing gonna be all right.

—"THREE LITTLE BIRDS" (BOB MARLEY)

Following Ben's seizure, Shawn and Deanne wanted Ben to enjoy a peaceful, carefree time with their family. DDad and Grammy, Shawn's parents, generously offered to treat the entire family to a vacation on scenic Lake Powell in Utah that summer. The trip had already been planned for a year, but after the recent trip to the ER, Shawn and Deanne felt torn. Nothing sounded better than some rest and relaxation on the lake with their family, but nothing sounded worse than spending a week in a remote location with no medical care available for miles. Finally making a decision on faith, the Breedloves packed their bags for Lake Powell.

Shawn, Deanne, Ally, Ben, DDad, and Grammy were joined by Aunt Kim and Uncle Dave, Uncle Rusty, cousins Amber and

Zach, and Great-grandmother Evelyn. Ben anticipated turning five years old during this trip, and the family had much to celebrate.

Lake Powell soon became the family's favorite destination. The enormous, pristine reservoir straddling the states of Arizona and Utah comprises the headwaters to the Grand Canyon. Majestic sand sculptures and cliffs tower over deep, glassy crystal water that seems to stretch endlessly in every direction. The Breedloves rented a seventy-five-foot houseboat for the week, complete with a hot tub and waterslide on the upper deck. During the day, the family enjoyed fishing, exploring caves and rock formations, cliff jumping, and evening fish fries. At night, they dragged mattresses, sheets, blankets, and beach towels up to the top deck to sleep underneath the night sky; bats swooped down over their noses while they gazed at shooting stars. The lake was illuminated by so many shooting stars, it seemed they couldn't all fit into the heavens at once. The trip was an opportunity for the family to bond on deeper levels than ever before.

Upon returning home, however, the family found the stresses of life awaiting them. Since his first day of college, Shawn had allotted time every week to balance his checkbook, and had done so almost religiously. But now, as he began to open the towering stack of medical bills from Ben's recent hospital visits, medical tests, and appointments, he was at a loss. There was simply no way he could pay them. The medical bills had already mounted into the tens of thousands of dollars, and because Ben had a heart condition, he was uninsurable at the time.

Shawn was overwhelmed. His entire adult life, he had meticulously managed his finances to ensure that he would not bear the burden of accruing debt. Now, for the first time, Shawn's finances were out of his control. In fact, his *life* was out of his control. For once, neither planning, nor saving, nor working tirelessly could change his circumstances. Shawn had a son with a serious heart condition. He now had a financial burden and an uncertain future, and all of it was out of his hands.

Fear began to set in. Staring at the insufficient funds in his checkbook, he realized there was nothing he could do. He decided that rather than let this uncontrollable burden loom over him, he would let go of his anxiety. "God," Shawn said aloud, "you are going to have to help me here, because I can't do this anymore. I'm giving this to you. . . . This is yours now." And Shawn never balanced his checkbook again.

In the coming months, the financial burden that seemed insurmountable became manageable. Ben and Ally's private school learned of their family's circumstances, and offered to temporarily reduce their tuition by fifty percent. An anonymous family delivered a very sizable sum of money to their home. Unsolicited, some doctors and hospitals offered to reduce their bills. One hospital even called and offered to reduce one of their largest bills by nearly ninety percent!

"Why are you doing this?" Shawn asked the woman on the phone, perplexed.

"You have been consistent in making monthly payments, and we appreciate that," she responded. "If you are willing to pay twelve hundred dollars of this bill in cash, we will cancel the balance of the eleven thousand dollars owed."

Shawn couldn't believe his ears, and accepted her offer eagerly. Other medical creditors were not quite as forgiving, but Shawn found the doctors and hospitals willing to work with him in return for his open communication and his relentless commitment to making the monthly payments. The overwhelming stress of debt was soon alleviated by the grace their family received. Shawn believed he was not on his own, and he believed his life—and his family's well-being—was in good hands.

• • •

Already, Shawn and Deanne realized they had to make tough decisions regarding how they hoped to raise Ben. Were they going to be overprotective and force him to live in a bubble? Or were they going to let him live his life, and allow him to experience all that he wanted, within reason and medical boundaries? They chose a tack somewhere in the middle. It was a conscious decision to which they would adhere throughout Ben's lifetime, although it was a constant struggle trying to maintain the balance between heeding warnings about his health parameters, and letting him live his life with joyful abandon.

This would especially play out in years to come, when all the boys in the neighborhood or at school were signing up for sports. *HCM patients should not exert themselves physically.* Or when Ben wanted to jump into the cold waters of Lake Austin. *The cold water could make him faint.* Or when he wanted to run in races on the playground. *Physical exertion was not advised.* Or visit the haunted houses at Halloween as a teenager. *Startling could cause sudden death.* Or stay up really late during friends' sleepovers. *Lack of sleep tempted arrhythmia.* Or when he would later want to ride roller coasters at Disney World. *Heart patients are always warned to stay off those rides.* And especially when he wanted to take up wakeboarding, weight lifting, or martial arts, all of which demanded intense levels of physical endurance.

Ben even had to be careful to not eat foods containing certain ingredients, such as MSG. Some of his favorite foods—football-season chicken wings and Flamin' Hot Cheetos—had too much MSG for Ben, but he sometimes indulged in them anyhow, always at a great price. He would end up with an arrhythmia for twenty-four hours or more after eating these things!

Even though Ben had informed the family that he had been accompanied by an angel while in the hospital, Deanne's comfort level hadn't improved commensurately with his. At times, after the kids were in bed, she and Shawn would be sitting in the living room watching television when her mind wandered back to the frightening moments that they had experienced in the ambulance and in the ER, and she would shudder at thoughts of Ben's fragile health. Sitting quietly next to Shawn, without the kids needing her attention, Deanne would spontaneously burst out crying. She needed no prompting by an event; merely her own thoughts and memories could suddenly evoke and release a well of tears. Although she tried to evade her fear, it attacked any area of vulnerability, attempting to creep into her heart and mind. She wondered whether Ben's small body could handle all the stress. *Will he live through the night with his heart bumping? Will he be forced to endure painful procedures and surgeries? What does the future hold for him?*

When Shawn heard his wife sniffling in the middle of the evening news one night, he turned to her with compassion and said, "Let's not worry about something that may not ever be an issue. We can't live our lives allowing something that hasn't happened to steal the joy and good in life that we have with Ben today. Let's thank God for every day with Ben, and savor every minute we have with him."

Shawn's reminder penetrated Deanne's heart deeply, and it helped assuage her fears. The words remained a source of comfort, hidden securely in her spirit. Over the years, they rose easily to the surface anytime Deanne or one of her loved ones faced a challenging day.

# CHAPTER 6

# IT'S IN THE WATER

It's in the water
It's where you came from

—"RADIOACTIVE" (KINGS OF LEON)

Six-year-old Ben bobbed up and down on the waves in the frigid Lake Austin water, wakeboard extended in front of him and ski rope in hand. He felt the rope pull tight, then the pressure of the water against his board, and he was up. A wave of accomplishment washed over him as the boat full of spectators erupted in cheers and applause. This was Ben's first time on the wakeboard and he *loved* it.

Ben relished going out on the family's boat on Lake Austin, a local jewel comprising part of the Colorado River. Shawn loved the water as well, and enjoyed teaching Ally and Ben—and eventually their younger brother, Jake—how to drive the boat and Jet Skis, and to enjoy various water sports. Ben especially took to wakeboarding, riding a small board similar to a snowboard, pulled behind a boat by a ski rope.

Wakeboarding involves a combination of skills and techniques drawn from waterskiing, snowboarding, and even surfing. Similar to skiing, the real fun is "jumping the wake" created by the boat. More avid wakeboarders—and the more adventurous— learn to do complicated tricks, including 360-degree "whirly-birds," "S-bends," and backflips known as "tantrums."

An entire wakeboarding culture grew up around Lake Austin, due to the smooth, calm waters, drawing both professional boarders and novices alike. Austin is home to professional wakeboarders Billy Garcia, who coached Ben one summer, and Holland Finley, as well as the Shred Stixx professional wakesurfing team. Former Austin resident Chase Hazen, from whom Ben also took lessons, is considered one of the best wakesurfers in the world.

For some reason, wakeboarding and wakesurfing—surfing the wake behind the boat without a rope on a board with no boots—didn't seem to tax Ben physically quite as much as other sports, seeing as the boat or its wake did most of the work. Despite his limitations, wakeboarding and wakesurfing were both sports at which Ben could excel.

• • •

Every summer, Deanne and the kids, along with cousins Tommy, Shawn, and Nikki, traveled with Gee Gee, Deanne's mom, to Garner State Park in Concan, Texas. The park was a popular destination for vacationers wanting to camp, hike, fish, shoot the rapids on inner tubes, or simply relax in the cold waters of the Frio River.

Camping at Garner had been part of the family's history ever since Gee Gee made the first trip with her parents when she was twelve years old. The annual summer highlight included sleeping under the stars, hiking up to Crystal Cave, making dinners on open fires, dancing at the outdoor pavilion to the tunes of the old jukebox, and most of all, spending lots and lots of time floating on the Frio River.

When Deanne eventually had a family of her own, she was thrilled to initiate them into the Garner tradition. Although she looked forward to some good family time, Deanne was always nervous about being out in the middle of nowhere, at least forty miles from the nearest hospital, should an emergency arise. As much as the family fought against such concerns, they always lurked in the background. The family's new normal dictated that wherever Ben traveled, they needed to be aware of medical facilities nearby.

During the camping trip, Deanne tried to relax and have fun for the family's sake. She was delighted when she discovered, perhaps providentially, that she had pitched their campsite right next to that of Francine, a pediatric nurse who worked in the cardiac unit at the children's hospital in Austin! Nurse Francine's presence helped allay some of Deanne's concerns, mainly for Ben, but for herself, as well. She was, after all, very pregnant, a few weeks away from her delivery date. She thanked God each night during that camping trip for allowing the family to have their special campsite neighbor. Years later, Nurse Francine would comfort Ben again when he became her surprise patient at Brackenridge Hospital in Austin.

For his part, Ben was his normally happy-go-lucky self all week long. After a week of adventure and shooting the rapids by himself for the first time, Ben was presented with the nickname

"Floating Bear" at the annual family powwow. This traditional closing ceremony took place around the campfire on the last night of the trip, the kids festooned in makeshift headdresses and vests blazoned with tribal paint. The next morning, Ben celebrated his sixth birthday at a picnic table, enjoying his favorite snack—pecan halves sent to him by his DDad.

When the time came to pack up camp and return home, the family was reluctant to leave their favorite camping grounds. The next summer would be even more full of adventure. The Garner gang was due to grow by one more.

On the car ride home, Ben eyed Deanne's pregnant belly suspiciously.

"Mama?" Ben piped up from the backseat.

"Yes, Ben?" Deanne replied.

"What are we going to do if this baby is black?"

Deanne tried to stifle a laugh before addressing his question seriously. "Well, Ben, we are going to love him exactly like we love you and Ally! But Daddy's not black, and I am not black, so I don't think this baby is going to be black."

Ben looked out the window, considering Deanne's logic. After a while, he looked back at Deanne with a big smile. "I think it would be neat if he's black!"

The following month, on August 31, 1999, baby Jake Harrison was born. He was not black, but Ben was just as excited to meet him, and the two soon grew to be close companions.

• • •

From their early family beginnings, Shawn and Deanne decided to acknowledge God's presence in their lives, and to be thankful every day. Shawn was raised in a family that embraced faith in God, and Deanne found her own faith after meeting him. They naturally passed along those values to their children.

When Ally was eight years old and Ben was nearly six, both children decided to be baptized in response to their individual decisions to invite God into their lives. Ben had requested that his dad baptize him. Concerned that having her dad baptize her might make it somehow less official, Ally opted to have their pastor baptize her.

It was a poignant moment on that hot afternoon in August when the family gathered in their backyard on Lake Austin to watch Ally and Ben be baptized. Shawn and their pastor gently eased each of them backward, down into the water, and then up again.

While most people think of baptism as a pastor's job, Shawn knew that the person who performs the baptism has no impact on its officiality. Ben's request made Shawn feel particularly loved, appreciated, and honored by his son. Several years later, Shawn would have the same privilege when Jake chose to be baptized at the age of eleven in the same spot along the shore of Lake Austin.

CHAPTER 7

# LIE LOW

It's funny how life can go
First you ride high then you might lay low

—"THE LOVE SONG" (K-OS)

W hen Ben was barely six years old, his doctors in Austin recommended that he be taken to Cook Children's Medical Center in Fort Worth for a cardiac ablation, performed by the renowned Dr. Paul C. Gillette. Cardiac ablation works by scarring or destroying faulty tissue in the heart that triggers an abnormal heart rhythm. So far, nothing had worked well in smoothing out the arrhythmia in Ben's heart, so the doctors felt the ablation might help.

Most patients who undergo cardiac ablations wake up after surgery with only small bandages at the catheter insertion site, usually the inner thigh, and often don't even require stitches. At the time of his ablation, Ben was one of the youngest patients ever to receive this procedure. The success—or failure—of Ben's procedure would later be written up in several articles.

Shawn and Deanne were prepped to expect a surgery requiring approximately two hours, possibly three, but the operation took much longer. Those first two hours dragged, then doubled, then almost tripled. Throughout the surgery, a nurse called the waiting room to provide the family with updates. During one such call, the nurse explained that the doctors had been working inside Ben's heart for a long time, and they didn't want to stay inside much longer. Since Ben was not experiencing an arrhythmia at the moment, Dr. Gillette was forced to pump adrenaline through his heart to aggravate an arrhythmia, so its route could be detected, and they could ablate it.

When Deanne hung up the phone, it hit her hard that Ben was really going through a lot. Troubling thoughts overwhelmed her, so she slipped into the bathroom and cried alone. As she often did, she prayed for Ben, asking God to see him through.

After nearly seven hours, the surgery was completed. Ben woke up with a 103-degree fever that the doctors could not explain. It eventually subsided, but the high temperature, like so many of Ben's medical conditions, remained an enigma.

Deanne had been assured that one of the positive aspects of this procedure was that Ben would wake up with an incision in his thigh so small that he wouldn't even need stitches. The doctors and nurses failed to mention the truly painful part of the procedure—removing the pressure bandages. Ben had extremely tight, adhesive pressure bandages wrapped around his tiny thighs during the surgery, and when it was time for the nurse to remove the bandages, she had to rip them off. It was almost as if his skin was coming off with each bandage. During the removal, Ben looked straight into Deanne's eyes and yelled, "No! Stop! Mama, please. *Make them stop.* No, Mama!"

To hear his plaintive cries was absolutely heartbreaking for Deanne. She had not anticipated this procedure, and she felt as if she had betrayed Ben. She never overcame that feeling of knowing he had to endure a pain for which she had not prepared him. Ever after, Deanne always made sure to ask the doctors extensive questions and presented the full picture to Ben before going forward with medical procedures.

• • •

Dr. Gillette was the first doctor to emphasize transplantation as a treatment for Ben's HCM. "The prognosis ultimately brings you to transplant," he said gently, but straightforwardly. The doctor briefly explained the process: Ben would have to live and stay within three hours of the chosen transplant facility. Another child approximately Ben's age would have to be pronounced "brain-dead," and the family would have to decide to donate the child's heart immediately after death. The donor's heart then had to be harvested and transferred to Ben's body within four hours while Ben's chest cavity lay open, his heart ready to be removed. It was a critical, time-sensitive procedure, and there were no guarantees of success.

Since Ben was so young, Shawn and Deanne chose not to dwell on the possibility of a transplant. If it became necessary at some point, they would consider that option. But not until then.

Human heart transplantation, although still a high-risk procedure, had been totally unheard-of before the late 1950s. It was then that Dr. Norman Shumway and his research collaborator, Dr. Richard Lower at Stanford University Medical Center, first successfully removed the heart from one dog and transplanted it into another. The dog with the transplanted heart lived for eight days, proving that such a procedure could work.

Almost forty years after that primitive procedure, Shawn and Deanne were grappling with the thought that their son might have to undergo the same surgery. Dr. Gillette was suggesting that Ben could possibly live a normal life if he received a heart transplant. At this young age, Ben still had options such as medication and a pacemaker implantation before considering a heart transplant, which was an extreme measure. It seemed that if a heart transplant was ever going to be a reality for Ben, it would be much further down the road. Not to mention that there were already numerous hopeful recipients waiting for hearts, and for every one of their hopes to be fulfilled, someone else had to die. It was all very sobering news to take in, but the Breedlove family made a decision to be content for the time being. Although they never ruled out the possibility of a transplant, the probability seemed rather remote.

• • •

On the way home, Ben's head nodded forward as he drifted off to sleep in the backseat of the car. Deanne sat in the back with him, carefully laying him in her lap so that she could keep an eye on his bandage over the incision site. After the surgery, the discharge nurse had warned them that Ben's femoral artery could possibly reopen, leaving Ben with only minutes before he would bleed out.

The drive home from Fort Worth felt long and tense, and Deanne and Shawn worried the entire way. Little Ben was so exhausted from his surgery that they wondered whether they should have kept him in the hospital one more night. But Ben, like Ally, was beginning to develop an aversion to hospitals. Although he didn't feel well, Ben was heartened by precious handmade "get well" cards from his kindergarten buddies. He settled into the car and was glad to be heading home.

The dichotomy of the parent-child relationship seems even more blurred in such times. Devotedly, children believe their parents' primary role is to protect them. Indeed, Shawn and Deanne were doing their best to do just that, but although they knew the ablation procedure was vital to Ben's well-being, they didn't feel much like protectors as they traveled back to Austin. On the contrary, their hearts and minds were fraught with consternation about Ben's future. The continuous threat of losing Ben loomed above every decision they confronted. They exchanged knowing glances and wondered how they could best care for him as they watched over their weak, exhausted son in the backseat.

# CHAPTER 8

# ADVENTURE

Spinnin' and monsoonin',
Grinnin', it's high octane

—"MY LIFE BE LIKE" (G.R.I.T.S.)

Ben and Ally removed the tissue paper from the gift bags Shawn and Deanne had set out for them in the living room, wondering why they were receiving gifts on such a random day in the spring, and why they were being videotaped. Reaching their hands into the paper bags, the kids each drew out red autograph booklets with various Disney characters printed on the cover. Ben and Ally looked questioningly back at their parents. "Does this mean . . ." Ben began, and Shawn nodded, smiling.

*"We're going to Disney World!"* Ben and Ally exclaimed in unison, jumping up and down with joy.

Shawn and Deanne had kept the trip a secret literally until

the last minute. After many somber conversations, they had faced the truth that Ben's time with them might be limited. If they were to ever plan a family vacation to Disney World, now was the time. They worried that Ben might not fully recover from the ablation in time for a trip. If plans had to change, the kids wouldn't be disappointed, because they didn't even know about the surprise vacation.

With the added protection that the ablation afforded in managing Ben's arrhythmia, Shawn and Deanne felt more confident to let him branch out and try some new experiences that other kids often take for granted. For instance, during the Disney World trip, Ben was able to enjoy his first chocolate candy bar ever—a king-sized Three Musketeers bar. The chocolate bar was fun enough, but then Ben wanted to ride Disney's popular Space Mountain roller coaster.

The rip-roaring ride is meant to simulate a blast into outer space, so each roller-coaster car is shaped like a rocket with three passenger compartments. After climbing 180 feet inside the mountain, passengers suddenly blast off into the dark, illuminated only by "falling stars" and other "celestial bodies" on a twisting, turning, careening ride, replete with gut-wrenching turns and drops that reach speeds of twenty-eight miles per hour, but seem much faster in the dark. Because the ride consists of such tumultuous thrills, Disney prominently displays a number of signs outside the building, and even inside before the ride begins, warning passengers not to ride Space Mountain if they have back or neck problems, heart or blood pressure problems, or other conditions that could be aggravated by being jerked around at high speeds in the darkness.

To casual observers, and especially to Disney ride attendants, Ben, of course, looked perfectly healthy. They may have noticed his slight build, but with his boyish grin and ebullient personality, nobody would have considered him anything other than another excited six-year-old, anxious for the ride of his life.

Deanne and Shawn guessed they wouldn't win any parenting awards for letting their heart-patient son ride Space Mountain, but after much debate and conversation, Ben's doctor decided Ben should be the one to set his own physical limits. As long as he felt okay, he could participate within reason. The first test was this roller coaster.

Deanne stayed behind to hold baby Jake. She watched nervously as Ben walked inside the space age–looking building to board the ride along with Dad and Ally. The sounds of surrealistic music emanating from hidden speakers all around Space Mountain did nothing to calm Deanne's butterflies. With the anxiety getting the best of her, Deanne's stomach tightened into knots; she felt as though she wanted to throw up. It had been a weighty decision to allow Ben to go, a choice that came with enormous risks. Had Deanne felt strongly opposed or had any sense of intuition that Ben should not go on the ride, she would have protested. So now she waited right outside Space Mountain while Ben went on the ride, wondering whether they had made the right decision, watching constantly for his face to appear at the exit.

Meanwhile, Ben was indeed having the time of his life, riding in the front rocket seat, whisking through the air, whipping back and forth through the dark, with his hands raised high over his head the entire time!

When he finally emerged from Space Mountain and Deanne saw him smiling from ear to ear, she knew at once it was worth it. She was overjoyed to see the elation on his face as he came off that ride. Deanne carefully listened to Ben's heart, and everything seemed perfectly fine. She felt such relief, as well as joy that Ben was getting to experience normal, fun things in life. A candy bar and a roller coaster all in one day! She hardly had time to celebrate, however, as Ben wanted to ride the rocket again. And again! Over and over Ben rode Space Mountain, enjoying the last ride as much as the first.

· · ·

As Ben grew older, the family's responses to his condition evolved as well. They coped in the best way they knew how, given the inherent tension between their resolution to let Ben experience life as he desired and the reality of his heart condition.

For the most part, they functioned in the realm of hope, trusting that Ben would learn his limits, and ultimately that he would be okay. The alternative was to allow themselves to wallow in despair and constant anxiety. When Ally, Ben, or Jake had questions or concerns about Ben's health, Shawn and Deanne attempted to answer them forthrightly, without holding back any secret information.

An old soul from her earliest years, Ally developed a watchful awareness of Ben's condition. She could gauge not only Ben's demeanor, but his overall sense of well-being. Occasionally she might notice that Ben's skin coloring was off, or his energy level wasn't good that day, and she helped call those things to her parents' attention.

Throughout Ben's early childhood, he continued to be asymptomatic, and apart from the regular cardiac checkups he had to endure, the HCM didn't impede him from having a good time.

# CHAPTER 9

# DREAM ON

Dream on
Dream until your dreams come true

—"DREAM ON" (AEROSMITH)

As Ben grew into his elementary school years, both teachers and students alike noticed and appreciated his buoyant personality. Near the end of every school year at Regents School—where Ally and Ben and later Jake attended—each student received a special stone called a "character rock" from his or her teacher. The awards were presented by the teacher during a classroom ceremony. The students typically sat in a circle and then the teacher presented each with his or her stone, one by one. Often the teacher might give a brief speech, or offer a few complimentary statements about the child, or recite an especially appropriate Bible verse, as she presented the stone to the student.

The purpose of presenting the rock was to show the students

which character traits they most consistently exemplified through-out the school year. Some examples of character traits noted were kindness, gentleness (which Ally received every year), thoughtful-ness, and others. The students' faces lit up when they saw how they had been perceived by their teacher. All the other kids usu-ally nodded in agreement as each child's special character trait was recognized.

Every year, with the exception of one, Ben received a charac-ter rock denoting some version of joy! He received joy, joyfulness, joyful spirit, or something similar. Interestingly, the teachers never conversed or collaborated with one another regarding their selections.

When Ben was in sixth grade, he did not receive a character rock signifying "joyful" for the first time. When he jumped in the car on rock day, the first question Deanne asked was, "What did you get?"

Ben wasn't too happy; he was not nearly as pleased as he had been all the other years when he had received "joy rocks." He mumbled something about "honesty."

"Honesty? That's an extremely admirable trait, Ben," Deanne said. "I'm so proud of you."

"Yeah, it's a good thing," he replied, "but it isn't true." Ironi-cally, Ben's statement was honest! He recognized that he didn't al-ways tell the whole truth, and to Ben, even a "white lie" was a big deal.

Ben's compassion and generosity toward his friends helped him to develop truly deep and rewarding friendships. Not sur-prisingly, when it came to his heart condition, he was also priv-ileged to receive the prayers of many people. One of Ben's closest childhood friends, Alex Hayes, became the first boy their age to begin praying for Ben's healing. Every night, beginning in preschool, Alex offered up prayers for Ben's heart. Alex's friendship, as well as his prayers, remained constant throughout Ben's life.

• • •

Ben was always a performer, the consummate entertainer, throwing himself into everything he did with all his might.

He made his earliest debut into the world of entertainment on home video in the Breedlove living room. Ben and Ally were initially the only kids in the neighborhood, and they became the best of friends. On long, uneventful days before either of them was old enough to attend school, Ally would devise a grand performance, creating some fantastic plot and putting together costumes, with her and Ben as the stars of the show. Ben always went along enthusiastically, delivering his part with gravitas.

Ben also mastered a number of magic tricks by the time he was seven or eight years of age. He practiced and practiced, then gathered the family in the living room for shows. He donned a cape and a large black magician's top hat, and waved a wand as he performed his tricks, providing a solid thirty minutes of entertainment. Ben took the quality of his tricks quite seriously, but he smiled and laughed the whole time he was performing. He learned numerous card tricks as well, really good ones, too. People who saw him perform were often surprised at how polished his magic shows actually were.

Eventually, Ben carried his performances over to the stage. By the time Ally reached middle school, she'd struck an interest in competitive theater. Every day after school, she spent hours rehearsing for a play, usually not returning home until after dark. The diligent rehearsals culminated in a regional tournament in which various Texas schools each performed a one-act play. After attending the performance and watching Ally and her cast members receive awards onstage in front of hundreds of people, Ben was sold. The next year, he accompanied Ally to the auditions. The following week, Ben became part of the cast of *Macbeth*, loving every second of the spotlight as Servant #2. He brought such energy to rehearsals, both on- and offstage, that the director often commented, "Ben, I just want to shrink you down to miniature size and keep you in a jar on my desk, so you can entertain us all day long!"

Ben carried his showmanship into most areas of his life. During middle school, he went through a phase of solving Rubik's cubes, always delivering his fastest performance in front of an audience. He had three-, four-, and five-row cubes, and he learned to solve them and make patterns with them by ordering and reading books detailing various solutions. Later, he would watch YouTube videos to get solutions. He could solve a difficult Rubik's cube puzzle in less than a minute, and he was always trying to beat his best time.

• • •

Ben was barely four years old when Sheri and Kirk Miller moved into a home on Lake Austin, and down the street from the Breedloves. Sheri noticed children's toys in the Breedlove backyard, so she stopped over to introduce herself and her son, Justin, a year younger than Ben. As the kids played in the backyard, Sheri and Deanne got to know each other. It was the beginning of a friendship that would last throughout their lives.

When Ben wasn't performing, he and Justin were outside making all kinds of contraptions to ride on. They created "chariots" made by duct-taping ice chests or laundry baskets to skateboards or office chairs and pulled by a jump rope. They pulled each other on inner tubes behind a golf cart—similar to tubing on the lake, but done in the yard—dragging each other as fast as they could, hanging on for dear life as the tubes skimmed across the lawn. Younger brother Jake enthusiastically volunteered to be the guinea pig for the test rides.

Ben and Justin searched for all sorts of creatures, the kinds usually found under rocks. Ben loved every creature he could find. He even hand-bathed his pet corn snake and applied medicine to its scales for almost a month. Ben took his creature collecting seriously. At first, he and Justin were content to collect scorpions. Once, they collected seventeen scorpions and froze them in Justin's mom's freezer. Later that day, they pulled the Baggie out of the freezer to inspect their scorpions without fear of getting stung. They dumped the frozen creatures onto a paper plate. As they were examining them, the scorpions began thawing out, crawling off the plate and falling off the kitchen table! Ben and Justin scrambled all over the kitchen floor collecting the scorpions again. When they felt sure they had recovered all of them, they released the scorpions outside—far, far away from the house.

Before long, Justin and Ben graduated from chasing scorpions to hunting down coral snakes, relatively small but potentially deadly vipers due to the neurotoxins in their venom—at least until their moms found out and put the kibosh on that adventure. Eventually, Ben collected alligator lizards, selling them to the local reptile store for fifteen to twenty dollars each. The expert at the reptile store, an unusual man in his own right, nicknamed Spider-Man, asked Ben to find a certain type of brown tarantula that thrives near Lake Austin. Ben succeeded in finding several of the unusual tarantulas. He delivered them to Spider-Man and received a small payment in return. It was not uncommon for Deanne to return home from running errands and find a menagerie of animals and insects living in various boxes, jars, and cages on the kitchen counter.

Ben's entrepreneurial side blossomed early. By the time he was eleven years old, in addition to hunting tarantulas and alligator lizards for pay, Ben and Jake earned money by manning a lemonade stand at the end of their driveway. Most of the neighbors stopped and made a purchase as they passed by, not so much because they were thirsty, but because they loved seeing Jake's and Ben's enthusiasm. When lemonade lost its appeal, the boys opened a fossil stand, earning about thirty-five dollars. They once ran a "pecan stand," from which they raked in about twenty-five dollars, despite the fact that most of the neighbors had pecan trees in their backyards. When pecans went out of season, the boys opened what they simply referred to as "the Stand," selling all types of things—sort of a semipermanent yard sale—from which they made more than seventy-five dollars. Deanne later discovered that some of the higher-priced items sold at the stand were family heirlooms, so she had the boys track down a few neighbors and politely request that they sell the items back to them. Ben loved coming up with new ideas for their "business," and

Jake loved having a "big brother" who included him in adventures like this.

• • •

Ben always dreamed big about his future. When Deanne asked him at age three what he thought he might want to be someday, Ben told her that he would like to be a monster-truck driver with a pink Mohawk haircut. He held on to this aspiration for years, until he noticed that the trashmen got to hang off the back of the garbage truck! Ben loved the idea of riding around like that all day in the outdoors, and decided that would be the job for him. Then with his first Holter monitor box came the dream of becoming a policeman. Later, he moved on to imagining he would become a great magician. And finally came his dreams to be an NBA All-Star. He didn't mind the fact that he was the shortest kid in his class. He dreamed of being a great athlete.

When Ben was eleven years old, he had received a notebook full of basketball cards from his cousin Zach, and began trading them with his friends. He begged Shawn and Deanne to let him try out for the middle school team, and since they were reluctant to tell him he couldn't physically handle it or that the game might be too strenuous for his heart, his parents allowed him to play. First, though, Shawn and Deanne talked to both his doctor and his coach. His doctor was hesitant to let him play initially, but his coach did not force Ben to participate in workouts if he wasn't up for it. Ben loved the game, and he was a fairly good player. Despite the fact that he was on medication that slowed his heart rate and made it impossible for him to keep up with the other kids,

Ben held on to his visions of becoming a professional basketball player. Shawn and Deanne encouraged him to dream big! After one season, however, Ben realized that basketball wasn't the sport for him. He would have to find something else at which he could excel.

• • •

During Ben's middle school and junior high years, like many boys that age, his friends became immersed in sports—sports in which, for the most part, Ben could not safely participate. He watched his buddies bond on the football fields, the basketball courts, and baseball fields, and in locker rooms. His friends naturally grew closer with one another through these activities, while Ben could only stand on the sidelines, watching, wanting to play, longing to be included, yet knowing it was too dangerous for him. Feelings of isolation from his more athletic peers grew almost imperceptibly, but Ben was adept at making new friends and seeking out his own interests.

Once football season was over and his friends became more available to hang out together, Ben was invited to spend a Friday night at one boy's house. He went.

That same afternoon, Ben had been fitted with another Holter monitor to record his heart rhythm, in what had become a rather routine cardiac exam for him. When he arrived at his friend's house that evening, the dad saw the Holter monitor and all its wires. He told his wife he wanted Ben to go home, because he worried about the responsibility of caring for him overnight. Ben overheard this conversation between the parents, and decided that going home early would not be a bad idea.

When Ben told Deanne about the incident, he insisted that it didn't bother him, but she could tell that he was grappling with larger acceptance issues. Ben was experiencing not merely the normal adolescent peer pressures, but deeper feelings that he was different, and wondering how he fit into this world. He didn't want any special considerations because of his heart condition. He wanted to be accepted for who he was. While his friendly smile and quick sense of humor created numerous social opportunities for him, Ben focused more on a few close friends with whom he felt comfortable being himself.

Justin Miller was that sort of friend to Ben. Indeed, Justin's entire family loved Ben and made him feel like part of their family. They included Ben on camping trips, and took him with them to the beach, as well as dirt biking, hunting, even on a family trip to California. They welcomed Ben into their family and never let go. They helped him to feel completely normal. He knew they loved him, and he loved them back.

## PART 2

# THE PASSION

## CHAPTER 10

# WHILE OUR BLOOD'S STILL YOUNG

While our blood's still young
It's so young, it runs

—"SWEET DISPOSITION" (THE TEMPER TRAP)

"I just saved tons of money on car insurance by switching to Geico!" Ben said with a wink as he pointed to the camera. Staging comedic videos during the summer of 2000 marked the beginning of Ben and Justin Miller's film entrepreneurship.

Justin's dad had given the boys an old video camera to use around the neighborhood, and they took to filming everything. They began by recording Justin's chocolate Lab, Boomer, dragging Ally and the two boys, all at the same time, around the house by a sock.

Then they got creative. Ben had the idea to fashion the video recorder into a sort of "helmet cam," his own precursor to the GoPro, by duct-taping the camera to his bike helmet. The boys filmed themselves jumping off their bike ramp, doing flips on the trampoline, and performing all kinds of other stunts. They soon discovered that comedy was their forte.

Ben and Justin continued making their own entertaining videos throughout middle school and high school, and even uploaded a few to the new original-content video website YouTube. One of their creations brought the guys more notoriety than they had ever imagined. During the Halloween season, Ben and Justin were trying to dream up something to do, but couldn't come up with anything original. They shared their frustration with Deanne, a Halloween enthusiast, and she offered them a suggestion: "When I was your age, my friends and I stuffed a pair of jeans with paper and put a pillow in a shirt, shaping it into a dummy that looked like a body. We poured ketchup all over the dummy and then left it out on the road, trying to scare people."

"Oh, wow, Mrs. Breedlove," Justin said. "That's awesome."

"Yeah! Let's do *that*!" Ben agreed.

Deanne felt satisfied that she had provided an innocuous idea to the boys to keep them occupied. What she underestimated was their incredible creativity and artistic ability to make the prank look realistic. In Deanne's version of the prank, which she had pulled as a kid, she used her mom's white Styrofoam wig head, which looked obviously fake. The guys went to work elaborately stuffing a pair of jeans and a hoodie to make the figure look like a real person. They attached gloves to the sleeves to appear as hands, added a pair of shoes, topped it off with a bike helmet, and then squirted it with watered-down ketchup for blood. They placed the "body" facedown on the street, with a mangled bicycle nearby, simulating a crash.

They then hid behind a tree and pressed "record" on the

video camera, hoping for a dramatic reaction. The first victim to drive down the street simply slowed down, chuckled, and kept going. All the neighborhood dads who passed by had similar reactions. When the neighborhood moms drove by, however, they were not amused. Another person stopped, got out, looked at the ruse, and then got back in the car and continued on. But then a landscape worker driving a white truck came down the street, slammed on the brakes, and stopped. The man jumped out of the truck and ran to the "body." He dived to the ground as though he were about to begin CPR on the dummy, and then realized it was fake. Just then a neighbor lady drove by and stopped her car. She was convinced the body was one of the neighborhood kids, and she began weeping hysterically.

About that same time, Justin's dad arrived home from work, coming on the scene of the truck, a car, the landscaping guy, a bloody body, and a hysterical neighbor. Justin's dad ran to see what was going on, and quickly realized they had been duped. With the video camera still rolling, Justin's dad attempted to calm the landscaper.

The boys were reprimanded for their outlandish prank, but it was difficult to be too hard on them, since the entire escapade had been Deanne's idea!

• • •

Ben and Justin did everything together, but one of their favorite activities continued to be making funny videos. Deanne had bought full-body-size bunny and gorilla costumes that Ben and Justin sometimes used to film their pranks. One day, they went Jet Skiing on Lake Austin—while wearing the costumes. The costumes were so heavy when wet, the boys would have sunk like rocks had they fallen into the water.

Ally had taken a job that summer at Ski Shores Cafe, a lakeside restaurant in the neighborhood. She was serving a hamburger and a Coke to a customer at the outdoor picnic tables when nearly everyone at the restaurant started laughing and pointing out to the lake. "Look at that!" one of her customers exclaimed, just as a big white bunny and a gorilla zoomed by on Jet Skis.

Ally took one look and rolled her eyes. "Oh, my gosh," she said, laughing and burying her face in her hands. "That's my *brother.*"

• • •

Of course, by the time Ben and Justin were getting their feet wet, offbeat videos similar to theirs were becoming the rage on YouTube. A few years earlier, Lucas Cruikshank, a fourteen-year-old living in Columbus, Nebraska, created a fictional video character known as Fred Figglehorn, a hyperactive six-year-old with a high-pitched voice and anger-management issues. The character's actions were loosely based on the antics of Lucas's younger brothers. Cruikshank introduced the "Fred" character in a series of comedic videos on YouTube beginning in October 2006, and they soon went viral. Ben's generation was watching and learning from this lowbrow, low-budget, but far-reaching video success.

YouTube was a huge success story in its own right, founded in 2005 by former PayPal employees Chad Hurley, Steve Chen, and Jawed Karim. By December of that same year, more than eight million views per day were logged on YouTube. In less than a year, that number skyrocketed to more than one hundred million video views per day, with more than sixty-five thousand videos being uploaded every day by what was now a worldwide viewership. In October 2006, Google acquired YouTube for $1.65 billion! Clearly people were watching—including Ben and Justin.

# CHAPTER 11

# SAY WHAT YOU NEED TO SAY

It's better to say too much
Than to never say what you need to say again

—"SAY" (JOHN MAYER)

T hroughout middle school, Ben's condition remained somewhat asymptomatic, but occasionally his heart would start "bumping," which was particularly inconvenient when he spent the night with friends. Once, he was several hours out of town at a friend's ranch, and in the middle of the night his heart began beating irregularly. Ben always felt more comfortable being at home during these episodes, so when his friend's parents called to inform Shawn and Deanne about Ben's condition, they drove the four-hour round trip out to the ranch to get him and bring him home. Unfortunately, as much as Ben just wanted to be a "regular kid," he had to skip a lot of sleepovers and other fun events with his friends due to difficulty with his heart.

During Ben's eighth-grade year, he began to experience heart failure. The doctors didn't use that phrase, but rather spoke about his condition in nondescript, sterile medical terms. But it was heart failure nonetheless. Deanne knew this because she had been researching it already once she started to notice Ben's symptoms. His stomach had bloated due to ascites, a backup of fluid in the abdominal cavity because his heart was not pumping it out effectively, causing discomfort and shortness of breath.

Ben's cardiologist explained the reason for the ascites, and said, "This is part of the process of this heart condition." He reiterated to Ben, "Someday your heart may quit functioning properly and we may have to replace it with a transplanted heart."

Ben sat smiling at the doctor, engaging him with his eyes. It was one of the more serious appointments he'd had to date. He learned that he might become so winded that he would have to spend much of the day sitting on the sofa with an oxygen tank to help him breathe. His breathing might become shallow and his stomach and ankles might swell. The heart failure might stabilize, or decline, but it would never reverse itself or improve.

Once Ben and Deanne returned to the car, Ben's stoic countenance alerted Deanne that he had taken the doctor's words to heart. Ben was never this quiet, and he had a reflective expression on his face. His jaw muscles were working. He was thinking.

*Should I draw his thoughts out of him?* Deanne wondered. *Or should I be more respectful and wait for him to give me the clues that he is ready to talk?* Ben was becoming a young man. Deanne knew that this meant he would want to tackle life on his own terms. Opting to remain silent and leave Ben to his thoughts, Deanne prayed inwardly and silently that God would comfort him. *Lord, give him peace and contentedness. Help him know which questions to ask. Give him hope.*

Deanne always encouraged Ben to ask the doctor questions. She wanted him to develop that direct relationship with his doctors so he could feel more in control, rather than always letting Mom and Dad do all of the questioning. Even with that encouragement, during most appointments Ben remained polite and listened. Then, when he'd get in the car, he'd have all sorts of questions for his mom.

After they left the appointment that day, they were both silent as Deanne pulled out of the parking lot. When they had driven about a block away, Ben turned to Deanne and asked straightfor-wardly, "Mom, am I going to die?"

Ben's attitude was not silly or flippant; he was serious.

Deanne drove a bit farther before answering. With her heart aching, she replied calmly, "Well, Ben, the answer is yes. We're all going to die, and none of us know when. I have asthma and I may be out on the boat tomorrow and have an attack and not recover. Your heart condition does give you a risk of having a problem. But only God knows when we are going to die. We don't need to live our lives like they're a death sentence; we need to *enjoy* our lives. I think you do a good job of that."

Ben remained quiet, sober, and thoughtful.

"Ben," Deanne said, parking at a stop light, "look at me."

He turned and looked deeply into her eyes.

"Ben, I truly believe you are going to live a long and fulfilling life," Deanne told him. "If I didn't believe this, I wouldn't say it to you."

His eyes welled with big tears, and Ben turned his head away from his mom and looked out the window. He seemed satisfied with Deanne's answer. But in reality, it was the beginning of Ben facing his own mortality. Like the sword of Damocles dangling by a horsehair, the specter of death hung over his head.

Ben rarely spoke openly about the fragility of his life, yet his awareness of it inserted itself into everyday events. Later that day, while Deanne was running a quick errand, he decided to remain in the car. Deanne left the engine running so Ben would have access to the air-conditioning and radio. John Mayer's song "Say" was playing as Deanne hurried inside.

When she returned to the car, Ben looked at her with utmost sincerity and deep emotion. "Mom, I love you," he said.

Recognizing that the lyrics to the song on the radio may have prompted him to say what he needed to say while he still had time on earth to say it, Deanne felt her heart flood with emotion as well. "I love you, too, Ben," she said. "Bigger than the universe!" She added the phrase that they had shared since he was barely able to talk.

CHAPTER 12

# WITH MY BROTHER STANDING BY

I said brother, you know, you know
It's a long road we've been walking on

—"ORANGE SKY" (ALEXI MURDOCH)

"You believe in God, don't you?"

Mark Kohler stared back at a flamboyant, fiery-haired woman in her late fifties with a gaudy Southwestern style.

"Yes, I do," Mark replied, taken aback by her question.

"I knew it. I love your artwork, by the way." Sue Raine, Ben's grandmother Gee Gee, had traveled to Arlington, Texas, to visit a friend, and had stopped by a local art show, one of her many spontaneous adventures. She had been musing about the various exhibits when she rounded a corner and fell in love with a watercolor entitled *Cowboy Prayer*, by Mark Kohler.

Shawn and Deanne always felt that it was no coincidence that Mark and his wife, Pam, met and became friends with the

Breedlove family. A professional artist specializing in Southwestern artworks done in watercolors, Mark had not yet sold a single painting when he and Pam set up a booth at the art show in Arlington that weekend. Sue bought the first piece of art Mark ever sold, and was delighted to learn that the couple lived in Austin. She became good friends with the artist and his wife, and introduced everyone back in Austin. The two families became close friends. Of all the gifts Sue gave to her family, the connection she forged between the Breedloves and the Kohlers was one of the best.

· · ·

Mark was an unusual mix—an artist and an avid outdoorsman who had grown up shooting firearms and hunting wild animals. "I was raised in Texas, where they present you with a gun when you are born," he joked. Early in Ben's teenage years, Mark and Pam moved to a 129-acre property in Sabinal, a small town west of San Antonio. When the Breedloves visited the Kohlers, Mark would take the kids out roughhousing on the property. He often invited friends to go hunting, to rid the property of destructive wild hogs. When the Breedlove kids visited, he literally let them run "hog wild." If it was muddy, he took them out on the four-wheeler and did doughnuts in the mud. When the kids were only eight or ten years old, Mark looked over at Ben and said, "Okay, it's your turn to drive."

Being with Mark gave Ben an opportunity to try adventurous and outdoorsy activities that he might never have tried on his own or with his own dad. Mark was a marvelous teacher, too, precise and meticulous, but patient and careful as well. Shawn appreciated Mark's willingness to teach Ben things that he might enjoy, especially the activities at which Shawn did not regularly participate.

Because guys tend to judge one another according to strength, athletic ability, and roughness, Ben usually was exempted from those criteria. Moreover, he wasn't allowed to test his strength and endurance because of the pressure it placed on his heart. But hunting and shooting allowed Ben to participate in a "man's" sport. With his dusty boots and old jeans, he headed into the woods, carrying his gun and ammo, with his sights set on dragging home an animal. He loved engaging in the ancient conflict of man versus nature. He always wore a satisfied grin on his face when he walked in with blood and dirt and the smell of nature on him.

• • •

A few years after his artistic career took off, Mark was planning to rid his property of the hogs, so he called Shawn and said, "Come on down. I have some nice hogs left. They're at a good size, about a hundred pounds each. Bring the boys and let's go hunt them."

Shawn, Ben, and Jake eagerly made the trip to Sabinal. Although the hogs were not tame, and they could be dangerous, Mark was careful with the boys, making sure that they maintained a healthy respect for the animals.

Wild hogs are among the most destructive, invasive species in the United States today. According to John Morthland, of *Smithsonian* magazine, "Two million to six million of the animals are wreaking havoc in at least 39 states . . . [H]alf are in Texas, where

they do some $400 million in damages annually. They tear up rec-
reational areas, occasionally even terrorizing tourists in state and
national parks, and squeeze out other wildlife. Texas allows hunters to kill wild hogs year-round without limits. . . . The goal is not
eradication, which few believe possible, but control."*

The guys hunted the wild boar with the dogs, rather than
shooting them. They tramped through the woods searching for
the hogs, with the dogs running in every direction, similar to a
foxhunt.

Once the dogs trapped a hog, Shawn yelled to Mark over the
noise and chaos, "Now what? How are you going to kill the hog?"

"I'm going to let Ben spear him," Mark replied, nonchalantly.

Shawn looked at Mark with a squeamish expression. "Oh, I
don't know if Ben will do that or not."

"Yes, I can, Dad!" Ben was already running toward the
trapped hog. Mark pulled out his boar spear and hustled into the
thicket.

The Cold Steel Boar Spear is a double-edged, thirteen-inch
blade, about three inches wide, on a six-foot-long shaft. Standing
perpendicular to the ground, the spear was taller than Ben.

The trick to killing the hog was to pin it right in the chest, so
the blade would sink all the way into the hog's heart. After the
dogs captured the hog, Mark grabbed the boar's hind leg so it
couldn't run. Taking the giant boar spear, Ben thrust it perfectly
into the hog's chest.

Killing the boar instilled a tremendous sense of empower-
ment in Ben. It had required a split-second decision, striking at

---

* John Morthland. "A Plague of Pigs in Texas." *Smithsonian* magazine, (January
2011): http://www.smithsonianmag.com/science-nature/A-Plague-of-Pigs-in-Texas
.html#ixzz2Bkc5HbmP.

just the right time without hesitation, and he had done it without a bit of reluctance.

Mark dipped his thumb into the hog's blood and put a mark on Ben's head, a classic rite-of-passage symbol indicating a hog hunter's success in his first kill. The blood on Ben's forehead proved that he had the intestinal fortitude to spear the hog. He was now initiated into the world of boar hunters, and wore the blood on his forehead all day long. He was not about to wash off that blood! Mark also allowed Ben to "notch" the shaft of the spear with a hunting knife, making a small hash mark on the shaft along with the other notches Mark had made every time he'd scored a kill with the spear. Ben carefully carved his mark on the shaft, feeling accomplished.

Mark then helped him clean the hog, and Ben took home some of the best ham and bacon he'd ever eaten.

• • •

Ben enjoyed hunting, but he was especially fascinated with target shooting, using Mark's collection of guns. Mark taught Ben how to carefully handle a gun, how to carry it, clean it, and care for it, and Ben was a quick study. He followed Mark's instructions to a T. At first, Ben was interested in pellet rifles. Then he moved up to a .22 caliber, and eventually graduated to military rifles.

Over the years, Ben took advantage of any opportunity to go to Mark and Pam's to shoot. He loved being with them, and they loved having him. Not having children of their own, the Kohlers treated Ben as though he were their own son.

When Ben was fourteen, Pam and Mark moved from Sabinal to Yorktown, where they had access to more than 250 acres. Ben would sometimes spend an entire weekend with the Kohlers, honing his target practice with Mark. Never a teenager who sought to avoid adults, he also enjoyed long conversations with Pam.

For the most part, Mark and Ben simply shot paper targets, but since Ben and his friends had grown up playing the Call of Duty video game, he relished shooting military guns such as an AR-15, the modern version of the Vietnam-era M-16 rifle.

That fall, Ben took a trip to Yorktown; he wanted to shoot but also wanted to help the Kohlers get Mark's art on YouTube. During the drive from the Breedloves' home to Yorktown, Ben was rather quiet and subdued in the backseat, which was unusual for him. When he arrived at the ranch, he told Mark, "I don't think it's a good idea for me to walk very far today." Ben's heart had started bumping, and he knew his limitations.

"No problem," Mark said. "We'll stay close to the house and just shoot out back." As soon as Mark and Ben went out of the house, Pam called Deanne to alert her about Ben's condition.

"Ben knows his body pretty well," Deanne responded. "So just let him do what he thinks he can handle, and make sure he gets plenty of rest and water when he needs it."

Mark and Ben did some target shooting next door to Mark's art studio, where he had some steel targets and silhouettes set up. They shot all morning long, and Ben experimented with every gun Mark owned. Mark had recently purchased some four-inch steel paddle targets that swung back and forth when hit. The paddles were rated for handguns. Ben shot the paddles with a pistol, but then he wanted to try the AR-15. Mark knew that the bullets from the military gun would mangle the steel targets, but he couldn't say no to Ben. "Yeah, sure, go ahead," Mark said. "Cut loose on it."

Ben shot nearly thirty rounds with the scoped AR-15 and missed the four-inch paddle targets only twice from one hundred yards away. To say Ben was a budding marksman was an understatement.

Since Ben wasn't feeling well, Mark and Ben spent more time than usual inside that weekend. At one point, the guys sat down to watch a movie. Mark put in *No Country for Old Men*, a movie about a Vietnam vet who finds $2 million after a Texas drug deal goes bad. Laced with profanity, blood, and nastiness, the movie also has overtones of moral themes and was a big hit at the box office.

As they were sitting on the couch watching the movie, Ben observed, "I don't think my parents would really want me to watch this movie."

With a twinkle in his eyes, Mark said, "Your parents aren't here, so don't tell them." The guys laughed, and Pam gave Mark a dirty look. Ben enjoyed the bit of "outlaw" that he shared with Mark.

• • •

When they weren't out shooting, Ben helped Pam and Mark develop a YouTube site to promote their art business. "Let's do a how-to video of you painting a horse," Ben suggested to Mark. "You'll get thousands of hits on it."

Ben and Mark filmed a few outdoorsman videos, with Ben hunting for huge Texas sun spiders, some as large as four and a half inches long. Ben was chunking grasshoppers into the web and filming as the spiders latched onto them. They uploaded the videos to YouTube under the name "Best of Outdoors." Almost immediately, viewers began to respond, sending Ben messages extolling him for his bravery or excoriating him for being so mean to those poor grasshoppers.

Ben read many of the YouTube responses to Pam and Mark, and they all had a good laugh from the project, but decided not to film any more "outdoorsman" videos.

# CHAPTER 13

# SMILE

Hey, I've got nothing to do today but smile

—"THE ONLY LIVING BOY IN NEW YORK" (SIMON AND GARFUNKEL)

Ben smiled as a Mexican mariachi band approached the table singing *"Feliz Cumpleaños."* His entire family watched him turn red with laughter as one of the singers placed a giant sombrero on his head and, when the song concluded, smashed a plateful of whipped cream into Ben's face. Everyone clapped and cheered, opening the night before their favorite vacation to Lake Powell with a family celebration.

They spent the following week basking in peace and quiet on the lake. No telephone, no TV, no chores, no homework—just an endless stretch of blue water and smooth sand rock cliffs, with plenty of fish to catch and lots of family time. There was always something in that peaceful, placid water that could calm Ben's soul. He loved returning to his water.

• • •

A few weeks after turning fifteen, he left those peaceful moments of summer behind and geared up for the academic year. Ben began his freshman year at a new school, Westlake High. Until then, Ben had attended Regents School of Austin, a private, classical-education school, and he was eager to experience a more diverse environment. Ally had made the move earlier and she was flourishing at Westlake. She felt sure Ben would easily adapt as well. Best of all, as far as Ben was concerned, he no longer had to wear uniforms. And of course, he easily talked Justin into making the move along with him.

Westlake required students to take several credits of physical education classes. Most of the kids in PE were enrolled because they had no desire to play other sports, or they were unable to do so—the majority being unable. Always looking to encourage the underdog, Ben noticed a young man in class who was a special-needs student. Other kids teased the boy because he didn't have all the social graces that "normal" kids have. Ben loved him because he was honest and genuine. The young man was always so happy simply to be in the locker room. "Hey, guys!" he'd gush. "Don't you love that we get to be *guys* and just hang out and talk guy talk and *cuss* and just be guys in the locker room?" Some of the boys would snicker at him, but Ben thought he was fun to be around. Whenever he and Ben passed in the hallways or out on the school grounds, they always gave each other a high five.

When Ally received her driver's license, she began driving herself and Ben to school every day. On the morning of their first drive together, Ally was winding down a hill in a quiet neighborhood, focused on getting to school on time, when she heard sirens and saw flashing lights in her rearview mirror. She pulled over to the shoulder and put the car in park. Tears welled in her eyes as she dreaded confronting the lawman. As the oldest child, Ally was never prone to mischief, unlike Ben.

After the officer had returned to his vehicle, Ally inched her car forward, crying and still holding the speeding ticket in her right hand. "Ben," Ally said, sobbing, "what should I do!" Driving did not come easily for Ally, to say the least, and now she was a nervous wreck.

"Well," Ben replied calmly, "you should probably put that ticket down, so you can drive with two hands, and use a tissue so you can see where you're going."

"You're right," Ally said very seriously. "Thanks, Ben."

Ben tried not to laugh as Ally attempted to pull herself together. After turning onto the main road, Ally looked down for a moment to stick the ticket inside the center console.

*Bam!*

"Ohhh, no!" Ally said, beginning to cry again. She had hit the back of a Mercedes SUV. Ben concealed a smile with his hand as Ally climbed out of the car to speak with the driver. Luckily, the Mercedes drove off unscathed, but Ben and Ally would drive every day from then on with a severely dented bumper.

Despite the fiasco, that morning marked the first of many car rides to school during which Ben and Ally grew even closer. Through speeding tickets, wrecks, and even her first boyfriend breakup, Ben was always a source of encouragement to Ally. He was there to tell her that she still looked pretty on the days when she didn't have time to put on makeup, and he was there to tell her she was being dramatic by singing Taylor Swift at the top of her lungs after a bad day. With a forty-five-minute drive

together every morning, and more than an hour-long drive together in traffic every afternoon, Ben and Ally became closer
than ever.

And, of course, they bonded over their mutual love-hate relationship with the 1990 Acura Legend they shared. The old white
sedan was two years Ally's senior, and with its newly crushed
bumper, it was the perfect teenage clunker. Complete with ma-
roon leather interior, a cassette tape player, and a glove box that
had dry-rotted out of its compartment and onto the floor, it truly
was a gem.

Once, the hood started smoking and the transmission went
out while Ally was driving. She had lost control of both the steering and the brakes, and fearing that the car would catch fire, she
and Ben jumped out and watched it roll down the street to a stop.
After that incident, the Acura would start only half the time, so
Ben and Ally spent most of their afternoons trying to jump-start
the car in the school parking lot.

The Acura's finest quality, however, was the horn. On the
steering wheel were placed four buttons, each displaying the em-
blem of a trumpet. At random, whenever Ben was looking for a
laugh, he would yell out, "Rapid-fire honks!" and begin pressing
all four buttons as fast as he could, firing off honks that sounded
like something from a video game.

· · ·

Each year the school requested that medical forms be filled out
for every student, so Deanne meticulously completed the medical
questionnaire, writing in large, capital, highlighted letters describing Ben's condition. She also attached a copy of his cardiolo-

gists' most recent report. She then would call the school nurse to make sure they had everything they needed.

Over the years, as the school nurses grew to know Ben, they became proactive about calling Deanne at the beginning of the school year to check in. Any change in Ben's health status or medications warranted a new phone call and recording it in the health records. This happened several times a year.

During his elementary and middle school years, Regents officials even pulled Ben out of class before a fire drill or any situation that might be alarming to him, to avoid startling his heart. Regents was also one of the first schools in the Austin area to install an automated external defibrillator (AED), even before it became popular to do so in schools, airports, and other public places. They were very proactive in being prepared for an emergency.

Exercising their own precautions, anytime Shawn and Deanne went out of town overnight or longer, they left behind notarized paperwork designating which adults were in charge of their kids, detailed medical and contact information, and an explanation of Ben's health and medications. If Ben went out of town with anyone else, Deanne phoned ahead to find out all emergency information, which hospital was closest, and whether it was equipped to handle pediatric cardiac patients. She would then forward all Ben's medical information to the people in charge wherever Ben was going. Most important, she made sure to send along the family's personal AED in case of an emergency.

Back home, there wasn't a need to inform parents of anything, since most of Ben's friends' families knew of his condition. Beyond that, Ben was good about monitoring himself, so it wasn't necessary to give much information to the parents. Knowing that he always had his cell phone with him eased his parents' minds, as well.

· · ·

During the spring of Ben's freshman year at Westlake, his heart began bumping more frequently. Consequently, he missed fifty-two days of school out of ninety during the spring semester alone.

Keeping up in school became extremely challenging for Ben. Westlake is known for its rigorous academic program, and although Ben was a bright, highly capable student, when his heart started bumping, his energy level diminished, and it became a daunting task merely to maintain his physical equilibrium, much less his homework assignments and grade point average.

He was constantly seeking out friends from whom he could borrow reliable classroom notes in his attempts to catch up with the material covered. When he felt well enough to go back to school—which could be as long as nine or ten days later following a bumping bout—he would have to arrive early, prior to the start of classes every morning, so he could go to the testing center and make up all the quizzes and tests he had missed. Then, after school, he met with teachers or friends to go over other assignments he may have missed and try to catch up—and he did all of this while learning the *current* work! These would make for some long, wearisome days, especially coming on the heels of periods when he felt so weak and tired because of his heart bumping.

Some teachers were patient and understanding and tried to help Ben as much as they could. Others, not so much. After a while, the overload of schoolwork weighed him down, and Ben realized that trying to keep up with the rest of the kids was almost impossible. He found it easier not to prioritize his schoolwork. Some of his teachers understood his immense challenges, but the ones who did not tended to chalk up his falling behind to laziness. Nothing could be farther from the truth, but his losing the motivation to do well in those classes simply exacerbated the problem. He was still passing his classes and maintaining a good GPA, and was definitely on track for graduation, but he had to work twice as hard as other kids just to keep his head above water.

Deanne frequently interceded on Ben's behalf with some of his teachers who were less understanding. She tried to explain that Ben was doing his best and working under unusual duress. It was a constant balancing act for her, trying to convey vital information about Ben's condition and its effects on his academic performance to the faculty members and administrators without coming off as an overly protective mother.

Although driving did not physically affect Ben's heart, his parents were nonetheless concerned. Ben's doctor requested that the Texas Department of Motor Vehicles issue Ben a handicap placard that he could hang on the rearview mirror of his car, allowing him special parking privileges, because sometimes Ben was too weak to walk from his car across the long, steeply inclined parking lot into the school. Occasionally, just the cold autumn weather caused his heart to overexert itself, causing Ben to nearly faint. The placard permitted Ben to park in a "handicap" parking spot close to the building. But sometimes when Ben arrived at school, all the handicap spots were taken, so he parked in a visitors' parking place, which was also situated close to the front doors of the school. He'd hang his placard and go on to class.

The campus security guards repeatedly gave Ben tickets for parking in the visitors' spots. Ben racked up a number of parking violations, each one costing forty dollars, a hefty penalty for a high school student. It was not unusual for Ben to have a hundred and twenty dollars' worth of tickets on the books until he could go to the administrative offices, explain the situation, and have the tickets cleared. The administration was good about voiding the violations, but the inconvenience was an irritation Ben didn't need.

Adding to the pressure, Ben was forced to seek tutoring after school just to cope with his workload, as well as going to school an hour early for makeup quizzes and tests. Increasingly, Ben was physically and mentally exhausted simply from trying to maintain his regular routines. Many people didn't understand why he couldn't keep up.

He looked normal to fellow students who saw him as he slipped out of his car parked in the handicap parking spot. Some eyed him suspiciously, as if he were violating the rules. He looked normal while he talked to a teacher, asking whether he could have more time than other students were allowed to make up a test. Others just did not understand the internal battle in which he was constantly engaged. Being capable of good grades, but being labeled "lazy" by some teachers wore on him.

Few people apart from Ben's closest friends and family members saw the challenges he faced. Often, even sitting still at home, reading through a history assignment, Ben experienced enormous difficulty. His heart would be beating irregularly the whole time, unnerving and distracting him, making it hard for him to concentrate on his schoolwork, much less breathe. He tried his best to ignore his body's inconvenient interruptions; he had little choice. Ben wanted to excel and did, insofar as he could physically.

When the arrhythmia made Ben too fatigued to carry out his chores around the house, he knew he could always count on his little brother. After Jake had done Ben the favor of taking out the trash or dragging the trampoline out of the way of the lawn mower, Ben always presented him with a special reward, which they called "the item," at the end of the day to thank him for his help.

"Is it ready?" Jake squealed one night, anticipating the brotherly ritual. Lying in bed on the bottom bunk, Jake peeked out from under the covers.

"Here it comes!" Ben shouted from the top bunk.

Jake watched as a tiny box lowered down to his level, dangling from a string. He clasped the box in his hands and untied the surprise parcel. Inside, Jake found his item, a shiny, red Swiss army knife.

"Thanks, Ben!" Jake exclaimed, adding the gadget to his collection of other gifts he had received in return for his help. After the presentation, Ben always fell asleep with a smile on his face, heartened by the bond of their brotherhood.

•  •  •

Throughout Ben's freshman year, the arrhythmia continued.

It was frustrating and sad for Deanne to be caught in the middle, knowing better than anybody about Ben's difficult struggle to stay academically viable, yet trying to appease the teachers and make them understand that he actually cared about learning, but that he couldn't produce at his formerly high level anymore. He did his best to keep up, but decided it wasn't worth it to always give schoolwork his all. He still maintained a B average, and though he knew he was intellectually capable of making an A, the difference in grades cost more than he was willing to pay.

At times, when Ben missed school, because Deanne felt sorry for him she allowed him to spend too much time on YouTube or playing Xbox games. When Shawn noticed this, he became concerned. He wasn't upset with Ben, but as a businessman, he realized the highly competitive nature of the outside world. Shawn recognized that Ben would probably have a family to support someday. A college degree could help him secure a decent income, and to gain entrance at a good college, Ben needed to have good grades in high school.

His parents grappled constantly with how they could help Ben maneuver in this competitive world despite his physical limitations without setting him up to fail. How could they empathize with Ben, yet properly motivate him so they didn't enable him to become a victim and not try?

After taking these concerns to Ben's school counselor, Deanne learned about Section 504, an accommodation made by Texas public schools that allowed students with special needs or health impediments to request specific accommodations unique to each student to help them keep up with their schoolwork. Thanks to Section 504, Ben was permitted to receive classroom lecture notes directly from the teacher rather than relying on other students' notes. He could have as many days as he needed to make up assignments instead of only a few days. He was allowed to waive any "busywork" assignments as long as he could pass the quiz or test. This didn't solve all of his academic challenges, but it definitely provided a means of staying in the game.

College was going to be a tricky consideration. Pursuing a post–high school degree by attending a university did not rank high on Ben's priority list. But throughout his lifetime, Shawn and Deanne always talked as if each of their children would go on to college or some form of higher education. That was a given; everyone in the family assumed that Ally, Ben, and Jake would continue their education beyond high school.

When the time came for Ally to move away for college, she was heartbroken to leave Ben behind. Ever since becoming best friends during their early childhood, the two of them had shared life together every day. Ben missed Ally as soon as she left, but they texted almost every day, and talked on the phone nearly every week. When Ally visited home for the holidays, it was if nothing had changed and no time had passed. Ben would confide in her, and she would offer him advice from a female perspective. Distance could never change their close relationship.

• • •

As Ben's college days approached, he faced new challenges. Could he manage a college course load while missing half of the semester? His most likely college choice at the time was Texas State University in San Marcos. It had a good curriculum, it was close to home, and it was located near a team of medical caregivers he needed. Ben was also attracted to Texas State because a cable waterski park was located nearby. Clearly Ben intended to have fun while he was in college!

The drawback to Texas State for Ben was that the picturesque campus was poised on a beautiful hilltop. Moving around campus meant climbing hills all day, and Ben was no longer physically able to do that.

Consequently, he and his parents had not yet settled on a plan for his college. They were still looking at options. Because of Ben's love for making videos, one alternative was for him to possibly move to Los Angeles, take a year off before starting college, and work as an intern in the film industry with his high school best friend, Grant Hamill, whose uncle wrote and acted for the show *Scrubs* at the time. He wasn't sure how it would all come together, but Ben always spoke as though he believed he had a full and exciting future ahead of him.

# CHAPTER 14

# THE SHOW GOES ON

All right, already, the show goes on

—"THE SHOW GOES ON" (LUPE FIASCO)

Ben's family, as well as his doctors, constantly looked for ways to help Ben accomplish his goal of functioning normally, but the HCM didn't always cooperate. Just after Christmas 2008, Dr. Rowe suggested that Ben go into the cath lab, a specialized surgery room containing equipment used by cardiologists to insert a catheter into the heart, for a relatively routine surgical procedure to measure the pressures in his heart. The exam would determine whether Ben was a candidate for a heart transplant, or if he had passed the window of opportunity to be a transplant recipient. Once the pressures in the heart become too high, a heart transplant is insufficient; at that point, the patient requires a heart-*lung* transplant.

Undergoing the procedure was not exactly what Ben wanted to be doing during his holiday break. The surgery was scheduled to take place during the week right after Christmas and just before New Year's, typically a fun, relaxing week for most. Ben, however, would spend his holiday in the hospital.

Regardless of the disheartening situation, Ben walked into the cath lab with a big smile and the attitude, *Bring it on! Let's get this over with so I can get back to better things.*

In previous surgeries, Ben was allowed to remain with his parents in a preoperative room, and was administered medication to help him fall asleep before being wheeled back into surgery. He rarely saw the surgical room. The operative protocol was different for teenage patients. This time, Ben would be asked to walk straight into the surgery room, alone, and without any medication to ease his anxiety.

Dressed in his hospital gown, Ben said good-bye to his parents and walked through the giant doors, where he was asked to lie down on the surgical table. As he did so, anxiety caught up with him. His heart began to race and he became light-headed. The surgical staff could see on the heart monitor that Ben's heart rate had increased drastically, above two hundred beats per minute. The staff discussed whether they should even proceed with the surgery, but soon Ben's anxiety was soothed away by the anesthesia.

During the cath lab procedure, Ben's blood pressure dropped dangerously low. His heart was not pumping sufficient blood. The doctors were forced to cardiovert him back by using an electric current to restore Ben's heart to a normal rhythm. They had measured the pressures on one side of his heart and found they were still within a reasonable range for a transplant, but when

Ben's pressure dropped, they had to abort the procedure without having an opportunity to measure the other side of his heart.

Deanne was waiting alone in the surgery lobby when she got the news that Ben's blood pressure had dropped so drastically. She was immediately overcome with concern for Ben. This was supposed to be a relatively routine test. Dr. Johnson, an attending cardiologist involved with the surgery, called her immediately from the surgical room, and then met Deanne in the lobby to explain further. Speaking with deep compassion, Dr. Johnson said that Ben's heart was just too sensitive and reactive to the procedure they were doing, so they were not going to continue. He explained that it was a serious event that had occurred, but reassured Deanne that Ben had recovered and seemed to be doing well, even though he was still under anesthesia.

It was a full thirty minutes before Ben came to and Deanne could go into the recovery room to see him. Fortunately, he was okay. But this occasion was a strong reminder that there was no such thing as a "routine surgery" for Ben.

• • •

The following Friday, Ally drove over to her best friend Rachel's house to hang out. Most of their friends had vacationed out of town over the holiday, so the girls spent the night talking and spending time together at Rachel's home. Late that night, they were sitting on Rachel's bed, browsing StumbleUpon on her laptop, when Rachel noticed a tiny, silent tear trickling down Ally's cheek.

"Ally! What's wrong?" Rachel asked, concerned. She was taken aback by Ally's sudden change in mood. They had been laughing together just minutes before.

As Ally looked back at Rachel with watery eyes, her lips began to tremble. "Rachel, I'm sorry," she began, her throat tightening. "I was just thinking about Ben. You know he had that minor surgery last week, and he barely made it through. It was such a minor surgery, and he barely made it," Ally repeated the words, as if to herself. "I asked my mom about it when she and Ben came home from the hospital. Obviously, something went wrong—something went wrong with *Ben*. My mom wouldn't tell me much, other than that they had to abort the surgery, so I told her, 'Mom, I *know* something is wrong with Ben. I know that surgery shouldn't have been serious,' and I asked her to please tell me what was happening to Ben's heart . . . and if he's going to be okay. I eventually got her to tell me that Ben is beginning to experience heart failure. That doesn't mean that his heart is going to fail right now, but it's beginning to fail slowly. He went through a major growth spurt this year, now that he's in high school, and his body is starting to get too big for his heart. His heart is having to work twice as hard now. His heart is too weak for his body."

Ally paused, seeming to absorb the reality of everything she had just explained. She looked up at Rachel with fear in her eyes. "Rachel . . . I think Ben is going to die." Before Ally could take a breath, Rachel's arms were wrapped around her, and both of them were sobbing.

Holding hands, the two of them fell asleep as Rachel prayed for peace and healing in their lives.

• • •

By the spring of Ben's freshman year of high school, his arrhythmia became so persistent, his doctors suggested that it was time to consider implanting a pacemaker within his chest to automatically regulate his heartbeats.

Ben was normally quite compliant with the doctors' plans and his parents' concerns, but he hit a wall when it came to the pacemaker. For the first time, he expressed his opinion on medical treatments and strongly resisted the implantation of a pacemaker. Other treatments were internal; the pacemaker would be visible evidence of his condition. The pacemaker would be concrete, tangible—a constant reminder for Ben and everyone close to him that his heart condition had evolved from a concept to an everyday reality for him. What had previously been unseen would then be seen; what had been Ben's private battle would be on public display. And Ben recoiled from the idea.

The pacemaker issue was a tough one for Deanne and Shawn, sorely testing their commitment to allow Ben to make as many of the calls in his life as possible. They felt it was important that Ben feel ownership over his own body. They believed it was essential for his dignity to allow him to have the final say in this situation. It was his body, his life, and it would be his pain and inconvenience if the pacemaker produced adverse effects. They sincerely pondered, *Do we dare let him make the decision, realizing he doesn't have the life experience to know how important it is that he receive the pacemaker?* Detailed, serious, mature conversations took place around the family dining table, as they reviewed the benefits as well as the possible drawbacks and consequences of this decision.

This time of parental contemplation combined with Ben's ambivalence kept delaying the decision, stretching it from one month to another. Meanwhile, the doctors prescribed another drug, Sotalol, to help control Ben's arrhythmia, which continued to negatively affect his quality of life. The medication worked for a short while, providing the family with false hope that the pacemaker decision might be a moot point, but the arrhythmia proved persistent.

During one of Ben's many medical visits, the doctor reminded the family of the seriousness of atrial fibrillation. "During fibrillation, the heart cannot pump blood effectively, allowing it to pool in the heart and potentially form clots that can move to the brain and cause strokes."

Ben knew that he was at risk for sudden death with HCM, but now he was reminded he was at significantly increased risk for stroke, which could affect his basic body functions, such as movement, speech, swallowing, vision, cognitive abilities, and much more. The reasons for getting the arrhythmia under control were numerous, but Ben still did not like the idea of having to be dependent upon some strange internal machine to function properly.

Several people, including Ben's aunt Lois, suggested that Ben should talk to someone who actually had a pacemaker-defibrillator implanted—and they knew Matt Nader would be the right person to share some real-life experiences with Ben. Matt was a former student and stellar offensive lineman on the football team at Westlake High School—the same school Ben attended. Matt was young, six feet, six inches tall, and three hundred pounds of solid muscle, and was well liked by everyone at Westlake.

On a hot, humid Texas night in September 2006, with his sights set on a college scholarship and a future career in the NFL, Matt had trotted slowly to the sidelines after a long second-quarter drive during a high school football game between Westlake and College Station. He flopped down onto the bench, then collapsed backward. He wasn't breathing and his heart had stopped beating.

With Matt dying on the football field, some Westlake parents—including his own—who possessed medical expertise rushed from the stands and performed CPR. A cardiologist came out of the crowd and fortunately found an AED nearby, right on the sidelines. The doctor used the defibrillator to shock Matt's heart back into rhythm, reviving him. Matt was then rushed to the hospital, where it was discovered that he had suffered from ventricular fibrillation, a potentially catastrophic event. Had the defibrillator not been readily available, Matt's life would have been over. Three days after the harrowing episode during the game, surgeons installed an internal defibrillator in his chest.

Ironically, Matt had already been offered, and had accepted, a full football scholarship to play for the University of Texas Longhorns, but with this new health condition, he was unable to fulfill his part of the deal. The university honored their offer to him and created a position for him as a student assistant so he could remain connected to the team without ever playing a down. Matt was able to attend UT and help with the team. Everyone in Austin, it seemed, admired Matt Nader; he was known as the kid who died on the football field and was brought back to life.

Matt agreed to talk to Ben about what it was like to have a pacemaker. They met at Texas Honey Ham, a local hangout, and while they shared many similarities because of their heart problems, the visual contrast between the two young men was in stark relief. Matt was huge, healthy, and energetic; Ben was small, frail, and listless. His skin coloring was pallid, too, another effect of the arrhythmia.

Despite their differences, they shared a common bond, so Matt was glad to be of help, and Ben listened intently to all Matt had to say about the pros and cons of having a defibrillator implanted in his chest—even the scary parts.

For instance, Matt told Ben that he felt so good after the pacemaker was implanted, he was convinced he could still play football at the college level. He began training again, rebuilding his strength. He knew he was getting faster, stronger. The summer of his freshman year in college, Matt was running wind sprints during an unofficial workout with some Texas linemen when everything went dark on him. But the defibrillator detected the problem and sent a current to Matt's heart. Although that bittersweet experience ended Matt's dreams that he could continue his football career, a defibrillator had saved his life again.

Another incident, Matt told Ben, wasn't so positive. "The defibrillator is good; it is going to save your life. You don't have a choice, buddy. But I'll be honest with you: One time it went off and misfired. I was working out when something malfunctioned. I felt this shock, and it hurt so bad that I thought I had been shot. I looked around to see who had shot me; then I felt another shock, and because it had just started to rain, I thought I'd been struck by lightning. Then I realized it was my defibrillator going off and I couldn't stop it. It went off about eight times, and it hurt like crazy." He told Ben that his defibrillator had to be recalled and replaced, but it was still worth the trouble.

A few days later, Ben announced to his family that he thought he should go ahead with the procedure. The date was set for May 5, 2009. Dr. Arnold L. Fenrich, the newest doctor to join Ben's team, implanted a pacemaker/defibrillator in Ben's chest.

Ben's first postoperation comment upon being settled into his hospital room was, "Does everyone who gets a pacemaker always feel this refreshed?"

Everyone around Ben laughed out loud, relieved that the operation was already having a positive effect on him. Ben felt good; he was optimistic about his future, and he was ready to continue living his life.

# CHAPTER 15

# LIVE YOUR LIFE

Stop lookin' at what you ain't got
Start bein' thankful for what you do got

—"LIVE YOUR LIFE" (T.I. FEATURING RIHANNA)

"I'll give one hundred dollars to the first person in our family who learns how to do a flip on the wakeboard!" Deanne exclaimed with a big smile on her face.

Ben was up for the challenge. After his pacemaker implantation, he was rejuvenated by newfound energy, and he was ready to expend it. Ben became the first Breedlove to do a flip on the wakeboard that summer, and once he did, he couldn't be stopped.

By September, Ben had not only turned sixteen and was back on the lake wakeboarding, but he felt better than ever. Using a ski rope and the trampoline near the big tree in the backyard, Ally's boyfriend, Cameron Thompson, taught Ben all sorts of maneuvers. Ben practiced simulated jumps on the trampoline that he hoped to do on the water, and even taught himself how to do a back roll—first on the trampoline, then on the wakeboard. The pacemaker made this possible by controlling Ben's heart rate and helping his heart pump effectively, allowing his body to provide the oxygen he needed to have energy. Being able to athletically perform those difficult jumps and back rolls on the wakeboard was one of Ben's favorite milestones. He was so excited that he taught Jake how to do a series of complicated jumps on the trampoline as well. By the end of the summer, Jake looked like an Olympic gymnast, doing amazing twists and turns and flips on the trampoline.

That summer, Ben had taken lessons from professional wakeboarders and wakesurfers Billy Garcia and Chase Hazen. The pros loved Lake Austin, so the placid cool water was popular for wakeboard competitions as well as the filming of commercials. One of the pros with whom Ben became friends was Holland Finley, and they loved getting out on the lake together.

Ben had received his wakeboard as a birthday gift that summer. It was a Liquid Force board, with his favorite Shane Bonifay boots, named after another professional wakeboarder. Following each run, Ben would bring his board inside and lean it against his bedroom wall.

Wakeboarding and wakesurfing were Ben's release. He could decompress out on the water. He could leave behind his anxieties of deadlines, schedules, and to-do lists. He could spend time with his friends, competing with his peers on the same level, and he excelled, boosting his self-confidence and vastly making up for the opportunities he missed by not being able to play other contact sports. Skimming across the water on a wakeboard, Ben felt free. He could feel his body working, flexing, moving, stretching. He pressed the outer limits of what his body could endure. He was living on the edge of his physical limitations, and he loved it.

Two weeks earlier, Ben had been wakeboarding and had injured his right knee. The knee was swollen so badly that he couldn't straighten out his leg. He had just recovered from walking with crutches, so he really wasn't supposed to be wakeboarding again so soon. Although he felt revitalized by his pacemaker, his new physical limits remained uncertain.

Nevertheless, when Ben and his friend Grant Hamill had a chance to host Holland Finley for a day of wakeboarding on the lake, they weren't about to miss that opportunity. With Grant driving the boat and Holland "spotting," Ben was jumping over the wake when he landed in just the wrong way. His tibia fractured right at the top of his boot. He could feel the break as soon as it happened. He later said that while lying in the water waiting to be rescued, as the waves moved his leg, he could feel the bone grinding inside.

Seeing the accident, Holland immediately dived into the water and pulled Ben to the boat and up onto the platform. She had seen numerous similar wakeboarding accidents, so she knew that despite the pain of a broken leg, the stiff, tight wakeboard boot needed to come off before the leg began swelling.

Shawn had left the house and was driving up City Park Road when he received a call from Grant.

"Mr. Breedlove, we're getting close to the dock, and I think Ben broke his leg."

"Okay, Grant. Have you tried to reach Mrs. Breedlove? She's there at home."

"I called the house and nobody answered the phone."

"Okay, I'm turning around, and I'm coming back to the house right now," Shawn said. "Try Mrs. Breedlove again." Shawn drove home and went straight to the boat dock.

About that time, Deanne happened to look out her bedroom window and noticed the boat floating in the water near their dock. *Awesome! Looks like they are having a great time this morning!* she thought.

Just then, her telephone rang. "Mrs. Breedlove," a familiar voice said.

"Yes?"

"This is Grant."

"Hi, Grant! I can see you guys out by the dock," Deanne said, looking out the window. "Looks like you're having fun. What's up?"

"Mrs. Breedlove, I'm sorry to tell you this, but we think Ben broke his leg."

The three wakeboarders were still in the boat right behind the Breedlove home, so it took only seconds for Deanne to get to the dock after receiving Grant's call. She found Shawn already there and Ben sitting on the back of the boat platform, watching his leg and ankle beginning to swell and discolor. He was shaking, because the water was so cold at that time of year, and he was grimacing in pain. Deanne threw a towel around him and called for an ambulance. As they waited for the paramedics to arrive, rather than try to move Ben, they all huddled on the back of the boat, attempting to calm his shivering and keep him warm. Suddenly, Ben stopped shaking, turned, and, with a straight face, looked at Deanne and said very seriously, "I'm just joking. My leg isn't broken."

*What?* Deanne stared back at Ben, stunned, not knowing whether she was relieved or angry. "Ben!"

"No, I'm kidding. It really is broken, Mom, and it hurts like crazy!" Ben returned to shaking, satisfied that he had pranked his mom and momentarily relieved the pain.

Later that day, Grant visited Ben in the hospital. Ben's leg was in a cast and he was disappointed that he was missing a school dance. To commiserate with his buddy, Grant skipped it, too, and hung out at the hospital with Ben instead. But that didn't mean they couldn't have some fun. They soon convinced the nurse to find a wheelchair so that they could do tricks with it out in the hall. Not even a broken leg was going to keep Ben down for long.

Ben's wheelchair was an item of interest when he returned to Westlake. He loved trying to do wheelies going down the hall. His buddies enjoyed watching him, so naturally Ben willingly shared the wheelchair with them, allowing them to attempt tricks in the halls and in the school parking lot. In no time at all, he and the guys destroyed the wheelchair and Ben had to get a new one.

Within a few weeks, he graduated from the wheelchair to using crutches. He hoped to be free of the crutches by homecoming, but he wasn't. No problem. Dressed in a formal suit, Ben joined a group of his friends, including Katelyn Brooks, Alex Faglie, and Grant Hamill, and went to the homecoming dance anyhow. Ben couldn't really dance due to his heavy cast, but he gamely got out on the dance floor and wobbled back and forth on his crutches.

• • •

Grant and Ben were the best of friends, but they always made room for Alex—a talented female dancer who aspired to perform professionally. Ben and Grant often attended her dance recitals to support and encourage her. The three of them were constantly together, hanging out. When the guys talked about moving to California and trying to get an internship with Grant's uncle on the *Scrubs* set, they naturally assumed that at some point, Alex would join them and pursue her dancing career in LA.

Alex's sense of humor matched Ben's so well, they frequently joked that she was the female version of Ben. They connected on both meaningful matters and mundane.

• • •

"Mom, can we go get some Wally's fried chicken for Alex?" Ben asked.

Deanne had picked up Ben from school for a midday appointment with his cardiologist, and they had just hopped in the car to return to Westlake. "Ben, Wally's is on the other side of town," Deanne responded.

"I know, Mom, but you don't understand. Wally's would make Alex *so* happy. Literally, it would make her day." Ben turned to Deanne with a smile so big, she couldn't refuse.

"Okay, fine. You win," Deanne said, shaking her finger at Ben. "But it had better make her *really* happy!"

Ben and Alex had found that good fried chicken could make most bad days seem okay. Whenever Alex had a bad day, Ben would take her to one of his favorite fast-food restaurants, where they would talk through their stresses and concerns. As their trust deepened, Alex admitted to Ben that she lacked confidence in her ability to one day make it as a professional dance performer, and that one of her greatest fears was being held back from pursuing her passion. Always sitting in their favorite booth, where they would munch on chicken fingers and shakes, Ben and Alex opened up to each other. Together they began to realize how to let go of their anxieties, and what really mattered in their lives.

CHAPTER 16

# WHO SAID WE'RE WACK

Who said we're wack?
You said we're wack?

—"WHO SAID WE'RE WACK" (THE LONELY ISLAND)

P ranks were part and parcel of Ben's personality. Ben Breedlove was rarely serious; far from it, he loved to make people laugh. His lips turned quickly into a smile, and his mind was constantly thinking up some new prank he and his buddies could pull.

A few weeks before Halloween, during his sophomore year of high school, Ben found a scary rubber clown mask that attracted his attention. Since most of his family members were not fans of clowns *at all*, they found Ben's fascination with the frightening clown mask all the creepier. Despite their protests, Ben loved the mask and donned it often during the Halloween season.

His goal, of course, was not to scare people but to evoke a response. One day, for example, Ben put on the mask and then sat in a chair at a busy intersection in Westlake. While he was sitting there with his face completely covered by the mask, a woman stopped her car right next to him and called out of her window, "Can you tell me where the closest gas station is?" as if everything were perfectly normal. Without removing the clown mask, Ben obliged her and gave her directions. She pulled away, never addressing the fact that a guy wearing a clown mask might not be the most reliable source of information.

Ben also received a text from one of his female friends, who said, "Ben! We just saw you sitting at the intersection in your mask!" People recognized him even inside that mask.

On Halloween, he was coming home from a neighbor's house. While driving through the neighborhood, he decided to wear his mask. A car filled with teenage girls was in front of him, driving slowly, so Ben turned on the overhead light inside his car to better illuminate his mask. When the girls saw that a creepy clown was following them, they started screaming and ducking down in the car! Just the reaction Ben was hoping for.

• • •

Ben, Justin, and their friends would sometimes dress in the life-size gorilla and bunny costumes and stage "incidents" around town. Usually Ben was the guy behind the video camera, filming the event and the reaction of the people who witnessed it. Once, he, Justin, and their friend J.P. staged a wrestling match between the bunny and the gorilla right in front of the doors of a Randalls grocery store, tumbling around in the entrance and spilling out into the parking lot. Ben pretended to be an innocent bystander, shocked at the altercation. In actuality, he was staying close to the action so he could film the incident on his phone.

The fight went on, with people in cars honking their horns, as other people stood by laughing hysterically, or appalled. Finally, the gorilla—Justin—wrestled the bunny—J.P.—into the traffic lane, blocking traffic and causing even more havoc. The fight culminated with the gorilla snapping the bunny's neck and leaving him in the middle of the intersection as customers tried to get by. Ben, of course, captured the entire escapade on video.

In the same shopping center, Alex Faglie was copying some photos at Kinkos, working on a project, when she received a text message from Ben. "Where are you?" Ben asked.

"In Kinkos," Alex texted back, and resumed her copying.

A few minutes later, someone in a giant white bunny suit burst through the Kinkos entrance, hoisted Alex over his shoulder, and carried her out, leaving her school supplies at the copier.

"What's going on?" Alex screamed, laughing hysterically, assuming that Ben was involved somehow. Alex began kicking and squirming, trying to get out of the bunny's grasp, all to no avail. The bunny ignored her, whisking her away before a storeful of astonished Kinkos patrons.

Once outside, Alex saw Ben laughing and filming the "kidnapping."

Another time, Ben and Justin drove around town wearing the costumes, just talking to anybody who would stop and listen to them. Dressed as the bunny and the gorilla, they would go through fast-food restaurant drive-throughs, ordering food as if nothing were out of the ordinary. Amazingly, most people who saw them acted as though what they were doing was perfectly normal, that there was nothing unusual about a huge white bunny and a gorilla ordering some tacos!

Of course, Ben was always up for a taco, with or without a costume. In his senior scrapbook—which he never had time to finish—Ben expressed his love for his favorite food. *Taco Bell! Where to begin? Definitely my favorite place to eat. All my family gives me gift cards to Taco Bell for birthdays and stuff. It's only two months into school and I have already gone through $60 worth! I will stop by Taco Bell almost every day after school and sometimes go there for lunch, too. My friends think it's so weird, but I don't care!*

Ben even made going to Taco Bell an event, rapping his order, freestyle, into the drive-through microphone:

> *I'd like two tacos,*
> *chicken and cheese,*
> *I don't need lettuce,*
> *And no tomatoes, please!*

Ben's sense of humor knew no boundaries. Ben and a friend were driving around town one day when they randomly came across a local Ferrari Club. The Ferrari owners had their immaculately clean and shiny cars parked in a long, neat row, with the cars' hoods popped open to display the amazing engines. Each beaming owner proudly stood by his or her car, ready to talk with other owners, admirers, or auto aficionados.

Ben and his friend couldn't resist. They drove to the end of the long line of beautiful cars, where Ben parked his own luxurious auto—the twenty-year-old Acura Legend, now even more dilapidated than when Ally first drove it. Ben popped his hood and proudly took the appropriate stance, with his hand on his waist, his head slightly cocked to the side, as he stood in front of his car. Several Ferrari owners loved his sense of humor, so they came over and asked him questions and talked to him about his old beater! One car buff even took Ben's photo with his "vintage automobile."

• • •

Ben could win over almost anyone with his humor, even some of the toughest crowds. His football buddies were usually too occupied with practice and schoolwork to ever make plans, but one weekend when practice had been canceled, they all ended up hanging out together. Although Ben was glad to see a few of his close friends, he didn't have much in common with most of the other players, and they didn't have much to say to one another.

They had all been sitting around on the couch on this particularly boring night, complaining about having nothing to do, when Ben received a text from one of his girlfriends. "Hey," Ben spoke up to the guys, "I can invite some girls over, if y'all want."

"Yeah, do that," one of the football players responded. About ten minutes later, an enormous party bus pulled into the driveway. The doors opened, and twenty-one girls, all wearing white dresses, filed out of the bus and into the house. "*What* is happening!" the same football player shouted, looking incredulously at Ben. "Dude, you got *all* of those girls to come over?"

Ben didn't tell the guy that he had no idea that twenty-one girls were going to show up. He had invited the one girlfriend he had been texting, but she didn't tell him that she just happened to be driving home from a retreat on a party bus with all of her best friends. Regardless, Ben was happy to take the credit. Nonchalantly, Ben responded, "Oh, yeah. That was me."

# CHAPTER 17

# LIFE KEEPS COMIN'

Been gettin' tired of my motor runnin'
Feelin' overheated 'cause my life keeps comin'

—"SAD SAD CITY" (GHOSTLAND OBSERVATORY)

Even with the pacemaker, Ben's arrhythmia eventually broke through, disappointing Ben and threatening to break the family's spirits as well. During the spring of 2010, Ben's heart bumped for nine straight days, causing him to miss school again. Dr. Fenrich decided to take him into surgery and use his own implanted defibrillator to shock his heart rhythms back to normal. It worked. But both Ben's doctors and his family members were discouraged to learn that the pacemaker wasn't a cure-all.

In many ways, Ben was unusually mature for his age at every stage of his life. Perhaps constantly dealing with a life-threatening disease caused him to cultivate more of an adult perspective on life than some of his peers. Maybe that's why he rarely obsessed over who won the big game, or what the world was currently preoccupied with. Or possibly it was because Ben was emotionally and spiritually grounded. Whatever the reason, he didn't resort to impulsive emotional outlets. He managed his emotions with maturity and in an appropriate manner. He would just go have a lot of fun to release some energy. He enjoyed hanging out with friends, temporarily escaping the world of schedules, doctors, and medicines.

Occasionally Ben pushed back against his parents' desires to protect him, but always in a benign manner. Rather than overtly disobeying their instructions, Ben asked their opinions about certain activities he wanted to do. If he was across town at a friend's house for the night, and he had forgotten to take his medicine, he would ask whether it was okay that he skip the medication for that night. He appreciated Shawn and Deanne's protection.

As he grew older, he questioned his parents' advice and protective prohibitions more vigorously. *Why would it be so bad to eat some pot stickers with soy sauce? What's wrong with wakesurfing early in the morning when the water temperature is a brisk sixty-five degrees? How is this new treatment going to help me or make a difference?*

Where he formerly had an attitude of acceptance and acquiescence regarding the medical protocols administered to him, he slowly evolved into wanting more control of his own destiny, and more say involving the decisions made on his behalf.

For their part, Shawn and Deanne constantly struggled to maintain the balance between wisely overseeing Ben's activities and allowing him to engage in the more adventurous and potentially dangerous activities that he loved.

In his later teens, Ben joined Gold's Gym, with Shawn's full knowledge. Shawn even went so far as to help him pay for the membership! Deanne, however, was not thrilled with the idea, and let everyone know every night at dinner.

Ben worked out most days after school, insisting that he knew his own body and would listen to any signs of stress. He met with a friend, Shaddy, a weight lifter who worked out several times a week at the gym. Ben frequently overextended himself in his exercise regimen—against his parents' wishes.

Deanne and Shawn suspected that Ben sometimes exceeded the weight limits prescribed to him by his doctor—a measly twenty pounds. The doctor cautioned that working out with more than that amount of weight would put too much pressure on Ben's heart, and the act of lifting the weight could even move his pacemaker around inside his chest, away from his heart. Nevertheless, Ben decided to test *all* of these limits.

At one point, he even took Brazilian jujitsu lessons. Although his parents discouraged strenuous workouts and full-speed contact, Ben loved the self-defense techniques he learned, especially those that, despite his size, would give him a distinct advantage in a physical skirmish. Even though he wasn't anticipating a fight, knowing how to handle himself in such a situation gave him an increased sense of confidence and accomplishment.

Allowing Ben to take any chance at all was more than some parents might have advised Shawn and Deanne. They knew some of Ben's activities were risky, but they also knew they could not micromanage every moment of his life. Yes, they wanted to keep him safe, but they also wanted him to be able to *live his life*. Armed with frequent updates and information gleaned from discussions with his doctor, Shawn, Deanne, and Ben approached each decision individually, trying to determine the best choice with the knowledge they had available.

• • •

When the pressures of life weighed on him, Ben escaped into his music. He would just take some time, go into his room, lie on his bed with his eyes closed, and listen. He loved all kinds of music. Skrillex, Coldplay, Empire of the Sun, Muse, Johnny Cash, and Kid Cudi were a few of his favorite music artists.

Although Ben controlled his emotions regarding the risks and dangers threatening his heart, consistently maintaining a stoic attitude about medical matters, when it came to other things he let his fear show. For instance, he did not like flying in airplanes or encountering dangerous weather—even on the ground. When he flew, he became anxious about all the things he had learned about 9/11. He had just turned nine years old the month before 9/11, and, like so many others, the images and scenes of that horrible attack were indelibly impressed in his mind, forever affecting his comfort level when he flew in an airplane. Anytime the family was traveling, Ben always asked whether they could drive instead of fly.

His emotions also sometimes got the best of him if bad weather was predicted. When Austin was under a tornado warning, Ben would run back and forth throughout the house, straining to see out the windows, and keeping the family updated on any changes he noticed in the sky. He tuned every TV to the

Weather Channel so the family could keep up with the most current weather alerts. His anxiety level stayed high until the bad weather blew over. Ironically, when he saw a real tornado off the coast of Destin one year, he remained amazingly calm and loved experiencing the sight of it.

# CHAPTER 18

# ORIGINAL

Come on, show 'em what you're worth

—"FIREWORK" (KATY PERRY)

Throughout his early years in high school, Ben didn't have a steady girlfriend, but he often spoke openly to Deanne about his dreams of getting married and going on a honeymoon to Venice, Italy, or Greece, and how he envisioned having a family. His one concern in that regard was whether it would be wise to have children, since his HCM condition was so highly hereditary. He told Deanne that if he and his wife decided not to have their own kids because of his heart condition, they would adopt a lot of them! And, of course, he looked forward to taking them all to Lake Powell someday.

Justin Miller, however, began dating a girl named Megan Parken during his freshman year. Megan had developed a large following on YouTube, where she regularly posted videos concerning girls' makeup, clothes, hairstyles, and other matters of interest to teenage young women. She developed her own channel, and by the summer of 2010 she had garnered approximately sixty thousand subscribers—regular viewers—and the numbers were still rising. Her channel attracted advertisers, and Megan was actually earning a steady income as she produced the fun and informative videos.

One night when Megan was traveling in New York City, Ben and Justin were hanging out in the Millers' boathouse when Megan posted a video saying that her boyfriend and his friend were back in Austin, and perhaps they would make a video for her and her viewers. Justin and Ben took the challenge and made a silly video of themselves goofing around, eating ice cream, and just hanging out. Apparently, the boathouse had not been stocked with silverware, so they found some old saltine crackers, which they used in lieu of spoons. Megan's viewers loved it and started sending in comments and asking the guys questions.

Megan encouraged Justin and Ben to develop their own channel, where they could answer the girls' questions. Although they had dabbled with making YouTube videos before, with Megan's help, the guys learned the "how-tos" of making better videos and how to best function on YouTube. Justin and Ben launched their own YouTube channel, GuyAdvice4Girls, on July 23, 2010. They quickly began attracting subscribers. Megan helped immensely by occasionally encouraging her viewers to check out Ben and Justin's channel. "Remember, though," she cautioned the guys, "anything you put out there is a reflection of me, because I'm sending my viewers in your direction."

Ben and Justin shot their initial videos on Justin's small flip high-definition video camera, the same one they had used to film some of their bike and skateboard tricks, as well as their favorite pranks. In the beginning, it took the guys as long as three to four hours to film a short five- or ten-minute video, but they soon learned how to be more productive and proficient. At first, the videos were simply Justin and Ben sitting in front of the camera, talking between themselves, joking around, and offering their opinions and answering the questions they received from their viewers, many of whom were female.

Due to a technical problem in November 2010, Google shut down GuyAdvice4Girls. If they wanted to stay in business, Justin and Ben were advised to create a new channel. OurAdvice4You was born on YouTube. The guys asked their previous subscribers to meet them on the new channel, and many of them did. They provided their opinions on everything from "ten signs a guy likes you" to "great Christmas gifts" to "how to sustain a relationship" and "the question of the day." The questions ranged from funny and lighthearted to sometimes sad or delicate.

By this time, the boys were receiving questions from girls all over the world. They decided to address the questions that were asked most frequently. For instance, Justin and Ben did a video on the subject "does size matter?" after many of their followers had asked whether guys really cared about girls' bra sizes. Regardless of the questions, Ben and Justin answered honestly, yet they were surprisingly tactful and sensitive, and rarely offended anyone. Most young women greatly appreciated Ben's and Justin's forthright answers. Moreover, their responses usually built confidence rather than denigrating the questioner's self-esteem.

Once, however, one of Ben's YouTube videos did not receive such great feedback. He had filmed himself sitting in an armchair that happened to be draped with the hide of the first deer he had ever killed. He received condemnatory comments from antigun and antihunting people from all over the world. Although the criticism didn't change his opinions, it did help Ben to be more aware of other people's sensibilities as he created his videos.

At one point, Ben and Justin were filming and uploading at least one video every week. They spent the majority of their spare time producing videos, but it didn't feel like work to them. They loved it! They moved to a more elaborate camera borrowed from Justin's dad and their production quality improved dramatically. After so many years of relying on Mr. Miller's generously lending his video equipment, Ben eventually received his own camera as a Christmas gift from his parents during his sophomore year. He began saving up his money to buy tripods, microphones, and other accessories, all of which littered his room and car. Megan gave Ben a green screen, a flat wall screen used in television production and in movies on which digitalized computer or video images such as weather maps and other "on location" scenes are projected. With green screen matte technology, Ben could appear to be broadcasting from downtown Austin, New York, Washington, DC, or the Eiffel Tower in Paris—all without leaving his bedroom, where he filmed and produced many of his later videos. Ben loved interacting with the audience and began envisioning possibilities of working in the film industry, either as an entertainer or as a producer.

One of Justin and Ben's favorite videos they produced was titled "Asking the City, Part One." For this video, Ben and Justin, along with female interviewers Megan Parken and Devyn Brown, went "on location" to downtown Austin's Zilker Park on Sunday night during the finale of the Austin City Limits music festival, a three-day music fest featuring more than one hundred bands, including artists as varied as Arcade Fire and Muse, to Willie Nelson, to Ghostland Observatory, Coldplay, to Damian Marley, and more. At the close of the concert, Justin and Ben arbitrarily selected people in the crowd to do "man-in-the-street" interviews about relationships. Megan and Devyn did the same. As the huge crowd dispersed from the park, the guys and girls randomly pulled teenagers and young adults aside and interviewed them. They asked questions as mundane and meaningless as, "Do you prefer blondes or brunettes?" to more serious queries such as, "If you cheated on your boyfriend one time only, would you feel obligated to tell him or her?"

The guys spent more than three hours filming and then another several hours editing the tape that same night. Justin did a stellar job adding music and special effects. Even Megan was impressed with her understudies' improvement.

Eventually, Justin and Ben's OurAdvice4You channel attracted more than sixty thousand subscribers. Because of the large number of viewers, they also attracted the attention of some advertisers, and in February 2011, Ben and Justin received their first paycheck for OurAdvice4You ads, about thirty-five dollars each. They could have done yard work in the neighborhood and earned more money, but as far as the guys were concerned, it wasn't about the money. They were having fun, and they were on the cutting edge of an entirely new way to reach the world. Ben was particularly fascinated with the potential of the new communication medium.

Prior to the end of Ben's junior year in high school, Shawn asked, "Have you considered where you want to work this summer?"

"Work? None of my friends have to work!" Ben answered mischievously.

Shawn smiled. "Maybe not, but you do. You can get a summer job earning seven dollars an hour working for someone else, doing things that other people want you to do, and not having any fun. . . ."

Alluding to the job Ben had picked up a previous summer, Shawn's statement evoked stressful memories for Ben. As an ambitious fifteen-year-old, Ben had taken a position as a busboy at Ski Shores, the neighborhood lakeside café, before he could drive. Assigned with tasks such as lifting heavy boxes and taking out the garbage, Ben soon found the position too strenuous on his heart, and was forced to resign. Neither Shawn nor Deanne wanted to put Ben in a position of committing to an employer, then proving unable to fulfill his responsibilities by not being able to lift boxes or even show up every day for work. They realized many summer jobs given to teenage boys required some form of physical labor.

"Or you could work for yourself," Shawn continued. "You could build on your YouTube success and take it to the next level."

Ben's interest was piqued immediately.

"But you will need to work on your channel full-time," Shawn told him. "That would be a job you would enjoy, and you might be able to turn your video channel into an income stream that could pay you all year long, not just in the summer. It's something you can include on a résumé for future work or college applications. It might also give you some insight into what you want to do for a living someday."

Shawn could tell that Ben was sold on the opportunity of focusing on his passion, so he included a reality check as well. "You can work on your own schedule, but if you choose to work for yourself, you need to regard your YouTube channel as a job, not just a hobby. You need to be committed to working six to eight hours a day, five days a week."

A few weeks later, Shawn asked for Ben's decision.

Not surprisingly, Ben said, "I think I'd like to work for myself."

"I thought you might," Shawn said with a hint of a smile. "Okay, get to work."

Ben did. He worked hard at making videos, and he relished the feedback from his viewers. As he became more creative in his approach, he watched the number of his viewers increase every day, and he experienced a monthly rise in income and personal satisfaction. Ben had found his niche.

Justin and Ben continued to make videos, sometimes with Megan. Her YouTube success made her channel quite attractive to advertisers. She was so successful, she invited Justin and Ben to join her and Devyn and the girls' parents on a Caribbean cruise, all expenses paid.

It was one of the most fun-filled weeks of their lives. Ben and Justin roomed together, and Megan and her friend Devyn roomed with each of their parents. The cruise stopped at ports in Grand Cayman, Jamaica, and Cozumel. They went Jet Skiing in Jamaica and parasailing in the Caymans. Ben and Justin joked that it was the most extravagant double date they'd ever been on!

But because of a dramatic breakup between Justin and Megan later that year, the couple preferred not to appear on camera together anymore. Ben and Megan remained good friends, but she continued her independent YouTube channels apart from the guys.

When Justin's family moved to a home closer to the school, he was no longer able to join Ben as often on-screen, so Ben involved some of his other friends and continued to make videos for Our-Advice4You. Justin and Ben still created occasional videos together, but Justin sensed that Ben wanted to do more.

One night when they were working on a video, Ben surprised Justin. "We've made a bunch of videos about relationships and giving advice," Ben said to his friend. "Maybe we should move on to something deeper, something more meaningful."

Justin was quite content doing the relationship-advice videos, even though he and Ben both knew they had no real expertise in that area. But they kept their viewers entertained. So Ben's comment about doing something deeper caught Justin completely off guard. "What do you mean?" he asked.

"Oh, I don't know; maybe we should do something to tell our viewers more about ourselves," Ben responded.

Justin later realized that Ben had a genuine desire to convey something more than mere relationship advice. That's why Justin wasn't offended when Ben eventually decided to develop his own channel, BreedloveTV, which he launched on May 23, 2011. In his videos, Ben sat at a desk with a fake stationary microphone, offering his opinions, similar to the news desk on *Saturday Night Live*. Ben regularly watched the show starring his comedic idol, Andy Samberg.

He went solo with the advice videos, offering suggestions on the subjects of confidence, appearance, what girls should expect from guys, how guys should treat girls, what guys find attractive about girls, and all sorts of other matters pertinent to his peers. Much of his advice was surprisingly mature, especially considering Ben didn't date a lot, and had never actually been in a long-standing romantic relationship. But the camera loved him, and his thoughtful consideration for the feelings of others and his friendly upbeat personality came through in every video, and his viewers responded positively.

In a major departure from OurAdvice4You, Ben ventured into some new territory, addressing deeper issues, including his family and his faith. When Gina Corbet, an elderly neighbor who lived down the street, passed away, Ben wasn't reticent to deal with the subject of death. In a poignant on-screen moment, Ben expressed an appreciation for Gina, one he had never shared with her while she was alive. He ended the video by encouraging his viewers to take time today to tell someone they loved them or appreciated them. A quintessential entertainer, although in fledgling form, Ben had a natural way of not only making people smile, but also making people think.

# CHAPTER 19

# LOOKING FOR A REASON

Now I'm looking for a reason why
You even set my world into motion

—"BLACK AND GOLD" (SAM SPARRO)

On the first day of summer vacation 2011, Ben cheated death for a second time.

Ally sensed a presence at her bedroom door. She opened her eyes to see the silhouette of Grant Hamill standing in the doorway.

"Ally . . . I think Ben's having a seizure." Grant maintained his composure, but Ally could sense the nerves behind his voice.

Before Grant could offer a word of explanation, Ally was out of bed and bounding into Ben's room. She hastily peeled back the covers draped over her brother to assess his physical condition.

"Ally, s-s-s-stop it! I'm f-f-f-*freezing.*" Ally shot a curious glance at Ben, wondering how he could be cold on a Texas summer morning.

Ben had startled himself awake with his own shivering that morning, almost three hours earlier. The cold was paralyzing; he couldn't even bring himself to reach a few feet over and nudge Grant awake. He was shivering violently now, so much so that he couldn't get a word out without stuttering through his chattering teeth. His skin wasn't radiating its normal summer glow, and his fingers were icy blue to his knuckles.

"He's not having a seizure, because he's conscious," Ally said to Grant, trying to remain calm. "Stay right here with Ben while I go get my parents."

"Ally, I'm fine," Ben protested.

"Ben, you are not fine," Ally replied. She kept calm, but her mind was racing. She ran up the stairs to her parents' bedroom, softly cracking the door open. "Mom, Dad . . . Ben's shivering really badly. He's not having a seizure, but I don't know what's wrong with him." Without a word, both of Ally's parents threw back their covers and made their way down the stairs. Once they reached Ben at his bedside, they were beside themselves. None of them could explain Ben's violent shivering.

"What's going on, Ben?" Shawn asked. He worried that Ben might be experiencing some sort of heart failure.

Deanne was equally distraught. "Ben, what's wrong?" she asked as she pulled the comforter back to put her head to his chest so she could hear his heart.

"I'm fine; I'm f-f-f-fine," Ben said through his shivers. He reached for the comforter, pulling it up again. "Put it back on, *please!*"

When Deanne laid her head on his chest, she'd discovered that Ben's heart was beating regularly, but she was nonetheless shocked. Ben was ice-cold. She also noticed that his fingers were blue. Ben pulled the blankets back up around his chin. Amid all the fuss, Ben wanted only not to be bothered, and not to have his blankets pulled away from him.

Shawn dialed 911 while Grant called his mother, an anesthesiologist. Grant woke his mother with a phone call, briefly explained the situation at hand, and answered a series of questions before his mom could draw a conclusion.

"She says that usually people's body temperatures drop really low before they're about to get a really high fever. She says y'all should probably take him to the hospital if he's about to get a fever that high."

Knowing from previous experience that an ambulance would take forever to find their house out in the hills, Shawn and Deanne walked Ben out to the car with Grant and Ally in tow. Grant said a quick good-bye, then reluctantly drove home to wait for the diagnosis. Shawn and the others drove off to rendezvous with the ambulance on the main road. About ten minutes down the winding pavement, with Ben still shivering beneath his sweats and a sleeping bag, they heard the ambulance's siren. Shawn pulled over to the side of the road, and Deanne scrambled around to the backseat to assist Ben into the ambulance. Shawn and Ally followed them to the hospital, praying all the while that Ben's condition wouldn't worsen on the way.

Ben was disgusted to be going back to the hospital again. Though he never complained, his misery and frustration seemed almost palpable. Due to his constant heart arrhythmia, paired with a case of tonsillitis, Ben had already missed several crucial weeks of classes preceding finals at school. His throat ached so badly that his mom couldn't even bribe him to eat with Taco Bell. By the end of the week, Ben had already lost seven pounds. At five-foot-eight and a slight 137 pounds, that was weight he couldn't afford to lose.

Although a veteran at playing catch-up, Ben had really challenged himself by declining his teachers' offers to let him take late finals, which meant he would be taking his finals unprepared *and* virus-ridden. But his best friend, Grant, had returned from his yearlong exchange program in Germany that evening, and Ben would *not* have their summer reunion sabotaged by makeup exams. The boys had been counting down the days until Grant's return, Skyping for hours on end, devising their next pranks, and arranging outings on the lake. Now, at last, morning had dawned on the first day of summer vacation, but instead of spending the day on the lake, another trip to the ER had ruined Ben's plans.

• • •

Once in the emergency room, Ben's fever spiked at 103 degrees. A nurse promptly administered medication to reduce Ben's soaring temperature. After a quick examination, an ER doctor determined Ben's fever to be the result of an abscess on his left tonsil. Apparently, what an ENT (ear, nose, and throat doctor) had diagnosed as tonsillitis the week before was, in actuality, an ugly, festering abscess. That morning, Ben had narrowly escaped septic shock.

Ben was now perspiring with fever beneath his paper-thin scrubs, wondering how he could have possibly been begging for more blankets just a short while earlier. He hadn't had even one day to catch up with Grant after he had been gone for an entire year, and now they were once again restricted to text messaging—

and one-handed at that, since Ben was hooked up to an IV on his left side. And it was the very first day of summer, which he would now be spending in his least favorite place on earth, the hospital. Making matters worse, the medical team had cut off one of his prized hoodies in the emergency room. This was not going to be a good day. But rather than wallowing in his misfortune, Ben put his one good arm to use by playing a one-handed game of Angry Birds on his iTouch.

Reassured that Ben was not experiencing heart failure, and that the abscess could be dealt with easily, Shawn felt comfortable enough to go in to work for a while. "I won't be long," he said. "Maybe an hour or so at most. I doubt much will happen before then. It will take that long to get Ben prepped." Shawn hugged his family good-bye and promised to be back as soon as he addressed some business matters he had ignored that morning because of the emergency.

After a while, an orderly peered from behind the white privacy curtain. "Mr. Breedlove, if you would, please follow me to the CT scanning room," he said matter-of-factly. "You can have one family member accompany you."

Ben compliantly slid off the hospital bed and followed the orderly down the hallway. Ally accompanied Ben, quietly slipping behind him and the orderly into the silent scanning room. Before them loomed an ominous, otherworldly contraption into which Ben would be inserted. The orderly beckoned Ally behind a glass-paneled control board as Ben slipped off his UGG slippers and tiptoed across the ice-cold tile.

Ally held her breath as Ben slid through the humming contraption. She marveled at her brother, wondering how he always had the courage to endure everything the hospitals put him through. If he was ever in pain, he suffered in silence. If he was ever afraid, he never showed it.

Once they returned to the emergency room, the ER doctor scheduled a minor surgery in the ward upstairs to drain the nasty, fever-inducing abscess. As the doctor and nurses hurried away to tend to their other patients, Ben finally began to feel relief. Just as he was pulling the sheets back over his body to rest, his face contorted into a peculiar grimace. "Gahhh, I am itching all *over*." Ben rolled up the sleeve of his scrubs to reveal an inflamed red rash creeping up his left arm from where the IV had been inserted. "Great. What now?" Ben rolled his eyes in exasperation.

Concern flooding back into her eyes, Deanne stepped out to summon the nurse once again. The nurse returned to reassess Ben's condition.

"It looks like Ben is experiencing an allergic reaction to the contrast dye used for the CT scan," the nurse observed. "We'll give him a dose of Benadryl, and the rash should clear right up."

"No!" Deanne said emphatically. "He can't have Benadryl. It's on his list of prohibited medications."

"Well, we have to give it to him," the nurse replied, looking at Deanne condescendingly, as though to say, *We do this every day. Please don't tell me how to do my job.*

"He hasn't had anything to eat yet," Deanne protested, grasping at anything to prevent the nurse from administering the Benadryl. Deanne's cautions fell on deaf ears. The nurse insisted that Ben take two Benadryl tablets. Deanne was especially concerned because Ben had recently begun a new medication. Combined with the Benadryl that she knew he was not supposed to have, the results could be problematic. She was getting the feeling that the medical staff wasn't paying attention to important details regarding Ben's medical history.

Deanne and Ally cast pitying looks toward Ben. They had a long day at the hospital ahead of them.

· · ·

After the ENT surgeon arrived on-site, Deanne and Ally accompanied two nurses as they wheeled Ben in his hospital bed up to the surgical ward. With a kiss on the forehead from his mom, and an encouraging smile from his sister, Ben was sent off to be prepped for surgery.

In a small, nondescript hospital room, the anesthesiologist and surgical nurse briefed Deanne and Ally on the procedure. It all seemed routine. The smiling nurse handed Deanne a clipboard clasping a thick stack of papers. Deanne thumbed through them, initialing here and there. Her eyes perused warnings of brain damage, loss of limbs, paralysis, and even death. Before handing the clipboard back to the nurse, she hesitated.

"Now, what *exactly* are the chances of any of these emergencies occurring that are listed in the fine print? I always just sign off on these things to save time, but I feel like I should be fully aware of the circumstances, since we were not prepared for this procedure today." Deanne knew she was asking unwelcome questions, but her guard had been raised due to the way they had handled the Benadryl issue.

The nurse lifted her pleasant gaze from her own paperwork. "Not to worry, Mrs. Breedlove. As standard protocol, we are required to list the emergencies that might occur during any surgical procedure, but these are highly unlikely to happen. Very rarely do patients experience such emergencies."

Deanne responded with an unconvinced smile. "Okay. I had to ask just to make sure I understand what I am signing." Deanne had always placed full trust in the medical staff who tended to Ben throughout his life. She knew Ben was dependent upon the expertise and experience of his doctors. She felt privileged that he had access to some of the best medical care in the world. Even though Ben had previously received excellent treatment at this same facility, Deanne intuitively wrestled with her thoughts and emotions. Something wasn't quite right. She couldn't put her finger on it.

Soon the paperwork was completed and the anesthesiologist and nurse left Deanne and Ally in the room by themselves, closing the door behind them.

For Ben, this was nothing. After braving several major and potentially life-threatening cardiac surgeries, a minor throat surgery was the least of his worries. He remained calm on the surgical table, entertained by watching the medical team move in slow motion as the anesthesiologist administered the sedative. All he worried about was getting back on the lake the next day.

Although Ben was undergoing a relatively brief, so-called routine surgery, Deanne and Ally were surprised that barely ten minutes had passed when they heard a soft rap at the door.

"Come in," Deanne answered.

Ben's surgeon stepped gingerly into the room and closed the door. Departing from his usual detached demeanor, the surgeon knelt before the two women with concern in his eyes. Deanne and Ally sat up in riveted attention. Lowering his register, the surgeon spoke with hushed sensitivity. "We aren't sure what happened, but Ben's blood pressure dropped. We had to do chest compressions to bring him back. He is being taken to ICU right away."

*What?* Deanne stared back at the surgeon in shock. This was supposed to be a *routine* surgery. *Tonsil* surgery. What did this have to do with Ben's heart? "Why are you taking him to ICU? What happened?"

"They aren't sure. They'll know more when he gets there."

Deanne felt her eyes burn with an instant well of hot tears; she could feel a knot forming in her throat and tightening as she tried to remain calm. "Uhh, okay," was the only response she could muster. With watery eyes, Ally grabbed her mom's hand and held her breath to hold back the tears.

The surgeon turned swiftly from the room, and Deanne broke down. "Dad is never here when these things happen!" she lamented through her tears. With Shawn at work during the day, Deanne was accustomed to braving Ben's medical scares alone, without Shawn's stalwart emotional strength. "We always think things are going to be fine, and then something happens!" Ally stretched her arms around her mom to comfort her, not knowing what to say.

A few minutes passed, and they heard another gentle knock at the door. A man with soft features and kind eyes slipped through the doorway and knelt before them.

"Hello, I am the hospital chaplain," he said quietly. "Is there anything I can do for you? May I pray with you?" The chaplain looked up at Deanne with concern.

Deanne shot Ally a sharp, disconcerted glance.

Ally stared back in frustrated bewilderment. As much as she appreciated the chaplain's good intentions, she was wary of any behavior that deviated from what was normal; abnormal behavior meant abnormal circumstances.

Deanne's imagination was similarly piqued. In all of Ben's hospitalizations, some at this same facility, they had never previously had a chaplain visit with them. Why now? Deanne looked at the chaplain, attempting to read his expression.

"Well, yes, I do want to pray," she replied. "But is there a specific *reason* why we would need to pray? Do you know what happened?" she asked the chaplain, not really expecting a medical answer. "The doctor who just left here couldn't explain it. Ben is going to be okay, isn't he?" she asked, her voice revealing her fear.

The chaplain broke eye contact, searching for words. "Let me see if I can find the doctor for you." After offering a prayer, the chaplain stood and eased out the door. Deanne and Ally sat in tensed silence.

After what seemed like an eternity, the surgeon reappeared in the waiting room doorway. "Ben has been stabilized," he said. "But we are keeping him in ICU to monitor his vitals. He will need to stay overnight."

The typical nuisance of an overnight hospital stay did not even register in Deanne's mind. She succumbed to her emotions once again, but now she wept tears of relief. Ally felt as if she could breathe again. "When can we see him?" Deanne asked.

"A nurse will be along to escort you to the ICU shortly," he answered. Bowing his head with what looked like a cross between pity and embarrassment in his eyes—Deanne couldn't tell—the doctor slipped from the room.

When Shawn returned, he found Deanne and Ally visibly shaken. Deanne informed him of the aborted tonsil surgery. "Ben is stable; he's okay," she said, but then she broke down. "But he went into cardiac arrest, and they had to do chest compression. He's in the ICU."

Shawn was shocked at the news. When he had left, the plan had been for a quick, routine procedure. Now his son was in another perilous medical situation.

After a while, the family received a report that Ben was fine, but still unconscious due to the anesthesia. Shawn went to get some overnight things for Ben and Deanne, and to pick up Jake from school, while the girls waited.

• • •

When they were finally allowed to see Ben, Deanne and Ally anxiously rushed down three floors and through the hallway of the ICU. Arriving at Ben's room, Deanne hesitantly cracked the door open. Inside, he lay unconscious and entangled in a mess of medical tubes. The fluorescent lighting accentuated his sallow skin and his perspiration-matted hair. A breathing tube protruded from his parted lips.

Deanne and Ally dropped their purses to the floor and slumped down into the visitors' chairs, pulling them close to Ben's bedside so they could hold his hands. Their hearts ached for Ben. Trying to block out the activity all around them, Deanne spoke gentle, reaffirming words to him, wondering whether he could even sense that they were there with him. A team of intensive-care nurses bustled about the room, observing monitors, filling out charts, and changing IVs. On a day when Ben had been expecting to make a quick video in the morning, then be wearing only a swimming suit and a life jacket for the remainder of the day, he was now encumbered with three IV lines in his arms, a femoral arterial line in his groin, a urine catheter, a large breathing tube inserted into his lungs, and a ventilator to aid his breathing.

Deanne caught the attention of the nurse nearest Ben. "Um, excuse me. Why isn't he awake yet?" She recalled that following previous surgeries, recovery took a much shorter time. Ben would usually be speaking by now.

The nurse stopped abruptly just as she reached to adjust Ben's IV. After a thoughtful pause, she resumed her work. "Well, Mrs. Breedlove, your son has just been through a very taxing event. We were able to get him stabilized, but his body is going to need some time to recover before he can wake up again. We wouldn't want him to wake up before the medicine kicks in, or for him to be alarmed by the breathing tube when he wakes up and have his heart rhythm spike. We need to keep him as calm as possible. Our hope is that he will be able to breathe on his own after we remove the breathing tube."

Deanne contemplated the nurse's response for a moment, her expression becoming more furrowed as she tried to read between the lines. "Well, what if he doesn't start breathing on his own?"

The nurse paused again, offbeat, then busied herself with the tubes again. "Let's just hope that he does."

Her words were anything but comforting. As Deanne sat in silence, awaiting an explanation from the doctors, questions continually raced through her mind. *Why did Ben go into cardiac arrest? Was it the combination of the high fever, weeks of undiagnosed illness, and the Benadryl, combined with anesthesia? Was it all too much for Ben's system? This was supposed to be a routine surgery. And now he might not wake up?* Neither the surgeon, nor the anesthesiologist, nor the clinical registered nurse of anesthesiology, nor the pediatric intensive-care-unit director, nor any of the cardiologists could—or would—satisfactorily answer Deanne's questions. One by one, each of the medical staff left the room, leaving the family with their unresolved concerns.

Four hours, two iced lattes, and seven phone calls later, the girls were greeted once again by the nurse Deanne had questioned earlier. "Okay, ladies, I think we can finally try waking him up now." All of the nurses, the PICU director, a cardiologist, and the breathing technician all observed with hushed intensity. Deliberately, painstakingly, the nurse removed the breathing tube from Ben's throat.

A gag, a gasp of air, and then words: "Guys, I need to get back to work!"

Ally and Deanne were overcome with laughter at Ben's untimely statement, but mostly by the joy of seeing him alive and breathing. Deanne gazed with affection into her son's eyes. "You don't need to worry about that right now, bud. Trust me; you'll have plenty of time to work once you get back home."

Ben stared back, perplexed. "How long have I been here?"

"Since this morning. And you're going to have to stay here tonight."

Ben was immediately animated. "What! No. I am *not* staying here overnight. I have to get back to work."

Deanne smiled to see her son's determined personality returning. "You have to, honey," she said. "You can get back to work when you get home."

Later, Ben would find out just how lucky he was to be able to spend one more night in the hospital. Apparently he did indeed have work to do, much more than he knew.

• • •

The Breedloves' annual trip to Destin, Florida, had been scheduled for June 4, a mere four days after Ben was released from ICU. He came home from the hospital with the abscess drained, but not removed. The simple solution would have been to extract the tonsils, but doctors felt a tonsillectomy was too risky. They discharged Ben with prescriptions for more antibiotics.

A more timorous family might conclude that they should forget about going on vacation for a while, but the Breedloves' hearts said go! They took a family vote and decided. Ben included, they wanted go to Destin. Why skip it? They would be relaxing, sleeping, eating, and relaxing even more. There would be medical help all along the way if needed. Deanne even planned ahead to make sure where hospitals were located and whether or not they could handle Ben's condition.

With waffling confidence, they pulled out of the driveway early the morning of June 4. They made the thirteen-hour trek to Destin without event, checked into their condominium on the beach, and walked out onto the balcony to smell the ocean air. It felt good to be back in a familiar place, where they could enjoy a few days without stacks of mail, homework, or business phone messages. It would be just family on the beach that week.

Ben spent the week soaking up the salty air, the sunshine, and all the king crab he could eat. He even made a few OurAdvice4You videos from the condo's balcony, with gorgeous ocean vistas in the background.

The family decided to go parasailing in tandem chutes. Jake rode with Shawn and Ben rode with Deanne. Ally chose to remain safely on the ground. Once they lifted off the boat, rising into the cloudless blue sky, Ben and Deanne were overwhelmed by how peaceful and beautiful it was above the noise of the crowd below. As they rose even higher, many things dissolved completely—the sound of the waves, people's voices, the hum of songs on radios, the cry of seagulls, and even Deanne's intense fear of heights. Deanne and Ben comfortably floated in the warm breeze; it felt almost *heavenly*. They could make out shapes in the aqua ocean, and see the curve of the horizon off in the distance. They remained silent, each enveloped by a quietness and peacefulness. It was so special that when they landed, Ben suggested that they do it again the following year. "Let's make this an annual tradition!" Ben said as he and Deanne high-fived in agreement.

# CHAPTER 20

# FEELING GOOD

It's a new dawn
It's a new day

—"FEELING GOOD" (MUSE)

A few weeks after returning from the reinvigorating trip to Destin, Ben was on his sixth round of antibiotics for his tonsil issues, and feeling no better. But when it came time for his long-awaited Alaskan cruise with his grandfather DDad in July 2011, tonsillitis or not, Ben was not going to miss that trip. It was the most recent in a lifetime of adventures and trips that brought Ben and DDad together.

Ben and DDad were really close from Ben's earliest years. Because DDad's great-grandmother was part Cherokee Indian, DDad registered Ben in the Cherokee tribe of Oklahoma before he was one year old. Ben's certified degree of Indian blood came back listing him as being 1/128th part Cherokee. That was good enough for DDad.

Ben was Cherokee, and DDad was proud.

When Ben was five years old, DDad and Grammy even took the family to Tahlequah, Oklahoma, to attend a Cherokee pow-wow so the grandkids could get more familiar with that part of their heritage. About one hundred of the Indian men were dressed in full feathered and hand-beaded costumes as they danced around in a big circle. Even though Ben was half their height and lacked a costume, he couldn't help himself from joining in. Stepping in perfect rhythm, Ben danced around with the Cherokee men to the beat of the drum.

• • •

Later that same year, Ben and Ally rushed outside their house to watch DDad's familiar, enormous RV pull into the driveway. After making a cumbersome turn and putting the vehicle in park, DDad stepped out of the driver's seat and immediately snapped into action. Handing a walkie-talkie to five-year-old Ben and giving him careful instructions, DDad climbed back into the RV to commence perfectly positioning and parking the vehicle.

Ben took his responsibility seriously, feeding DDad encouragement and precise directions through the walkie-talkie. The RV was nearly settled, and DDad was still intently focused on the task at hand when Ben's little voice rang through his speaker.

*Cshh,* the static crackled through the walkie-talkie. "DDad?" *Cshh.*

"Yes, Ben?" *Cshh.*

*Cshh.* "DDad. I love you." *Cshh.*

For a long moment, DDad couldn't answer because he was so choked up. Finally, he responded, "Ben, I love you, too."

• • •

DDad and Grammy lived more than six hundred miles to the west in Las Cruces, New Mexico, and Ben loved to visit there. He especially enjoyed DDad teaching him how to play poker and Texas Hold 'Em card games, and quickly learned that it wasn't luck that shaped one's destiny around the card table, but probability and strategy.

When Grammy passed away, after a thirty-month battle with cancer, Ben asked whether he could recite a passage of Scripture from memory at her funeral, which he did. That Ben would honor Grammy in such a manner meant the world to DDad.

After some time, DDad met and married Corine. Ben was only nine years old when he first met her in New Mexico. Walking into the kitchen, Ben approached Corine and said, "Excuse me, but I just need to know what to call you."

"Well, Ben," Corine answered, "my best friends always call me Corine."

Ben nodded. "Okay." He called her Corine ever after.

For Christmas of 2010, the entire Breedlove family celebrated the holiday together at Aunt Kim and Uncle Dave's house in Pueblo West, Colorado. Deanne had encouraged the kids to write special notes to Corine and DDad for presents, expressing how much they meant in their young lives. Ben's letter to Corine reveals as much about him as it does Corine.

> After Grammy had passed away and I heard that DDad
> found someone who made him happy and that he loved, a lady
> who is truly amazing and brings out the best in him, I was
> unsure of this sudden addition in life, someone I didn't know

Ben wakesurfing on Lake Austin.

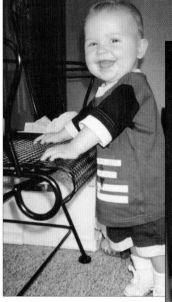

A very happy toothless Ben.

A three-year-old Ben enjoys some of his birthday cake.

"Floating Bear" on the Frio River at Garner Park.

Ally, DDad, and Ben on a road trip in the grandparents' RV.

Best friends, Ben and Ally, at ages two and three.

Ben and Ally welcome newborn baby brother, Jake.

Jake and Ben enjoying one of their many moments fishing on Lake Austin.

Ben, Jake, and Shawn on the shores of Lake Powell with a lizard.

Steering the ski boat that was pulled behind the seventy-five-foot-long houseboat on Lake Powell during a family vacation.

Ben and Jake with their first lemonade stand.

On his annual camping trip to Garner Park.

Ben's homemade "helmet cam."

Hiking the creek with his friend Justin at the Millers' ranch.

Shawn, Jake, Ben, Deanne, and Ally get away to Universal Studios.

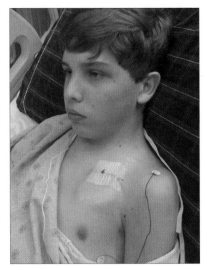

Still groggy from the anesthesia, Ben is about to find out how much better he feels with his newly implanted pacemaker-defibrillator.

One of Ben's many hobbies: playing electric guitar.

Ben, Grant Agatston, and Grant Hamill just driving around on a sunny day . . . laughing.

Ben goofing around with Grant's camera.

Ben with BreedloveTV fans at IHOP, enjoying his favorite banana and Nutella crepes.

A family vacation to one of Ben's favorite spots, Destin, Florida.

Neighbors Kyle, Benji, and Nate having fun with Ben and Jake on a typical summer day.

Teaching Jake how to wakeboard.

Another day on the lake!

Cameron Thompson and Ben messing around on Lake Austin.

Ben's turn to wakeboard!

Ben and Grant host Manu and Celia Kraus, exchange students from Germany, to a day on the lake.

Part of Ben's regular daily practice on the trampoline.

Ally and Ben on an evening boat ride on the Fourth of July.

Ben's mentor, Mark Kohler, with his wife, Pam.

Ben and Jake running into their favorite wakesurfers/skaters, Rusty Malinoski, JD Webb, and Danny Hampson, in the Seattle Airport, on Ben's birthday.

Erik Ruck (professional wakeboarder), Cameron Thompson, Ben, Grant Hamill, Parks Bonifay (professional wakeboarder), and Nick Weinacker (professional wakeboarder).

Photo shoot for BreedloveTV.

Ben's first successful back roll!

On the family boat
on Lake Austin.

Ben and Justin
on the lake.

Grant Hamill, Ben, and Grant Agatston after school.

Alex Faglie and Ben, with Parker Medford goofing around in the background.

Madeline Nick before a school formal.

Jamie Buchsbaum and Ben at a WHS football game.

Justin Miller, Megan Parken, Devyn Brown, and Ben at WHS Homecoming.

Ben and Jake during a guys' four-wheeling trip in Colorado.

Cameron, Ally, Jake, Ben, Aunt Kim, Uncle Dave, Deanne, and Shawn on an annual Destin, Florida, vacation.

Ben, Jake, and DDad about to board the float plane in Alaska, 2011.

Ben and Jake take a break in front of the stream where they watched bear catch salmon in Alaska.

Jake, Shawn, and Ben hone their snowboarding skills in Brighton, Utah.

Ben, Ally, Jake, and Chica. The last Christmas photo of the kids from 2011.

and had never met. A part of me, secretly excited inside, yet not sure of the outcome, I was honored and blessed to finally meet you, and right then I knew and could see how wonderful and sweet you are, and what I realized the most is how much love you have in your heart, to be able to accept all new family and show the amount of love you always share with me and everyone, but most of all towards DDad. You helped him get through some of the toughest times in his life and I don't think anyone could have done it with as much commitment and love as you had for him.

After getting to know you and spending more time with you, I've learned more about you and more about life. I am really fascinated and enthralled with the determination you have about telling me to do the things in life that I enjoy and make me happy. I am blessed to have someone that encourages me as much as you do, and makes me feel good about myself and how important my future will be.

I am glad to say I'm honored to have been given the chance to have met you, and would not trade it for anything. I Love You!

Ben

• • •

Ben loved traveling with DDad. In addition to the family trips to Lake Powell, DDad, Ben, Jake, and Shawn took several "guy trips" together. They attended the world-famous Albuquerque balloon festival, and rode the gondola up the side of the Sandias mountains, despite high winds. Because of Ben's love of magic, DDad arranged a trip to New York City to see the Steve Cohen magic show at the Waldorf Towers. DDad bought the boys seats on the front row so they would not miss a trick. They waterskied together in Austin, and even rode all-terrain vehicles together in the mountains of Colorado.

But of all the trips Ben and Jake took with DDad and Corine, the Alaskan cruise during the summer of 2011 was a high point. Deanne made sure Ben traveled with medical instructions and release forms, and Ben visited the onboard doctor and nurses as instructed, just to make them aware of his condition.

Besides enjoying the breathtaking Alaskan scenery around Glacier Bay and the sumptuous dining aboard the ship, Ben, Jake, and DDad took a floatplane ride to a mountain lake where salmon swim farther upstream to spawn and die. The boys watched in awe as black bears attempted to snatch the salmon out of the streams. Corine joined them on a whale-watching trip, and on another excursion they went to the Iditarod training camp for sled dogs. Ben and Jake got to experience what it would be like to have dogsleds as their primary means of transportation.

In his senior scrapbook, Ben wrote:

I used to travel with my grandpa and grandma a lot, but once my grandma passed away, my grandpa stopped traveling. However, this summer I got to travel to Alaska with my grandpa, his wife Corine, and my brother, Jake. I really enjoyed it and am very lucky I had time with him (my grandpa) again. We got to do a lot of neat stuff on the trip. We went on a floatplane and flew to this remote place where we saw bears. We also went dogsledding and whale watching.

Amazingly, Ben's recurring fever and sore throat disappeared while he was in Alaska. Whether the medication had finally kicked in, or another factor was in play, the family's prayers were answered, and the sore throat never bothered Ben again.

On their way home from Alaska, Ben, Jake, Corine, and DDad were going through the security checkpoints at the airport. Having a pacemaker, Ben had to be manually patted down. All the members of the party went through security and were gathering their belongings, returning their belts and shoes to their proper places. Corine looked back and saw that Ben was still standing in line, patiently waiting for the security officers to allow him to pass.

Corine and Jake shared a bench as they put their shoes back on. Corine said to Jake, "You two sure are close, aren't you? You are such good brothers to each other. Jake, do you ever worry about Ben?"

Jake's immediate and firm reply was, "Nothing is going to happen to Ben."

Corine took that as Jake's way of saying, *End of story. Do not ask any more questions.* That was Jake's coping mechanism, and perhaps even his way of expressing a deeper contentedness and faith. He believed, *This day is okay. Let's not worry about tomorrow or the next day.*

Indeed, Jake rarely raised questions regarding Ben's health. He took everything in stride. Whenever Deanne or Shawn specifically asked Jake whether he had questions or concerns about Ben's condition, Jake responded confidently that he did not.

He loved his brother and, even at his young age, Jake had no thoughts of losing his sibling mentor anytime soon.

Ben received an added highlight on the last day of the Alaska trip, which fell on his eighteenth birthday, when he ran into several professional wakeboarders in the Seattle airport. The guys all posed for a photo together, and to Ben that was better than any birthday present. He treasured the many photos taken during that trip, but the one he showed the most when he got home was the shot of him and the wakeboarders.

# CHAPTER 21

# THIS IS NOT THE END

The memories in my head
Are just as real as the time we spent

—"THIS IS NOT THE END" (THE BRAVERY)

Grant held the trash bags stuffed with pillows as Ben finished wrapping the last strip of duct tape around the bags. Grant hadn't been home from Germany very long before he and Ben were up to their usual antics.

"I don't think this is a good idea, guys," Deanne admonished them, looking on skeptically as they set the stage for their master prank. "And if anything happens, I am not going to bail you out."

"Don't worry, Mom," Ben assured her. "We'll make it funny." Deanne wasn't so sure that pretending to bury a dead body in the woods by a busy street could turn out to be funny. Nevertheless, Ben and Grant stuffed their "body bag" in the trunk of Grant's SUV and proceeded undeterred.

They felt confident that people who saw the gag would have

a sense of humor about matters once they realized the body was a hoax. They filmed each detail as they meticulously prepared the "body bag," attaching the white trash bags together, stuffing them with paper and pillows, and wrapping the bags strategically with silver duct tape. When they lugged the body bag out to the car and put it in the trunk, it really looked as though they were carrying some sort of clandestine cargo.

Dressed in athletic shorts and hoodies—in broad daylight during the middle of a hot Texas summer—the guys grabbed a shovel and Ben's video camera. They found the perfect location along City Park Road and parked Grant's car near the woods, where they could spot vehicles coming over a hill and around a turn. They placed the camera on a tripod and positioned it out of sight behind a sign, catching the action as cars slowed down to navigate the turn.

Then they waited. As the first driver approached, Ben and Grant hauled the "body" out of the car's trunk, along with the shovel, while wearing the hoodies pulled up over their heads. Pretending to struggle with the heft of the body, Grant and Ben looked like thugs. It certainly appeared to passersby that they intended to bury a dead body. As cars drove by, some drivers slowed down and gawked, while others circled back around several times to take another look. Nobody stopped to ascertain whether the situation was a genuine crime scene. Perhaps the neighbors were afraid, or more likely the locals recognized Grant and Ben's modus operandi.

Every time they saw a car coming over the hill, Grant and Ben dragged the body bag out of the trunk toward the woods, carrying along the shovel. Although their hoodies concealed their facial expressions, they couldn't keep from laughing as they did their best to look like thugs.

One woman drove by several times, so the guys knew she had taken the bait. Once as she drove by, Grant saw the woman talking on her cell phone.

"She's been by here so many times, she's probably called the police by now," Ben said, half seriously.

During a brief lull in the traffic, Ben rested on the back of the tailgate while Grant, in his boredom, flung rocks into the woods with the shovel. When the next car finally swerved around the bend, they hustled back to the SUV. Feigning strenuous effort to heave the body bag out of the trunk, they began re-creating the crime scene—then stopped short. Suddenly, a police cruiser with screeching siren and flashing lights skidded to a halt behind Grant's SUV, stirring up a cloud of dust between them.

As far as Ben and Grant were concerned, the video camera was located in the perfect spot to capture the police car slamming on its brakes. The camera continued filming as the police officer jumped out of his car, drawing his gun out of the holster and holding it ready at his side. Quickly sizing up the situation, the policeman pointed the gun at Ben and Grant and shouted, "Drop it!"

Ben and Grant dropped the "body" and stretched their hands high in the air. "It's just a prank!" they both called out simultaneously to the lawman. "There's nothing in the body bag! It's a joke."

The officer wasn't taking any chances. With his weapon raised and pointed toward Ben and Grant, he nodded toward the body bag on the ground. "Open it," he commanded.

Ben and Grant slowly moved toward the taped-up garbage bags and nervously opened the top, letting the pillows fall out on the ground. The officer glared at them and lowered his gun. Speaking into his radio, he growled, "Just a couple of kids pulling a dumb prank.

"All right, get up," he said gruffly. He then reprimanded them for their foolishness. Suddenly he had an epiphany, and asked, "Are you guys filming this?" He must have realized this was exactly the kind of thing you would do to get reactions on tape.

Ben and Grant looked at each other, trying to suppress huge, guilty smiles. "Yes, sir," Ben replied, desperately trying to address the situation seriously. The officer glared back with disapproval.

"We'll give you the camera; we'll give you the film, anything you want!" Grant blurted. "You can have it!"

*What!* Ben stared incredulously at Grant, disappointed that he surrendered so willingly. "No, dude!" Ben muttered under his breath. "He is *not* taking my camera."

The officer didn't confiscate the camera or the film, but he continued to lecture Ben and Grant, reminding them of all the potential disasters that might have occurred, and cautioning them to be wiser in their choices of fun.

And then came the phone calls to their parents.

As soon as Deanne heard the serious-sounding male voice on the phone, she knew the prank had not gone well. The policeman said, "Mrs. Breedlove, this is Officer Stone."

"Oh, I'm so sorry," Deanne interrupted him, rolling her eyes and feeling completely embarrassed. "Let me pass the phone to my husband." Covering her mouth with her hand to conceal her own guilty smile, she handed the phone to Shawn, effectively evading the problem.

Laughing at Deanne's prank, Shawn looked at her as if to say, *You owe me*, and then took the call.

"These guys aren't in any trouble," Officer Stone began, "because they weren't breaking any laws, but I just want you to know that what they did could have turned out very badly. Besides disturbing somebody driving by, I could have shot them, not knowing what was going on. Or someone passing by could have decided to be a vigilante and do something crazy to stop the boys. This was not a good idea."

Shawn listened patiently to the officer's lecture, understanding his concerns, yet finding the situation humorously predictable. When the officer finally paused for a breath, Shawn asked, "So, Officer, do you need anything else from me?" He meant no disrespect, but simply wanted assurance that he would not be bailing his son out of jail that day.

The officer again confirmed that no laws had been broken, and wished Shawn a safe day. Ben and Grant were off the hook this time.

Even Grant later agreed, "That probably wasn't the best idea . . . but I'm so glad we did it!"

The officer was definitely right. But Ben and Grant got the video, and while they didn't upload it on YouTube, they watched it regularly, always sharing a good laugh over the prank.

• • •

Like most guys their age, next to making videos, Ben and Grant's favorite activity was just hanging out, driving around in the car together, joking and laughing until they figured out something to do. As Grant recalls, "When we were in the car, we'd be laughing the *entire* time. We weren't that funny, but we cracked each other up." One night as Grant and Ben were driving around, Ben got the idea that they should go find a "coyote caller." Coyotes were relatively common in the outskirts of Austin, but coyote callers were not exactly a staple for most families.

Already late at night when the guys drove around to various stores, searching for a coyote caller, it was after midnight when they found one at a store that stayed open all night long. The caller was a sort of whistle, with a reed that caused a buzzing sound when blown. They read the directions for the caller, and eventually got good at producing the sound. In parts of Texas, it is legal to shoot a coyote if it is in a neighborhood, so Ben retrieved a rifle from home.

"What are you going to do with that?" Grant asked.

"If we see a coyote, I'm going to shoot it!" Ben replied.

"Oh, okay, dude." Grant laughed.

The guys went out calling coyotes in the woods near the lake. They called coyotes for several hours, and actually saw one, but Ben didn't get a clear shot.

• • •

One day as they were driving around, Grant showed Ben a song he had downloaded on his phone. "Check this out," he said. "I wake up to this every morning." Grant played "Mr. Rager," a song and video by their favorite rapper, Kid Cudi.

Ben really liked it and was intrigued by some of Kid Cudi's

lyrics referring to heaven. Ben wondered whether Kid Cudi might believe in God. Yet on the same album, the rapper included songs with lyrics that many people found offensive. Always open-minded, and with a keen ability to find the good in people, Ben connected to something behind Kid Cudi's music. He heard the hurt and the pain in Cudi's lyrics, but he also detected hope. Consequently, as Ben and Grant cruised around Austin, they usually had Kid Cudi music playing in the car.

Grant and Ben had all sorts of plans that common sense would tell you were not good ideas for a kid with a heart condition. For example, they had plans to go skydiving. Ben secretly purchased two skydiving tickets as a graduation present for Grant. He knew that skydiving was not an "approved activity" for him and that his parents would never have approved, but he always wanted to do it.

• • •

Ben and Grant's mischief making dated back to the beginning of their friendship. As Ben walked up the steep incline in the Westlake senior parking lot at lunch during his sophomore year, he felt the energy drain from his body, leaving him light-headed. A wave of fatigue washed over him in an instant. His face paled and his lips turned blue as his heart started bumping hard against his chest.

"I'm getting really tired," Ben said breathlessly. "Can you carry my backpack for a second?"

Ben's friend Allen Cho had been too busy joking around with the other guys to notice Ben's sudden decline in energy. Without realizing that Ben was having heart trouble, Allen thought Ben must have been kidding. "You want me to carry your backpack? No way, dude!" he replied.

The backpack slipped off Ben's shoulder and thudded onto the pavement. Ben didn't move to pick it up.

"Ben, we have to go," Grant called to him. "We're going to get in trouble. Thunder is going to catch us!"

Westlake seniors were permitted off-campus lunch privileges; however, whenever underclassmen attempted to sneak out, they would inevitably be caught by the campus security guard, Thunder. Thunder was well-known and loved by all the Westlake students, but she wasn't afraid to catch the troublemakers, and Grant was well aware of this.

"I feel like I'm about to faint," Ben said quietly, and collapsed in the parking lot.

Grant wasn't really sure whether Ben was fooling around or not. The guys and Alex Faglie joked so much that it was always hard to tell when one of them was serious, so they had devised a special code word—*pineapple*—that they would say when they were definitely telling the truth, or when something was really wrong. They had even whimsically made a pact that the penalty for breaking the code of *pineapple* was death. Sometimes, though, to evade their rules without penalty, one of them might respond, "Pie-apple," while carrying on with a prank.

Grant looked at Ben on the pavement and said, "Ben? Are you joking?"

No response.

"Ben? Pineapple?" Grant asked, concerned.

"Pineapple," Ben tried to say through a gasp.

Grant still wasn't convinced, since Ben hadn't really *said* *pineapple*.

Iker Uranga, another of their friends who had joined them and saw what had happened, called 911. He was trying to describe Ben's condition to the operator as Ben was fading in and out of consciousness. "Someone has fainted in the parking lot. . . . Oh, hold on—Ben, are you okay? Wait, yes, we're in the parking lot; hold on; oh, he seems to be doing better . . . no, he's not." Iker never got around to telling the operator that they were in a parking lot at Westlake High School.

"Iker, just tell them to come!" Grant shouted. "Even if Ben is okay, tell them to come."

While Ben was still on the ground, a senior drove by in his car, lowered the window, and called out, "Hey, are you guys okay? Do you need any help?"

"Yeah, we do," Grant yelled. "This kid has passed out."

The senior looked at Ben, sprawled out in the parking lot. "Ooh, I gotta go to lunch. . . . I was hoping you would say you didn't need any help. Sorry." And he drove off.

Grant dialed Ally's phone number. "Ally, Ben just fainted in the senior parking lot," he told her. At first she thought he was joking, but Grant quickly informed her that he was serious. Ally had been walking out the main entrance of the school, on the opposite side of the building, but when she received Grant's call, she dropped her heavy book bag and ran all the way up the hill to where she and Ben had parked that morning. She spotted the group huddled around Ben on the ground and hurried to them. She knew that anytime Ben collapsed, it could be life-threatening, but she was relieved to see that although his lips were blue, he had roused; his eyes were open and he was conscious.

After a few minutes on the ground, Ben was starting to get his strength back when the EMS crew showed up, as did Thunder. The 911 operator had somehow interpreted Iker's vague instructions and found them.

"I'm fine, guys," Ben said, as he sat up on the ground. "Really, I don't need to go to the hospital. I'm fine."

The EMS guys weren't buying it; they checked Ben's vitals and kept him in the ambulance until Deanne arrived and took him home. Ben was okay, but he never made it to lunch that day.

# CHAPTER 22

# STILL HAVE EACH OTHER

Now that it's raining more than ever
Know that we'll still have each other

—"UMBRELLA" (RIHANNA FEATURING JAY-Z)

B en wasn't the only person in the Breedlove family affected by his condition. Indeed, all of the immediate family and extended family members—from Shawn and Deanne, Ally and Jake, to DDad and Corine, to aunts, uncles, and cousins—lived with Ben's HCM and adjusted their lives accordingly, whether it meant altering daily activities, modifying their eating habits, or changing their vacation schedules. They wanted to stay close to him, to help him in any way they could, and simply to be with him. Everyone in the family recognized when Ben's health was deteriorating, and that spending time with him was a luxury that might not always be possible.

Ally and Jake lived with the constant tension Ben's HCM

brought to everyday life, but they never complained. They didn't feel unimportant or neglected. Nor did they ever express anything other than concern and love for their brother when so much of their parents' attention, out of necessity, had to revolve around Ben. Rather than focus on what they couldn't do because of Ben's illness, Ally and Jake sought out ways to help however they could. Although Ally was away at college for Ben's junior and senior years of high school, she prayed constantly for her brother, often asking other friends to join her in prayers for Ben.

Jake was present for day-to-day life as Ben's condition began to worsen, and he jumped into action to help Ben whenever he could. He carried Ben's suitcases for him on trips. He would run errands for him in the house if Ben was having a tough day or simply needed to rest. Jake frequently took upon himself some of Ben's chores if Ben needed extra help.

As Ben's conditioned worsened, he could no longer easily walk up the stairs in the Breedlove home. Part of his chores had always been to empty the wastebaskets, then take out the trash on Tuesday mornings, but when Ben couldn't even make it upstairs to empty the wastebaskets, Jake volunteered to help.

As far as Jake was concerned, Ben was his hero. To Jake, Ben was smarter, stronger, and wiser than anyone. He seemed to have all the answers, in Jake's world. Many of Jake's sentences often began with the phrase, "Ben said . . ." Ben was the one who had helped Jake learn how to ride a two-wheeler; Ben was the guy to bring the latest YouTube video to him, or teach him to wakeboard by taking him out behind a Jet Ski rather than the boat. Ben encouraged Jake on every level. Their love and support for each other were mutual.

• • •

Ben's condition brought Shawn and Deanne closer together, because they were forced to wrestle with tough emotional, physical, spiritual, and ethical decisions on a regular basis. There were no break times. Ben's condition didn't go away simply because the family went on vacation. The HCM was always there, coloring every aspect of their lives. It was not a "once-in-a-while" situation; it was every day, month after month, year after year.

Their marriage was strengthened because they shared the common bond of wanting to help their child. They prayed together for Ben regularly. They celebrated health victories. Each year, on Ben's birthday, after all the celebration, Shawn and Deanne prayed together before falling asleep, thanking God for giving them one more year with their beloved Ben. They loved all of their children, of course, but they regarded each added year with Ben as an answer to prayer.

CHAPTER 23

# SHOW ME WHAT I'M LOOKING FOR

Save me from being confused

—"SHOW ME WHAT I'M LOOKING FOR" (CAROLINA LIAR)

"I like a girl."

"Ha!" Ally laughed aloud at Ben's simple declaration, but she knew he was serious. Ben had always had *plenty* of admirers. His fame among YouTube fans had brought him adoring comments and even recognition as a local celebrity. Girls would spot him from afar at the movie theater, or at IHOP, one of his usual haunts, and want to take a picture with him. Even Ally had become accustomed to the occasional question from a stranger, "Are you Ben Breedlove's sister?" Ben regarded the attention lightheartedly. He had taken many girls on many dates, but he had always preferred to remain friends. Ben had never had a steady *girlfriend.*

Ally had just come home from college to visit, and she had been looking forward to catching up with Ben. Going back to school in the fall of 2011 to begin his senior year presented all the usual challenges for Ben. But there seemed to be one bright spot that lightened the load on his emotional heart, if not his physical heart. Infinitely curious, but wanting to come across as nonchalant, Ally casually asked, "So what's her name?"

"Madeline," Ben replied.

"Madeline what?"

"Nick." Ben, like most teenage boys, was well versed in the one-word response.

"Okay . . ." Ally fished, "so where did you meet her?"

"Spanish."

Ally thought for a way to press Ben into providing more detail. "What is she like?"

"Nice."

"Oh." Ally gave up for the time being. "Well, that sounds good."

"Yeah," Ben replied.

• • •

Actually, Ben was captivated by Madeline the moment he saw her in Spanish class. She had long, dark hair, with sparkling blue-green eyes, and lucky for Ben, she would be his *"compañera"* (Spanish partner) for the year.

Although they sat side by side from the beginning of the semester, they never officially met until October, when they were assigned their first group project. A Texan born and raised, Ben had been adequately immersed in Hispanic culture on both sides of the Mexican border. Nevertheless, despite his bright intellect, he still had trouble translating a menu at a Tex-Mex restaurant. Although he struggled, Ben was thrilled to work on a Spanish project with Madeline. And as an added bonus, he got her phone number.

After class, Ben caught up with Grant Hamill, as usual. But today, Ben was beaming.

"Dude, I just met the hottest girl at Westlake!" Like Ally, Grant was intrigued. Ben had never made a statement like that before. Ben couldn't contain himself, but he was apprehensive about the grade that he and Madeline had made on their presentation. Madeline routinely made As, but today with Ben as her *compañero*, they were given a B. Ben hoped it wouldn't hurt his chances.

Later that night, Madeline received her first text from Ben in an apology that said, "Sorry about that, that we got a bad grade." Lucky for Ben, Madeline didn't mind a bit.

Although unaware of Ben's feelings for her, Madeline was struck by his personality. She thought Ben was handsome, and she was familiar with some of the YouTube videos he had filmed with Megan Parken. She had also heard that Ben had a heart condition, but this made a negligible impression on her perception of him. What really struck her was Ben's compassion. Madeline had often seen him engaging in conversation at school with kids who had special needs, and she admired his consideration. And, of course, his smile. Ben was always smiling.

Madeline lived just across the lake from Ben, and to his delight, she had expressed an interest in wakeboarding and wakesurfing. "I've only done it a few times," she had admitted to him, "but I really liked it. I hope I can get up next summer." *Wow*, Ben thought. *She's pretty* and *she likes water sports.* He was sure he had met his dream girl.

Ever the encourager, Ben had told her, "Don't worry. You'll be really good at it."

Partnering in Spanish class eventually led to studying together at Barnes & Noble after school. Well, at least they had planned on studying. When they met, they talked for hours about water sports, film, and music. As their conversations and trust deepened, they began to share other aspects of their lives.

Ben opened up about his heart condition. Madeline confided in Ben about a conflict that hurt her deeply, and Ben listened.

"People don't know who you really are," Ben told her. "And they don't know my real story. They don't know the truth. They've just heard stuff and assume they know me. Same with you. Don't worry about being popular with everybody. You're a good person; just be caring, unique, and honest with yourself." Although Madeline didn't say so at the time, she knew she was looking at a person with precisely those qualities.

"You're right," Madeline said. "I tend to be a worrywart."

Ben smiled. "I understand. But don't worry so much; just enjoy the ride you are on."

• • •

"Hey, what's up?" While Ally was home one weekend, visiting from college, she stopped by Ben's doorway just to talk.

"Just looking up some Kid Cudi interviews," Ben replied, typing on his laptop. "Come watch." Ben seemed particularly fascinated with the videos and interested in sharing them. Ally hopped up on the bed next to him.

"It's funny," Ben began. "Kid Cudi talks about God and heaven in some of his songs. I know there's a lot of bad stuff in his songs, but I think he believes in God."

"Really?" Ally was genuinely interested in what Ben was telling her, yet even more intrigued by his curiosity about Kid Cudi's spirituality. Ben kept up with popular news about his favorite artists in the media, but it was unusual for him to be researching one of them in such depth.

"Like in 'Mr. Rager,' Kid Cudi talks about how there's all this bad stuff in life," Ben responded, "but he likes to think of a day when people won't have to deal with that anymore. To me that sounds like heaven. And I know that Kid Cudi said in an interview that he thinks his dad is in heaven. His dad died of cancer when he was a little kid."

"Wow, that's actually really interesting," Ally commented.

"Yeah," Ben agreed. "I really think he might believe in God. I hope he does."

Throughout the fall of his senior year, Ben regularly attended a Young Life group with one of his best friends, Justin Martinez, and some other friends from school. The group was led by Andrew Hayslip, a young college graduate who volunteered as a Young Life leader. He would have the guys over to his house, mainly to talk about life and matters of faith. Ben also attended the Austin Stone Community Church with his family, where he enjoyed music led by Aaron Ivey. Ben occasionally invited his friends to go along with him, but he was never offended if a friend declined his invitation.

Ben crossed all lines when it came to establishing friendships.

He didn't judge, but instead he accepted everyone unconditionally and looked for the best in each person. He wasn't naive or unaware that some of his friends were dabbling in drugs, or getting into trouble in other ways, but Ben chose to focus on people's best qualities, and could value those relationships. Ben knew that he was not immune to making bad decisions himself, and adopted a mind-set of encouragement rather than judgment.

Andrew Hayslip understood that Ben's faith would become evident through his actions, and advised Ben just to be a good friend. "Don't worry," Andrew said. "You'll find a way."

## CHAPTER 24

# COASTIN'

When life brings trouble
You can fight or run away

—"COASTIN'" (ZION I)

As the days approaching the Thanksgiving holiday became ever more festive, Ben became ever more miserable. There was an almost palpable tension in his every move.

"Deanne," Shawn began, his tone somber, "we need to do something about Ben."

"We are doing everything we know to do." Deanne was frustrated. She knew that Shawn was genuinely concerned about their son, but oftentimes she felt as if he were placing all of the responsibility on her. Deanne also acknowledged that ultimately there was no way, no matter how many appointments she scheduled with his doctors or how much research she conducted, that she could do anything to change Ben's condition.

"Well," Shawn continued, "we need to find something that works. This is bad. We can't let his arrhythmia go on like this."

"I know," Deanne replied.

A few years earlier, Shawn and Deanne had taken Ben to see a nutritionist, Dr. Glen R. Luepnitz, to seek alternative treatment for Ben's condition. Ben immediately took to the doctor and found him to be caring and attentive, in contrast to the blunt nature of some of his other physicians. Dr. Luepnitz prescribed an array of supplements that would hopefully improve Ben's quality of life, and Ben, as well as his parents, seemed content with the new regimen.

After a few weeks of popping almost twenty pills a day, Ben grew weary of the new routine. He was scheduled to take the supplements at all different times of the day, and some of the pills were so large they were cumbersome to swallow. Ben would sometimes feel nauseated just from the large amount of water he had to consume to wash them all down. He began skipping doses, eventually skipping whole days' worth of supplements altogether.

Shawn urged Ben to keep up with the supplements, and preferred that he take all of the pills, all of the time. Shawn believed that Ben would improve optimally if he kept a consistent routine with a more nutritious diet, which would improve upon his fast-food tendencies.

Deanne, on the other hand, understood his pill fatigue, and she didn't mind if he felt like skipping doses every now and then. Unlike his Atenolol prescription, the pills served only as a supplement to his health, rather than as a necessity. Although the supplements may have improved Ben's general well-being, nothing seemed to combat his failing heart.

Ben had tried medication after medication, and none of them had calmed the arrhythmia. The initial prescription made him feel so faint that he could barely make it partway through the school day. Walking from the handicap parking spot to the school entrance, Ben often felt as though he would pass out. Taking the school elevator to the second floor, he felt exhausted merely from standing. Trying to focus in class, he felt light-headed. He just didn't feel good.

Ben's medicine was designed to relax his heart muscle, but it drained him of energy to the point that he could barely walk from his bedroom to the kitchen—a mere twenty feet away—without feeling weak. Nausea caused him to lose his appetite. He was already thin enough, especially with a recent growth spurt that pushed his height to nearly five feet, ten inches without adding an ounce of weight.

The doctors continued to say, "If we can just get your body acclimated to this medicine, we think it will be good for you; it might help smooth out the arrhythmia."

As the situation continued with no change, Ben became more vocal about the problem. "This is not working," he said. "I'm not taking this medicine anymore."

Sometimes he texted Deanne from school, saying, "I don't feel good. This medicine is horrible. Can you call the doctor and ask him about it?"

Empathizing with his frustration, Shawn and Deanne attempted to be his advocates with his medical team, urging them to find something else that worked better. They appreciated the doctors' efforts, and they understood that their intent was to avoid the next level of drugs, which included even more negative side effects. Besides possible liver damage, the more aggressive drugs would affect Ben's countenance and appearance, externally changing his skin color to a sickly bluish cast.

Moreover, the doctors' primary concern was getting his heart rhythm under control. The frequent arrhythmia was not a safe situation and could turn catastrophic at any point. They knew that they needed to find something that worked, and time was not on their side. They discussed two other alternatives with the Breedloves. In the first option, they could put Ben under anesthesia and use his own defibrillator to shock his heart back into a smooth rhythm. But that was a surgical situation, and ever since the cardiac arrest problems during the "routine" tonsil procedure, they were reluctant to put him under anesthesia again.

The second option was also a surgery that would cause the heart to be completely dependent on the pacemaker, so it would never again be able to work on its own. That was a "no-turning-back" decision, and the doctors exhibited such a stern seriousness when they explained that possibility, Deanne and Shawn shied away from pursuing it until there were no other alternatives.

Ben *begged* Deanne to make the doctors take him off the medicine. He couldn't stand it anymore. At this point, he preferred the discomfort of his heart bumping over the harrowing side effects of the medication. Hating to watch her son suffer, Deanne consented. "We'll just have to work with your doctor to find something else for you," she told him. But even after trying various other medications, nothing helped Ben feel any better. To his chagrin, the doctors pressured him to try the original prescription once more, to see whether his body could acclimate to the medication over the holidays.

So Ben continued to take the medicine every morning and every night. And he continued to be miserable.

DDad and Corine had come to visit for the holiday, but contrary to his usual eagerness to entertain company, Ben secluded himself in his room throughout much of their stay. The family atmosphere fell limp without his witty humor and unpredictable mischief that were so beloved by them all. Deanne was a bit embarrassed by her son's lack of consideration for their company. She urged Ben to engage, but he was just not himself.

He would emerge from his room jaundiced and sickly-looking, with dark circles under his hollowed eyes. He would recede into a corner of the room and sit, listless and without speaking a word. When questioned, he would respond with a curt remark.

The family could sense his growing agitation and generously tried to give him the freedom and space to be cranky. Who could blame him? Everyone felt his frustration and had great compassion and empathy for Ben as they watched him struggle, and each one in his or her own way tried to be encouraging, but in truth, there was little they could do.

Corine was concerned. Having served as a dean of nursing in her earlier years, she knew that Ben's countenance was telling of more than just bad medicine. Toward the end of their holiday together, Corine knowingly remarked, "Ben, it must be the pits, feeling this bad."

"It is," was his response.

• • •

The Sunday following Thanksgiving, Ally attended the evening service at the Austin Stone Community Church with her boyfriend, Cameron. The two of them walked into the Austin High gymnasium, where the services were held, and took their seats as the lights faded and the band began to play. Moved by the soulful voice of Aaron Ivey, one of Ben's favorite worship leaders, Ally closed her eyes and let her thoughts fade away. As Aaron sang the lyrics to "Your Great Name," the words began to sink in.

> *All the weak find their strength at the sound of your*
> *great name . . .*
> *Sick are healed and the dead are raised at the sound of*
> *your great name.*

By the end of the service, Ally felt hot tears streaming down her face. She took Cameron by the hand and pulled him out of his seat before the lights came on, dragging him all the way out to the car.

As they climbed inside the Jeep, Cameron started the ignition and turned on the heater, then took Ally's hand in his. "Ally, what's wrong?" he asked, confused.

She took a deep breath. "Cameron, I don't know," she told him. "Those lyrics were just really getting to me. For some reason I just think . . . I feel like . . ." Ally burst into tears before she could finish her sentence. "Ben is going to die."

Cameron wrapped his arms around Ally, hearing the deep pain inside her as she buried her face in his shoulder. After a few minutes, she sat back in her seat, sighing heavily. "And I don't mean eventually," she resumed, dabbing her eyes with her sleeve. "I feel . . ." Ally paused, lowering her voice to a whisper. "I feel like it might be soon."

Cameron hesitated, breaking his gaze from Ally's to keep his composure. "Don't think like that," he whispered back.

"Maybe I need to think like that," she replied. "I don't know, Cameron. Maybe God is preparing my heart."

The two remained silent and contemplative on the drive back to Cameron's house. As he pulled into the driveway, Ally stared out the window at the stars, thinking. "Cameron?" she said finally.

"Yes?" he replied.

"Do you think we can spend a lot of time with Ben over Christmas break? I know we hang out with him a lot at home, but I mean, can we invite him out to do things with us?"

"Of course we can," Cameron replied.

Ally and Ben had always enjoyed spending time together, but now Ally felt an urgency to make the most of the time they had. What proved difficult for her was devoting more of her attention to Ben without making him feel like he was dying. He knew her well, and he could sense when his family was treating him with special attention. Oftentimes, Ally would refrain from telling him something that sounded too sentimental, or hold back when she desperately wanted to hug him. And ultimately, she didn't regret it. She knew that he wanted more than anything to live a normal life, and Ally wanted more than anything for him just to live.

• • •

Going back to school after Thanksgiving proved stressful for Ben. He was already far behind in his classes and hoped to work extra hard the following week to make up for it, and to begin studying for his finals, only two weeks away. Ben pushed himself, but couldn't make it through the week. He missed more school, got farther behind, and became even more demoralized. In most of his classes, reviewing for finals was scheduled to begin the following Monday, December 5. Ben still couldn't make it to school. He stayed in bed until three p.m. that day and didn't have much of an appetite. All the while, Deanne and Shawn were in contact with his doctors, who believed that if the new medicine worked, it could control the arrhythmias, which would prevent Ben from feeling so weak.

And if it didn't work . . .

## PART 3

# THE PURPOSE

CHAPTER 25

# DON'T FAIL ME NOW

*The only thing that I pray is that my feet don't fail me now*

—"JESUS WALKS" (KANYE WEST)

M adeline Nick was beginning to worry. Ben had been out of school almost all week. On Monday, December 5, a finals review day, he was absent again. Madeline wondered about him throughout the day, and was thinking about him that evening as she worked on her homework when she noticed a text message from him, asking what Ms. Albright had reviewed that day in Spanish. They texted back and forth for a while, and Madeline asked why he had been absent from school.

"I haven't been feeling well," he responded. Madeline offered a few words of encouragement, and then as Ben always did anytime they texted at night, he sent another message saying good night to her. She replied similarly, and then sat back in her chair, impressed again at Ben's thoughtfulness.

When Madeline spotted Ben in their first-period Spanish class the next morning, she noticed that he looked unusually tired. Wearing a warm black zipped-up North Face jacket, he seemed listless and lethargic when Ms. Albright asked him to step up to her desk to get some homework assignments.

Madeline's next class was in the opposite direction, so she didn't walk with him. That wasn't unusual, since often after Spanish, Ben met up with Grant on their way to film class.

Ben walked slowly up the crowded hallway, oblivious to the swirl of faces around him, as students and faculty members hurried to their destinations. Approaching "the commons," a large open atrium where students crossed paths and congregated for quick conversations between classes, he could feel himself becoming increasingly sluggish. He knew that weak feeling well; he'd experienced it so many times before. He had to get to a place where he could rest—soon. Several benches lined each side of the commons, so he headed for one of them and eased himself down. For a few moments, he sat there alone, his heart bumping, consciousness fleeing away from him.

Grant was looking for Ben that Tuesday morning, watching for him as he did every day after first period as he approached the commons. Grant looked everywhere for Ben, but didn't see him. Then he caught a glimpse of him coming up the hall, but at that moment, somebody said hello to Grant, and he turned his head. When he looked back, he didn't see Ben. Thinking that he might be pulling a prank, Grant went outside to the courtyard and couldn't find him, so he returned to the commons. There he saw a crowd of people gathering by a bench, so he hurried over to see what was happening. To his shock, he saw Ben on the floor, stretched out on his back.

• • •

Westlake High's school nurse, Holly Hubbell, had been an emergency room and an intensive-care-unit nurse since 1978, working in California for a number of years before moving to Austin. By Ben's senior year, she had been serving as Westlake's nurse for more than six years. She was accustomed to being called upon to treat classroom emergencies—everything from bloody noses to seizures—and had even been summoned to a classroom to help Ben on one occasion, back in November 2008, when he felt as though he were going to pass out in class during his freshman year. This was the first of many emergency situations in which Nurse Holly would come to Ben's aid. She was aware of Ben's condition, but he was not a frequent or fickle visitor to her school clinic. Ben was not the type of student to fake a sickness so he could go to the nurses' office simply to get out of class; if he went to the clinic, he had a real need.

When Nurse Holly got to the classroom in this first emergency encounter with Ben, she discovered that he was short of breath, and his face had a dusky blue appearance, his lips purple. She transferred him to the school clinic, put him on oxygen, and kept a close watch on his vitals; his blood pressure was especially low. The oxygen revived Ben, and he seemed to be okay, so Holly called Deanne rather than an ambulance.

Deanne drove to the school to pick up her son. She recognized immediately that Ben's heart was bumping. Holly helped Ben into a wheelchair and transported him out to the car. Deanne took him home, and, with some rest, his condition improved. Later, Deanne sent Holly a beautiful bouquet of flowers as a token of her appreciation.

That was the first of several incidents involving Ben that Holly Hubbell treated. It was never routine for Holly, but both she and Deanne had learned how to deal with it. When Ben had trouble, Holly called the Breedlove home, and Deanne hurried to the school to pick him up and take him to the doctor—again.

As she moved throughout the school, with its population of more than twenty-six hundred students, Holly regularly kept a keen eye out for Ben. She recognized that his condition was deteriorating and had commented to her colleague Marisa Garcia, "I'm afraid we're going to find him down in a bathroom sometime." By November 2010, the seriousness of his condition prompted Deanne to have Holly place a note in Ben's file to contact an EMS first if he was nonresponsive, even before contacting the parents for any heart emergencies he might experience. They both understood that if he should have another incident, time would be of the essence.

• • •

The coming finals week followed by the excitement of holiday break put the school in an energetic mood, but Tuesday, December 6, began as a typical, peaceful Westlake morning for Holly and Marisa. They were in the nurses' office, located just off the commons, when a student ducked into the office and frantically yelled, "There's a boy down on the ground in the commons and he's purple!"

Holly and Marisa dropped everything and ran out the door into the commons. The bell for the next class was about to ring, so although the commons was still crowded, the large number of students had already begun to thin out. But there was a circle of people staring down at the floor near one of the benches, so Holly and Marisa headed in that direction. As they were running, they saw Thunder sprinting toward them. Ordinarily, when there was a medical emergency, Thunder came calling for Nurse Hubbell: "Nurse Holly, Nurse Holly!" But Thunder ran right past Holly with a terrified look on her face, yelling into a radio, "Somebody get the AED!" She ran straight to the office and grabbed an AED, then bolted back toward Holly and Marisa. Thunder's radio announcement alerted the school administrators that an emergency was in progress, so the principal, Linda Rawlings, and an associate principal, Steve Ramsey, headed toward the commons as well.

A school security camera later confirmed that Holly and Marisa reached the circle of students surrounding Ben within forty-five seconds. Holly pushed through the crowd, looked down on the floor, and saw a familiar form. "Oh, my God, it's Ben!" she shouted. Holly took one look at his purple color and thought, *He's dead.* Nevertheless, as a certified CPR instructor, she wasted no time; she tilted Ben's head back and blew two breaths into his mouth, then went directly to doing compressions. "Go get the oxygen," she yelled to anyone who might respond. "It's in the clinic."

Thunder ran up to the group carrying a defibrillator. Officer St. Clair, the campus policeman, saw the commotion and joined the nurses on the floor. "I can help with the compressions," he said. "You monitor this." He nodded toward the AED. The officer took over pumping on Ben's chest.

Holly grabbed the defibrillator, pressing it into position, but as she was about to shock Ben, the defibrillator read, "No shock advised." Holly knew what that meant: The patient had flatlined. The defibrillator has to be able to read some movement of the heart muscle before it can shock, so Holly knew there was either very slight to no fibrillation in Ben, or he was dead. She and Aaron continued doing CPR anyhow. Another minute went by.

Linda Rawlings, the school principal, arrived on the scene and began conveying Holly's comments regarding Ben's condition and the compressions they were doing to a 911 operator and the EMS team that was on the way.

Just then Ben's body seemed to stir slightly. "Stop doing CPR!" somebody shouted. "He's moving!"

Holly knew better. She had seen reflexive motion too many times to interpret a body's movement as a sign of life. She shouted, "Keep going!" They continued doing compressions. Somebody brought the oxygen, so Holly held an oxygen tube to Ben's mouth and nose and poured oxygen into him.

"Clear the area!" somebody called out to student onlookers. "Go to class." Somewhere in the din, Holly heard the announcement, "Teachers, we are in 'stay put' condition. Stay where you are. Students, go immediately to class and remain there until further notice." All the while Holly and Officer St. Clair and Marisa continued doing CPR.

The EMS crew arrived, and Holly quickly briefed them. "This student has a known heart problem," she told them. "We found him in full cardiac arrest and have been doing CPR for several minutes and he has not responded." Holly, Marisa, and Officer St. Clair moved off to the side, giving the paramedics room to take over. Ben had been out for nearly three minutes.

A paramedic quickly cut off Ben's black North Face jacket and T-shirt so he could get the AED into better position on his chest. With her own heart racing, Holly sank down on a nearby bench. They had done their best, but she feared that they had lost Ben.

. . .

Grant had been standing nearby, concerned for his friend, and not willing to leave his side. He heard the assistant principal saying that he wanted to get the Breedloves' phone number, so, pulling his phone out of his pocket, he said, "I have it right here," and pressed send. Shawn answered, and in his nervousness Grant skipped any polite greetings. "I don't know what is going on," Grant told Shawn, "but Ben has collapsed."

CHAPTER 26

# MAD WORLD

The dreams in which I'm dying are the best I've ever had

—"MAD WORLD" (GARY JULES)

O n December 6, 2011, Ben cheated death for a third time. He awoke on the hard floor of the Westlake High commons, a blurred huddle of faces over him. His senses returning to him, Ben realized that he could neither move nor speak. As the image in front of him came into focus, he made out the figures of two paramedics leaning closely over him. On the bare skin of his chest, Ben could feel the two gauzy pads of a defibrillator. One of the paramedics pressed two fingers against Ben's jugular vein, holding his free hand in front of Ben's nostrils.

"He's not breathing . . . and he has no pulse."

As Ben lingered in a strange limbo of consciousness, he could hardly believe the words he was hearing. He listened to his last few heartbeats resound with an eerie thumping that seemed to echo inside his chest, then silence. *This is it,* he thought. *I'm dying.*

Somehow, Ben watched the paramedic who had taken his pulse place his hands on the electric pads stuck to his chest. Turning to his assistant, who apprehensively manned the defibrillator box, the paramedic shouted, *"Go!"*

In that instant, Ben could only anticipate the intense, electrifying pain about to sear through his body. He wanted desperately to steel his entire body in preparation for the jolt he was about to feel, but his muscles were useless. He was helpless and paralyzed on the hard floor. And he was about to experience the pain of death. Then . . . blackout.

White. Pure white. He could see no walls, only white, a brighter white than he could ever describe that seemed to engulf his surroundings in every direction. In the whiteness, Ben listened to the most quiet he had ever heard in his life.

As he stood entranced in that room, Ben was filled with an awareness that surpassed all understanding. It was the same sensation he had experienced in the presence of the bright light during the seizure he had when he was four. It was absolute peace.

In front of him stood a full-length mirror. Ben looked into the mirror to see himself handsomely dressed in a dark suit, with a hand resting on his shoulder. His eyes traced the hand's reflection up to its owner's face. Behind Ben, also suavely suited, stood his favorite rap artist, Kid Cudi. *What?* Ben wondered how he could possibly be staring into the face of a celebrity. *Kid Cudi*, of all people! Then Ben remembered: *I'm dead.*

Marveling at their handsome reflections, Ben thought to himself, *D\*mn, we look good!*

Staring at his reflection, he felt more confident than he had ever felt in his life. He couldn't stop smiling, and he was smiling *really* big. Something was different. Ben stared more intently into the mirror. He wasn't just looking at his reflection . . . he was looking at his entire life. In a sense of time that Ben could never explain, he stood in front of that mirror and watched his entire life, every moment he had ever experienced, play out in front of him in real time. Yet somehow it went by in an instant. In that incomprehensible moment, Ben felt proud of himself, of his entire life, of everything he had done. It was the *best* feeling. Ben knew he was ready for something more important.

Kid Cudi drew Ben away from the mirror and guided him over to an enormous glass desk. As they stood before the desk, the room suddenly began to resonate with music; Ben listened as the familiar lyrics from Kid Cudi's song "Mr. Rager" resounded throughout the room and inside his heart.

*When will the fantasy end?*
*When will the heaven begin?*[*]

As the music played, Kid Cudi asked Ben, "Are you ready?"
"Yeah," Ben replied. He was ready.
Kid Cudi urged Ben, "Go now!"
Ben really thought he was going to heaven.

• • •

Instead, Ben awoke to find himself back on the cold floor of the Westlake High commons. With the noise of shuffling feet and the

---

[*] "Mr. Rager," written by Emile Haynie, Scott Mescudi, © Sony/ TV Music Publishing, LLC.

familiar squeaking wheels of a stretcher rolling in his direction, he was ushered back into the world.

As he took his first breath, his chest ached with excruciating pain as his lungs expanded against his rib cage. Ben knew the feeling. *They must have bruised my ribs during CPR,* he thought to himself, catching his breath again.

"We have a heartbeat!" Ben heard someone shout. He reluctantly opened his eyes. Above him, two blurry figures came into focus, revealing the two paramedics who had tried to revive him from the dead. Expressions of immeasurable relief washed over their faces. The one who had taken Ben's pulse looked him over in wide-eyed wonder.

"Whew! That's one big smile you've got on your face!" the paramedic exclaimed. "Bet you're glad to be back, bud!"

Back? That was the farthest thought from Ben's mind. *Back?* If only the paramedic had known where he had *actually* just been. Ben didn't ever want to leave that place. His smile faded away with the dream. Ben wished he had never woken up.

He continued lying on the floor for a few more moments, observing the team of paramedics and the Westlake faculty collecting their wits and catching their breath.

"Where's my phone?" Ben asked, his first spoken words after returning from heaven's waiting room. The sea of faces around him broke into smiles. Nurse Holly burst into tears of joy. She had seen dead people before, and she understood how unusual it was for somebody in Ben's condition to come back.

"He must be okay if he's looking for his phone," someone chirped happily.

Ben remained motionless as the paramedics hoisted his body onto a stretcher and began wheeling him down the fluorescently lit hallway. The harsh light hurt his eyes, and his ears rang with the buzzing of electricity. His body seemed to weigh heavily on the stretcher. Nurse Holly leaned over Ben and whispered, "I was praying for you the whole time."

Ben smiled weakly at the nurse. "Thank you."

As the team approached the exit doors leading out to the circle drive where the ambulance awaited them, a figure walking alongside the stretcher in Ben's periphery caught his attention. "Officer St. Clair, I've been meaning to talk to you about all those tickets they've been writing me," Ben said with a sly smile. "Look, every morning when I show up at school, all the handicap spots are taken. *That's* why I've been taking up the visitors' spots. And you know I can't walk all the way from the senior lot." Again, Ben smiled mischievously up at St. Clair, waiting for his reaction.

Officer St. Clair looked incredulously at Ben. "Let's not worry about that right now," he said. "All right? You just worry about getting yourself to the hospital."

Even after facing death and being torn away from the peace for which his soul now longed, Ben remained lighthearted. He was destined to stay that way for all of eternity.

CHAPTER 27

# DON'T LET ME FALL

Just a moment ago
I was up so high

—"DON'T LET ME FALL" (B.O.B)

For most of Ben's life, Deanne Breedlove woke up each morning wondering whether he had made it through the night. Often, with great trepidation she peeked into his bedroom before dawn, hoping against hope that her son was still breathing. It was not until she saw his chest moving up and down in rhythmic motion that she could breathe easy along with him. She would then see whether Ben felt well enough to go to school that day. Every day was the same routine. *Is he alive? Is he energetic enough to get out of bed today?* Fortunately, most days Ben would be up and in the shower, getting ready for school before Deanne even checked on him.

Tuesday morning, December 6, was one of those days. Deanne was surprised, because Ben had felt so poorly for weeks leading up to this day. Nevertheless, she was relieved that he felt well enough to go to school. Although even after his shower, Ben did not look as though he were back to normal—at least, not to Deanne. To her, he looked tired. As he gobbled down a quick bite of breakfast, Ben said that his heart was bumping—his usual signal that he needed to stay home—but that he felt well enough to go, that he would just attend his finals reviews and then come home.

"Are you sure you feel okay to go to school today?" Deanne pressed him several times that morning.

"I'm fine, Mom. Really."

"Well, please promise me that you will come home right after your test reviews."

Ben smiled one of his signature impish smiles at his mom. "I will, Mom. Promise." Deanne and Ben hugged and he was out the door.

With Ben at school, Deanne's day opened up. She planned to do some much-needed Christmas shopping that morning. She hadn't been out of the house in more than ten days, so getting some errands done would be a welcome change. She left the house shortly after Ben and Jake were off to school.

Sometime around nine a.m., she called Shawn at home. When Shawn picked up the phone, he didn't even say hello. Instead, in a serious tone, he asked directly, "Where are you?"

"I'm shopping," Deanne replied.

"I just received a call from Grant Hamill, and he said that they were working on Ben at school and that we should get there."

Deanne didn't need any more details. She immediately pointed her car in the direction of the school, which was approximately thirty minutes away. Along the way, she called the school office, only to be transferred to a very shaken assistant principal, who didn't have much information to tell her. He was kind, but didn't know what to say. Deanne could tell he was searching for words. He said Ben had passed out, was given CPR, and was finally responding, and that he would be going by ambulance to the hospital. He asked whether she had a preference for which hospital she wanted Ben to be taken to, since the ambulance had not yet left the school property.

"Take him to Dell Children's," Deanne said. "They know him there." Deanne gave the administrator some brief instructions, turned her car around, and started driving toward the hospital. Just then Nurse Holly entered the front office, and the assistant principal passed the call along to Holly. "Yes, he's been in cardiac arrest, but he's awake and talking, and has a heart rate," she informed Deanne. "I'm on my way," Deanne replied, then hung up.

With horn blaring and her vision blurring from tears, Deanne prayed loudly as she careened through the busy streets. "Please comfort Ben," she prayed, "and let him survive. Please don't let him die! Not like this, not now! Let me hug him and tell him I love him." It was as deep and desperate a prayer as the one she had prayed when he was unresponsive in the ambulance at age four.

Deanne reached the ER before Ben did, so she was ushered into the examining room that Ben would be coming to once the ambulance arrived. When she saw the paramedics wheeling Ben into the emergency room, she was shocked by his appearance. He was tucked onto a gurney and was being wheeled in with several IVs trailing behind. She had seen Ben so many times before in various hospital settings, but never like this. He was blue. His earlobes had actually turned a dark purple, almost black.

Ben was talking, but he seemed groggy and out of it. When he saw Deanne, he recognized her, but had a confused expression on his face, as though he couldn't comprehend where he was and what was happening. "Mom? What are you doing here?" Ben asked.

Deanne grabbed his hand and tried to hug him around his IVs with her other arm. He was ice-cold. The nurses covered Ben with layers of warm blankets, fresh out of the warmer, and still he wanted more heat. Deanne was relieved to be able to talk to him and hold him, even though he was still strapped onto the ambulance gurney. Ben smiled at her, and said, "Don't worry, Mom. I'm okay." He had no idea how blue his skin was!

"Do you remember what happened at school?"

"No . . ."

"You passed out and Nurse Holly had to do CPR."

Ben didn't remember that. He did recall greeting Officer St. Clair, and hopefully getting the parking tickets worked out.

• • •

Back at school, the associate principal had found Grant Hamill and called him out of class. "Ben's gone," he told Grant.

"What!" At first, Grant thought the principal's words meant that Ben had passed away, and Grant's own heart nearly stopped.

"He's gone to the hospital, and if you want to go, you can."

Grant didn't waste any time. He headed for the hospital, where he found Ben still in the emergency room. By then Ben's coloring had returned to almost normal, and his sense of humor was definitely back. Ben stuck his fist out to Grant when he saw him. Grant bumped Ben's fist with his. Without even saying hello, Ben asked Grant, "Did you film it?"

"No! No, I did *not* film it," Grant replied, encouraged that Ben was okay. "Go get fixed. I'll wait here."

A short time later, Shawn arrived, and Grant had wrangled his way in to visit, the two of them now joining Deanne alongside Ben's bed. Now that he was settled into the usual post-incident pattern, Ben was more reflective about what he had experienced while he was unconscious, and technically dead for more than three minutes. He openly and enthusiastically shared his vision or dream—he wasn't quite sure what to call it—with Grant and his parents. They listened attentively, intrigued but not really knowing how to respond. Grant was especially befuddled, since he lacked the "faith context" in which he could process Ben's account. He and Ben had occasionally discussed their beliefs, more specifically Ben's belief in God and Grant's decision not to believe. But that was as far as they had gone. Grant could tell by Ben's expression, though, that his friend was being completely honest. There was no need to confirm with *pineapple* on this one.

Shawn was fascinated and intrigued. He knew Ben tended to be skeptical and not given to an easy acceptance of similar near-death stories. For her part, Deanne was convinced that what Ben had encountered was some sort of heavenly experience. She'd read and heard about numerous near-death experiences, and what some experts called "life-after-life" episodes in which a person encountered a bright light apparently on the borders of heaven. From her perspective, she had no problem believing that Ben had indeed touched the shores of heaven, and the fact that he had come back from the throes of death meant that he was alive for some very special purpose.

Before long, Holly Hubbell and Diane Carter, Westlake's assistant principal, arrived at the hospital, as did Grant's dad. "Ben," Diane commented, "you'll be happy to know that all of your parking tickets have been waived." The atmosphere was almost festive, as they all knew when they looked at Ben that they were looking at a living, breathing miracle.

# CHAPTER 28

# WHEN WILL THE FANTASY END?

—"MR. RAGER" (KID CUDI)

After spending a day and a half in the hospital under observation, Ben was itching to get back to school and be around his friends. Donning some scrubs that were given to him by a doctor upon his hospital release, he wanted to return to school Thursday morning. Deanne much preferred that Ben stay home and continue to rest. She really didn't want to let him out of her sight, so she decided to check with his doctors. Surprisingly, they said that if he felt up to it, he could go. Deanne reminded Ben that his grades weren't the top priority right now and that he didn't need to try to make it to the test reviews, but he had a strong need and desire to go anyway.

Ben seemed to appreciate his mom allowing him to make this decision for himself. Deanne desperately wanted Ben to have this freedom and be in a normal setting, but she insisted that they let the appropriate people know that he was going to be on campus that day, so she notified the principal, assistant principal, and the school nurse. Ben and Deanne had an extended visit with Nurse Holly in her private office before Deanne felt comfortable enough to release Ben into the hallways.

Nurse Holly, Deanne, and Ben concurred that it would be wise for Ben to take it easy his first few days back: to use the elevator rather than the stairs, and always have a buddy with him, even in the restroom. If at any point Ben decided he didn't want to push through the day, he could call it quits and go home. Nurse Holly encouraged him to simply show up in the nurse's office and rest on one of the couches if necessary.

Ben was excited about getting back to real life—his life— outside of the hospital. He loved his friends. He liked getting to be in school with everyone. Plus he wanted to show off his scrubs. He had earned them!

Halfway through the school day, the home phone rang. It was Ben asking to be picked up. He had expended all his energy. He was so glad he could go for that partial day. It would be the last day he would sit at his desk in his classrooms. He would never make it back.

•  •  •

Although Ben did not feel strong enough to return to school on Friday, he did, however, convince his parents to let him escape the house briefly to buy a new charger for his phone that had died. On the way down Westlake Drive, an oncoming car swerved into his lane. In an attempt to dodge the car, Ben also swerved, grazing the side of a beautiful, brand-new Jaguar XJL Ultimate.

Out of the driver's side of the Jag emerged a portly man in a suit, bedecked with gold rings and a gold chain. Ben instinctively reached for his pocket to pull his driver's license from his wallet when he realized he was wearing his hospital scrubs. *Oh, great,* Ben thought.

"I'm sorry, sir," Ben apologized. "I'm going to have to call my mom to bring me my driver's license."

The man was irate. "What do you think you're doing? You teenagers! You were texting, weren't you?"

"No, I wasn't. I—"

"Unbelievable!" the man interjected, and continued to vent.

Ben attempted to appease the man, but to no avail.

Waving his arms around with overdramatized gesticulation, the man hurled expletives and insults while Ben phoned his mom. "Mom, do you still have my wallet in your purse from the other day in the hospital?"

"Yes, I do," Deanne replied.

"Okay, I'm gonna need it," Ben told her. "I just got in a wreck. Can you bring it to me, please?"

"Ben, are you okay? Are you hurt?" Deanne's first and foremost concern was for Ben. Even if he wasn't injured, the stress of being in an accident might be too much for him.

Ben reassured her that he was fine, but said that the police had not yet arrived, and the other driver was yelling at him, making prodigious use of the F-word.

"Move away from the other driver," Deanne advised, "and just ignore him. I'm on my way."

When Deanne arrived on the scene of the accident, Ben and

the other driver were each standing by their cars. A policeman was pulling up in front of them.

Deanne walked over to see how things were going. Ben explained that the other driver had parked on the right-hand side of the lane in which he was driving. He was about to drive past him, but another car rapidly approached from the other direction. Ben decided he'd have to squeeze between the two cars: the one parked on the side of the lane, and the oncoming car. As he did, he made an error in judgment and he sideswiped the parked car.

Ben apologized repeatedly, but the Jag owner was irate. His wife then poked her head out of the car and started making derisive comments as well.

Being just days away from that peaceful white-room experience, Ben didn't find this place to be too peaceful. His apology was falling on deaf ears, and he could feel himself winding tighter. By the time Deanne got there, Ben told her that he really just wanted to punch the guy, but knew he couldn't do that. He had been accused of being one of those irresponsible teenagers who had no manners, and of texting while driving or making a phone call, neither of which he had done.

That peaceful white room was drawing Ben back.

• • •

Because Deanne thought Ben's vision was such an amazing story, she asked him to tell a few of her friends about it after he was discharged from the hospital. He was a bit embarrassed or uncomfortable at times in talking about his heavenly encounter, but he always complied. Ally was due home from college that weekend, too, and Deanne could hardly wait for Ben to share his experience with her. Later, the family would learn from Ben that this vision was so powerful and so real that he knew he was awake. In fact, he shied away from referring to it as a dream or a vision, because he knew he had really been there, one step outside of heaven.

• • •

Ben's fainting in the commons had brought Madeline Nick's feelings for Ben into better focus. When a student had barged into her second-period class that morning, telling everyone that Ben had collapsed, Madeline was deeply concerned. She realized that her crush on Ben was growing into something more significant, that she cared for him. After she found out that Ben was okay, she wanted him to know how she felt about him. Later that day, she sent him a text message—"I hope you're doing okay in the hospital"—and she let him know that she really liked him.

Ben had responded in a text: "Aw, thank you so much. We'll see how things go."

Ben remained home from school every day in December, except the half day that he attended classes following his release from the hospital. By Tuesday, December 13, he was feeling stir-crazy. After resting all day, Ben felt strong enough that evening to go with Madeline to Barton Creek Resort & Spa, one of Austin's premier country clubs, where they talked for several hours. He told her that he wanted to tell her about the experience he had the week before, when he had collapsed in the commons. He hinted to her that he believed in angels.

Ben and Madeline hung out for a while, enjoying a carefree time together. They laughed about guys who said their idea of the

WHEN WILL THE FANTASY END? • 199

perfect woman was one who would be willing to make a great sandwich for her guy.

Later that evening, at nine forty-six p.m., Madeline sent Ben a text message: "You're the type of guy I'd make a sandwich for."

He responded, "Ha, ha, ha, I can't believe you just said that. I wish I could screen-shot that. Okay. I want a sandwich."

· · ·

After the auto accident, Ben's spirits were often lackluster. Deanne, Shawn, and Jake seemed to radiate with the joy of having Ben back, and heartfelt messages from his Westlake friends bombarded his phone; even random kids from other Austin schools, having heard rumors, inundated Ben with conversations over Xbox LIVE. Still, Ben remained crestfallen.

Ben tried to appreciate their attempts to lift his spirits; he really did. And when his facade of good humor failed him, he hid behind literal humor. At home, however, Ben found that his family was not as receptive to the return of his prankster persona as he had anticipated.

Ben ambled into the kitchen one evening while Deanne was doing the dishes. Casually, she asked Ben whether he had been studying for his finals. Attempting to provide comic relief to yet another taxing day, Ben joked, "Come on, Mom. I just died last week; do I still have to study?"

Deanne glanced up from unloading the dishwasher. "Yes," she replied, smiling, "you do."

Overhearing the conversation while rummaging through the pantry, Shawn laughed at Ben's not so tactful attempt to evade his studies.

Deanne knew Ben was trying to make light of the situation. Placing a dish down on the counter, she wrapped her arms around him. "Ben, I know you are joking," she admitted, still embracing him. "But . . . " Her voice trailed off as her words were stifled by a knot in her throat. The reality of Ben's statement closed in on her. Deanne knew that, in fact, her son *had* died last week. The thought of losing—that she had lost—her son was far too grave to be the subject of humor.

Her eyes brimmed with tears. "I just don't want to lose you," she finally sobbed to Ben.

"Wow, Mom!" Ben replied, taken aback by her earnest sentiment. "You really are upset. Don't worry so much!" he said with a huge grin.

"Ben," Shawn interjected, "your mom is justified in feeling this way. You have to let her show her love for you, especially after such a serious event.

"And, Ben . . ." Shawn added, now also embracing him, "I want you to know I love you, too."

Shawn looked into Deanne's eyes, silently sharing her anxieties. They both sensed the gravity of Ben's condition, and they connected in a way that Ben could scarcely fathom.

CHAPTER 29

# ON THE LEDGE

I wish you would step back from that ledge, my friend

—"JUMPER" (THIRD EYE BLIND)

L ate on Saturday night, Ally searched for Ben inside the house. Their parents had asked Ben to stay home that night because his heart needed rest, so when Ally couldn't find him, she was concerned. She worried that perhaps he had collapsed someplace inside, so she checked every room in the house. Ben was nowhere in sight. Ally called Ben's cell phone, wondering whether he might have gone out briefly. She breathed a sigh of relief when Ben answered.

"Ben, where are you?" she asked.

"I'm out back, sitting on the dock," Ben replied.

She looked out the kitchen window and noticed him sitting on the back of their boat. The dock lights were off, so his form was barely discernible in the moonlight. "Are you okay?"

"Yeah, I'm fine."

More and more in recent days, Ben sought the solitude of the lake at night. The placid, starlit water surrounded by nature was a good place to think about life—and death—and to pray.

Ally hung up the phone, threw on her warm North Face jacket over her pajamas, and walked out toward the dock.

In the silent, halcyon night, Ben was perched on the platform of his docked boat. He was suspended just off the ground, his toes nearly brushing the water's surface. His mind was pervaded by his thoughts, but the world was silent. His heart was restless, but the world was still.

At the time, Ben was not aware of the Saturday-night carousing going on without him, or that his sister was searching for him inside the house. His mind was at ease; he was at peace.

It was not until Ally settled on the platform beside him that Ben realized he was not alone.

"You've been doing a lot of thinking, haven't you?" Ally asked.

"Yeah . . ." Ben replied, his eyes resting on the water's surface. "Recently I've been coming out here to ask God questions."

Ally stiffened against the stern of the boat, her ear alertly inclined toward Ben. He had rarely spoken overtly to her about God, much less divulged that he and God had been conversing together in a nearly literal manner.

Ben broke the silence.

"Remember when I went to the hospital when I was four? Well, it's weird. I don't remember anything about getting to the hospital or leaving it; I just remember being in that hallway and seeing that bright light above me. And it was like nothing else in the world mattered." Ben became still; in that moment, he *knew* that nothing else mattered. "I just kept looking at it, and I couldn't stop smiling." A reminiscent grin flashed across his face. "And that was the most peaceful feeling I've ever felt. I can't even describe how peaceful it was.

"Coming out here in the middle of the night when it's quiet and the water is so still," Ben resumed, "it's the closest I can get to that peaceful feeling. So I come out here and just ask God questions."

Ally hesitated for a few moments before asking, "What questions do you ask when you come out here?"

"Well," Ben replied, "I know this is bad to say, but sometimes I ask why I didn't just stay there. I haven't told you or Mom this, but when I got in that wreck with that guy after I got out of the hospital, after I got back in my car, I started crying so hard. I just started bawling." Ben let out a nervous laugh and looked up at his sister with a sheepish grin. He quickly returned his gaze to the water, his face becoming solemn once again. "And I thought, 'Why did I have to come back to this?'"

Understanding his frustration, yet wanting Ben to desire to live, longing to back him off that ledge, Ally was at a loss for words. She sensed almost instinctively—in a way that only a sister could know about her brother—that Ben was ready to cross over that thin line that separates the physical and spiritual worlds, that perhaps in some ways he already had, that in some ways he was already living in a new, elevated state of being—that for Ben, eternity had already begun. She knew his destination was secure, but she wasn't ready for him to leave.

As they sat together in silence, Ally's mind sought resolution.

"You want to tell me about your dream?" she ventured. "I know I heard about it from Mom already, but I haven't heard it from you yet."

Ben contemplated the question a few moments before answering. "Well, at first, when I passed out, I couldn't talk or move or anything, but I could still see and hear what was going on. So when I saw the EMS guys put the shock pads on my chest, I thought, 'Great, they're about to shock me, and I'm still awake.' And all I could think about was how much it was going to hurt."

Ben's eyes widened as if with the fear of anticipating the pain, revisiting the experience. "But right then I went into my dream. And I call it a dream or a vision, but I don't really know what to call it, because I was awake."

"It was real," Ally asserted. "Wasn't it?" She knew that Ben believed it was.

"Yeah . . ." Ben replied. "It was real."

Again they both sat in silence.

"So," Ben continued, "you know I was in that white room . . ."

"Right," Ally affirmed, "but with no walls?"

"It just went on forever. I can't really explain it. And I felt that same peaceful feeling I felt when I was four."

Ally marveled. "It was the exact same feeling?"

"Yeah," Ben replied. "And it was weird . . . I had never heard that much quiet in my life." Ben lowered the register of his voice. "It was so peaceful, like nothing else in the world mattered."

As Ben's mind drifted away from the conversation, Ally stared directly into his eyes, hoping to follow him into his receding thoughts.

"So," Ben resumed, "I was looking into that mirror, and . . ." He paused to throw his sister an *I don't know, so don't ask* sort of glance. "Kid Cudi was behind me. I still haven't really figured out why he was there, but we were both dressed in really nice suits, and—I know this sounds weird—but we looked *really* good,"

Ben noted with a nervous laugh. "And I felt more *confident* than I had ever felt in my life."

He paused, reveling in the thought. After a moment of musing, a telling smile stretched across his face. "And I just couldn't stop smiling, and I was smiling *really* big, and . . . I was proud of myself." Ben glanced back at Ally, attempting to gauge her reaction.

She was smiling at him, her eyes beaming with approval. Ben rested his eyes again on the water's peaceful surface.

"And when I was looking in the mirror, I know I was looking at myself, but I wasn't *just* looking at myself; I was looking at my entire life." Ben hesitated, evaluating the clarity of his statement. "And I was proud of my entire life, and everything I had done, and I just couldn't stop smiling. And . . ." He suddenly turned to face Ally, his eyes intent, looking deeply into hers. "I knew I was ready for something more important."

Ally stared just as intently back into Ben's eyes, absorbing his words in still silence.

Ben continued. "Then we walked over to this big glass desk. And Kid Cudi put his hand on my shoulder and said, 'Are you ready?' And I said, 'Yeah.' And then he said, 'Go now.' And the music started to play: 'When will the fantasy end? When will the heaven begin?' "

Ben paused, his animated smile fading. "And I really thought I was going to heaven."

Ally had *not* expected this. She sat motionless, staring back at Ben, astounded by his confession. Her lack of response was accompanied by a symphony of crickets.

Ben laughed abruptly, startling Ally from her pensive state. "And then I remember, those EMS guys must have thought I was crazy, because I woke up and I just couldn't stop smiling. And later this girl asked me, 'Why were you smiling so big when you woke up?' And I said, 'Well, I was just really happy.' And she looked at me like I was so weird." Ben and Ally laughed together.

Ally turned toward her brother. "Are you happy you woke up?"

With a deep sigh, Ben replied, "I guess." His hand pressed hard against his eyes; he was sobbing.

Ally could not suppress the sudden tears welling in her eyes. Throwing her arm around Ben's shoulder and drawing herself even closer to him, she tried to comfort him. But mostly she tried to convince him of his own desire to live.

"Ben, we are so happy you are still here with us. And I know you might not want to be here, but you have to know that *this life* is not our life. Our life is eternal, and that is God's gift to us. And *this life* is our gift to God.

"I don't know why God brought you back, and we may never know. But what you have to know is that if God chose to bring you back, he must have a *very* important purpose for you here."

Ally hugged Ben tighter, crying uncontrollably. For several minutes they remained in that same position, their shared tears communicating in a language they both understood.

When their breathing began to come more steadily, and their chests fell more softly, Ben broke the silence. "I think you're right. And I also think that God let me have that vision so I wouldn't be afraid of dying . . . And so I would know that heaven is worth it."

The silence this time seemed to echo throughout the entire lake.

After a long while, Ally lifted her head from Ben's shoulder.

Hesitantly pulling her arms from around his shoulders, she leaned forward to face him. "I love you, Ben," she said softly.

Ben tore his gaze from the water to meet Ally's. "I love you, too," he replied from his heart. Again, they embraced.

In an attempt to restore their usual lighthearted tone to the atmosphere, Ally added, "I'm sorry if I ruined your peace out here with my talking."

"No, that's why I come out here," Ben replied, "to talk."

Ally smiled.

"Well, I'm going inside now," she said after a moment, wanting to leave Ben in peace.

Without hesitation, Ben answered, "I'll come with you." He eased off the platform, and together, arm in arm, Ben and Ally walked the dock for the last time.

# CHAPTER 30

# I'M TIRED

A week before Christmas, Ben cheated death for the last
time.

Ben, Ally, and Jake all groggily emerged from their
bedrooms, yawning. Dawn had not yet broken, and a two-and-a-
half-hour drive to the Middle of Nowhere, Texas, awaited the
Breedlove family.

Eager to spend some quality time together, the Kohlers had
invited the entire family to join them for a daylong gun safety and
self-defense course at a shooting range near their home. Ben had
always taken advantage of every minute he could spend at the
Kohlers' ranch, so he was eager to gain some professional tactical
training for his target practice. With their duffel bags, guns, and

bullets loaded into the family SUV, the Breedloves headed off into the frigid December dawn.

Ben had awakened to find his heart bumping—again. It had been in a state of almost continuous arrhythmia since Thanksgiving. Adding the weather forecast of a cold, windy, potentially wet day, Shawn and Deanne thought seriously about canceling the trip. But Ben didn't want to miss out on a day of shooting, and he insisted that he felt fine. He really wanted to go, and because of his intense desire, Shawn and Deanne consented. They knew this was one of those times when their preference would have been to play it extra safe and stay home. But that would continue to isolate Ben and keep him from the things he loved to do. It seemed right to let Ben call the shots. He needed to enjoy life. This was a great way for the family to be together, with good friends, especially if Ben was feeling well enough to go.

Once outside Austin, they drove past boundless stretches of Texas pasture, passing barbed wire–fenced fields and Longhorn cattle in the blue dawn glow. While Shawn navigated the way, his four passengers snoozed against car doors and shoulders in the backseat. About an hour into the trip, they pulled into the parking lot of a Buc-ee's, the largest convenience store in Texas and a perennial favorite, where everyone could grab a quick bite to eat.

As they stepped over the threshold, the wafting aroma of freshly ground coffee, sizzling meats, and rising dough welcomed the new prospects. Inside the gigantic convenience store towered aisles and aisles of all sorts of goodies. Deanne and Ally gravitated toward the canisters of brewing coffee, while Jake and Shawn selected freshly made sausage-and-egg biscuits from a glass case.

Noticing that Ben had never left the car, Deanne walked back outside to check on him. She rapped on the window glass and motioned for Ben to roll it down. "Ben, don't you want to grab some breakfast while we're here? This is the only stop we'll make, and it will be about two thirty before we get a break for lunch."

Ben remained motionless in his seat, barely lifting his eyes in acknowledgment of his mom's words. "Nah. I'm not hungry. Thanks, though." He offered a faint smile of appreciation.

Ben was accustomed to waking up every morning feeling drained and depleted of energy. Oftentimes, his fatigue diminished his appetite. For him, it was just another one of those mornings. He decided to forgo breakfast and rest up for the long day ahead.

"Well, okay," Deanne acquiesced reluctantly. "But you really do need to drink some water. I'll go get you some." Deanne returned to the store to gather the stragglers. As she purchased bottled water for Ben on her way out, she decided to grab a sausage biscuit and some orange juice for him also, just in case he decided he was hungry later. She didn't want him getting low blood sugar before a taxing day out on the range. The Breedloves were soon back in the car and on their way, reaching the outskirts of the range before sunrise.

Just as the horizon began to glow orange, Shawn turned down a dusty dirt road marked by a small, blue-painted mailbox on the left. Shawn steered farther down the road until they arrived at a covered rest area, where the gun safety instructors and their trainees had congregated. The crowd huddled in groups, rubbing their hands together for warmth, and making small talk before everyone assembled for an introductory lecture.

Shawn pulled the SUV alongside a line of parked cars and turned off the engine. Scooping up their hats and boxes of nine-millimeter bullets, the Breedlove family clambered out into the biting air. It was a chilly but beautiful blue-sky day.

Spotting them from across the field, Mark and Pam Kohler walked over from a group of more experienced shooters to welcome the Breedloves with good-morning hugs. As Pam released Ben from her embrace and looked him in the eyes, she noticed they were lacking their usual spark. She thought he seemed strangely subdued, and she could tell he was not feeling well that morning.

Mark tramped over to Jake and Ben as they were unpacking the SUV. "Mornin', boys! Y'all got your holsters ready?" Ben and Jake lifted up their coats to reveal their holsters, strapped on and ready to go.

Ally, on the other hand, was not so prepared. She had adorned her shivering frame in two layers of hooded North Face jackets, offset by skinny jeans and cowgirl boots, making herself an easy target for Mark's banter.

Fluent in sarcasm, Mark teased her in his usual playful tone. "Think you got enough layers on there? Are you cold-blooded or something? You reptile."

"We are so glad y'all could make it!" Pam lavished her company with her natural warmth and amiability. "Just follow us right over by the picnic tables; our instructors will address the entire group, and then we'll split up the novices from the experienced shooters."

After a regulatory spiel from the instructors, the Breedloves broke away from the Kohlers to commence their first-ever gun safety and self-defense course.

Ally and Jake had brought twin .22-caliber Rugers, smaller handguns without a kick, fit for nervous, inexperienced hands.

Shawn and Deanne had each brought a Glock 19, and Ben sported a Springfield XD. All five of them were equipped with protective eyewear, earmuffs, and plenty of ammo. They stood at attention with their weapons before them.

"Now, listen up! Not a *one* of you will lay a finger on a trigger before we have fully learned and executed gun safety routine, and until we have done so to the point that each of you is comfortable handling a firearm," the instructor asserted in his native Texan drawl.

While Ally and Deanne heaved sighs of relief, Ben and Jake exchanged glances of disappointment. They weren't interested in speeches; they wanted to shoot! The instructor addressed the group for what seemed like hours on gun safety, etiquette, and the maneuvers that the trainees would be executing for the day, demonstrating each technique as he lectured. After a full morning of instruction, the trainees were granted permission to handle their weapons for the first time.

• • •

At lunchtime, ravenous from a long morning's activity, Shawn and Jake scrambled to the car to rummage through the cooler full of sodas and turkey sandwiches Deanne had packed. Ben lagged behind, then slowly meandered over to a picnic table under the covered rest area. After anticipating this day for weeks, all he wanted was to practice his aim over and over and race Jake to pick up the shells. He wanted to laugh, and pester Ally, and pull pranks on everyone else like his usual mischievous self. But today he just didn't feel good enough.

Ally noticed that Ben's energy had diminished considerably

after standing all morning, listening to the instructor. She walked over and sat down beside him. "You doin' all right, bud?" She was concerned about Ben's listless disposition, and worried about his blood sugar levels. "You haven't eaten anything all day. It's two thirty now."

Ben shot her a sideways glance, not bothering to face her. "I'm all right," he said nonchalantly. "My stomach kinda hurts. I'll be right back." Exerting himself even to stand, Ben trudged toward the restrooms across the field.

"Ally, do you think Ben's okay?" Deanne also had noticed Ben's weary demeanor.

Ally held her concerned gaze on Ben, who was still making his way across the field. "I think he's fine," she replied, her eyes never leaving her brother. "He said that his stomach was bothering him, so it must not have anything to do with his heart. It seems like he's been doing okay on the medicine he's taking now. It doesn't wear him out as much as the one he tried last week, so I think it's just his stomach slowing him down." Ally seemed to be convincing herself of these thoughts even more so than her mom.

By the time the half-hour lunch break had concluded, Ben rejoined the family to resume training. He was exhausted and desperately wanted to feel better, but he was determined to enjoy the day. Deanne found a folding chair for Ben, and he reluctantly sat down during the lecture portion of the session until it was time to shoot.

The instructor leaned casually against one of the center targets, waiting for the last lunchtime stragglers to make their way back to the tables. "All right, folks, *now* we get to shootin'." Brass shells spewed in every direction as the squad of trainees opened fire on their targets.

Despite his physical exhaustion, Ben's first two bullets shot dead center into his target. The rest of the Breedloves didn't do too badly, either. Ally and her parents each made one shot into the center of the target, and one skewed off to the side. Jake, however, had apparently been born a marksman. With the first bullet ever unleashed by his hand, *bull's-eye*. No one questioned his skill, despite his age, for the remainder of the day.

As the instructor wrapped up the course with a parting speech, the trainees began milling about the dusty grass, picking up expended shells and pitching them into the waste bucket. Before the ground was cleared, Ben wandered back over to the covered picnic tables and sat down. Tossing a last handful of shells into the bucket, Ally followed, sensing that he was not really all right. As Ben cast off his earmuffs and eyewear, Ally sat down beside him.

"I don't feel good," Ben mumbled.

In the split second it took Ally to look over her shoulder at her brother, Ben was lying down on the picnic bench. "Ben, are you okay?"

Without responding to Ally, Ben's head slipped off the bench in slow motion. At first, Ally thought he was playing a not so funny practical joke, but in an instant, his face flushed purple. This was no joke. Ben was in trouble.

Ally had never witnessed Ben during a cardiac arrest. She had heard about his collapse at Westlake, but now she was experiencing it firsthand.

Before the reality of the situation even registered in Ally's mind, her mom was there, at the other end of the bench, holding Ben's head in her lap. Deanne had been picking up spent shells when she noticed Ben walk over to the picnic bench. She saw him lie down, so she stopped in her tracks to watch him. She gasped as she saw his head and shoulders began to slide off of the bench. Deanne raced over to Ben, finding his face purplish blue and his eyes already rolled back in his head. She panicked. She grabbed his head and tried to shake and talk Ben awake. "Ben, are you okay? Can you hear me, sweetie? It's okay, Ben. You're going to be all right." It wasn't working. Ben was not all right.

Deanne cradled her son in her lap as Shawn ran to lift Ben's feet in the air, trying to induce blood flow to his head. Taking a firm hold of his shoulders and feet, they quickly moved him to the ground. Deanne looked up, her eyes frantic. "Shawn! Should we do CPR?"

A crowd had gathered around the picnic table by that time, looking on, stunned. The experienced-shooters group had noticed the commotion from across the field and rushed to the scene. Pam immediately dialed 911, walking briskly away from the crowd in search of cell coverage; Mark followed closely, feeding her the address and directions to the range.

A man pushed his way forward and knelt in front of Ben, ready to assist with CPR. Mark hustled up behind and motioned to the man. "Fifteen-two?" he asked, meaning fifteen chest compressions to two breaths, the former standard method of CPR. The man nodded, but administered only one chest compression, then sat back on his heels and waited. No response.

"Do more!" Deanne found herself shouting out her thoughts. Despite the many scares they had survived, and the multiple times Deanne had rehearsed emergency routines in her mind, she felt unprepared to handle the situation, and inept. She had taken CPR classes. She had even purchased and carried around an external defibrillator before Ben had his pacemaker implanted. She had always researched and practiced what to do in an emergency. She had played the scenarios over and over in her mind for years in preparation for just such an event. But now, with Ben's face a darker blue and his eyes looking lifeless, she was paralyzed by her own fear. Helpless thoughts raced through her mind. *Can Ben hear us? Can he feel anything? Please, God, help him not to be in pain.*

Shawn was not doing much better. He looked nearly catatonic. His hopes for Ben were heartbreakingly slipping away.

Ally distanced herself from the crowd, not quite sure how or when she had moved. She had wanted to get out of the way, to remove herself from being a useless bystander in the midst of the trauma. She wrapped her arms around Jake, who had also fled the scene, quivering in tears from a safe distance.

Ben's coloring had degraded to a deep bluish purple. He wasn't being revived. They were in the middle of nowhere. Helplessly, Ally watched the scene unravel before her eyes. She didn't move, or breathe, or think. She only stood still.

Just then, Ben sat up. Obviously disoriented, he asked Mark, "Hey, am I all right?"

"You're good," Mark replied, relieved to hear Ben's voice again.

One moment Ben had been limp and bluing on the picnic bench; the next he was sitting up with color coursing back into his face. Just like that.

"I'm okay. Just let me sit here for a minute," Ben said. He looked around as if he couldn't grasp where he was, then noticed the intense looks on Shawn's and Deanne's faces. "Hi, guys. I'm fine now," he said, almost as though he were talking about the weather. An ambulance sped around the berm and skidded to a halt in the dust.

Jake broke free from Ally's embrace and craned his neck

around a bystander to catch a glimpse of Ben. He peered at Ben sitting up and talking, then hurried back into Ally's arms.

"Are you okay, Jake?" Ally asked, looking into Jake's weepy eyes.

"Yeah," Jake replied, his voice quavering. "I just had to get a good picture in my head of Ben looking okay."

• • •

The EMS team set to work examining Ben, checking his vitals and jotting notes on their clipboards. One of the paramedics turned to Deanne. "So, Mrs. Breedlove, would you like to ride in the ambulance?"

Overhearing the conversation, Ben interjected. "Whoa, whoa, whoa! Hold on. I'm eighteen. I'm an adult. So that means I don't have to go to the hospital, right?" Ben looked directly at the paramedic, counting on his affirmation. After a lifetime of compliance with the cumbersome rules and regulations regarding his medical care, Ben had had enough. For the first time, he asserted his decision as an adult.

Caught off guard, the paramedic looked to Shawn and Deanne with an apology in his eyes for the answer he was obligated to give. "Well, um . . . that's right. Once you are eighteen, you can deny medical help."

"Well, I'm not going," Ben stated bluntly.

Shawn and Deanne exchanged astounded glances, taken aback by Ben's emboldened attitude. For eighteen years, Ben had always accepted his circumstances without much complaint. This time, Shawn and Deanne could sense a resolve in their son that they had never seen before.

They understood his reluctance to spend another night in a strange hospital. They had been through the routine before. They commiserated with him, knowing he did not want to go, because he realized he'd be spending the night with several IVs stuck in his arms, having lots of tests done, then just lying there, bored stiff, while being "observed," waiting for a doctor to discharge him the following day. Exacerbating matters, they were out of town, which meant they'd be dealing with an entirely new battery of doctors. Worse yet, as far as Ben was concerned, no friends other than Pam and Mark would be able to visit to break the boredom. Ben knew this routine well, and he rejected it. He didn't want to be poked, prodded, or examined anymore. He wanted to be home in his own bed.

Nevertheless, perhaps because this was the first time Shawn and Deanne had experienced one of Ben's episodes of cardiac arrest firsthand, they felt even more strongly that he should be examined at the hospital. "Ben, honey, let's just go to the ER and get checked out," Deanne implored. "Then we will drive home."

"I'm not getting in that ambulance." Ben sighed.

"Well, if you're not getting in the ambulance, then who's giving you a ride home?" Shawn cleverly countered Ben's argument. Shawn knew that Ben wasn't happy with his response, so he assured his son that they would do only what was necessary at the hospital to make sure he was not at significant risk, and then get him home as soon as possible. Neither father nor son wanted to fully understand how significantly at risk Ben really was. In the end, Ben succumbed to his hospital-bound fate.

CHAPTER 31

# HOW FAR IS HEAVEN

Save me from this prison
Lord, help me get away

—"HEAVEN" (LOS LONELY BOYS)

Reluctantly, Ben found himself enduring yet another monotonous evening in the ER. Fortunately, the on-duty ER doctor was from Austin and knew Ben's cardiologists well. Still, the debate about whether to keep Ben in the hospital, or return him to Dell Children's in Austin, or simply to take him home remained unsettled. Shawn and Deanne reasoned through the decision with both doctors for several hours, as the hospital staff monitored Ben.

Only one family member at a time was permitted into Ben's appointed section of the emergency room, so Shawn and Deanne took turns keeping him company. All the while, Ally and Jake made themselves at home in the dilapidated, tobacco-scented waiting room. The peach-painted walls were lined with wooden chairs covered in cheap-looking, floral-print fabric. Ally and Jake sat atop the sticky, protective plastic seat coverings and tried to keep their shoes from adhering to the unmopped linoleum floor. The whole place had a dirty feel to it.

• • •

Back in the emergency room, Ben lay exasperated in a rickety old hospital bed. Unlike the high-tech beds at Dell Children's Medical Center, if Ben wished to raise or lower the angle, he had to manipulate a catch on the back of the primitive bed, similar to a chaise longue. Making matters worse, he couldn't get a moment of peace with the constant whirring and buzzing of the ancient medical machines cluttering the room. Eventually, a nurse swept through the curtain to change his IV. She had a pretty young face and a naive look about her. Her eyes shone full of surprise as she looked down at Ben. "Honey! You are too young to have a pacemaker! Usually sick old men have pacemakers!" she remarked with a sweet country drawl.

Ben had had enough. He took to his cell phone with persistence, texting his parents in his *I'm joking but I'm serious* tone, "Let's go home! Get me out of here! Pleeeeeeaaaaaaase!"

Despite Ben's disregarded attempts to escape the emergency room, he did persuade his dad to break the rules in one respect: Ben devised a plan, and recruited Shawn as his accomplice. Deanne, Ally, and Jake would also be accessories to the crime. They would break into the ER with contraband: Taco Bell.

Shawn quickly pinpointed the nearest franchise on his smart

phone, and the mission commenced. Soon, Shawn, Ally, and Jake returned with the forbidden food, handing Ben's portion off to Deanne. As though smuggling drugs, Deanne stole down the hall to the ER, hoping her perfume would disguise the aroma of Ben's five chicken-and-cheese soft tacos. She slipped behind the curtain, and between nurse and doctor visits, she passed the tacos to Ben one by one out of her purse, then crumpled the wrappers and disposed of the evidence. Temporarily, Ben was satisfied. Taco Bell *almost* made up for his imprisonment in the hospital.

Ally and Jake grew weary as the night darkened. Finally, Shawn reemerged from a long visit with Ben in the emergency room. To the siblings' relief, their dad announced that they would finally be returning home. Ben's doctors had unanimously advised against the move, but Ben was adamant.

Ally assumed that Ben had taken advantage of his adult rights and had negotiated a ride in an ambulance to Dell Children's Medical Center in Austin. Ally and Jake eagerly made their way out to the car, happy for Ben that he would finally be able to go home safely. But when Ally opened the backseat door, she almost lost it.

There sat Ben.

*"What!"* Ally protested. "Ben is *not* riding two and a half hours back home in the middle of the night, through the middle of nowhere, with unstable vitals, against his doctors' wishes, and with no way for us to revive him if something happens along the way! *Why* is he not in the ambulance?"

"Ally," Shawn said firmly, looking somber, "this is the decision Ben has made, and we're going to honor his decision. We've already discussed the issue."

Ally grudgingly crawled into the backseat, terrified of the long ride ahead of them. Ben leaned, exhausted, against the backseat window, noting Ally's expression of reproach as she slid into the seat next to him. "I was *not* spending another night in the hospital," Ben asserted. "And I was *not* going to ride in another ambulance. I just want to get home."

Although Ally disagreed with his decision, she sympathized with Ben. She knew that the end of his patience had been a long time coming. He had been admitted to the hospital one too many times, and now he was drawing the line. Shawn pulled out of the circle drive and onto the dusty road. One hundred and twenty-two miles of deserted Texas highway loomed ahead of them.

As Shawn drove through the night, Ben drifted off to sleep. But sleep for him meant more tension for the other family members. In the darkness, it proved difficult to distinguish between his restful slumber and unconsciousness.

Ally was restless. She kept constantly trying to illuminate Ben's face with the faint glow of her cell phone to ensure that he was still breathing. Every now and then, Ben grumbled something under his breath about being woken up by the light, but Ally didn't care. She was not about to let her brother slip away.

Secretly, Deanne had used her smart phone to map out the quickest route to every hospital along the way. Not wanting to upset Ben by turning in her seat every few minutes, she strategically positioned the rearview mirror to keep Ben in her sight. She kept a constant eye on her son, noting each rise and fall of his chest. With every road sign, she updated her hospital routes, and cast a glance at Shawn to make sure he wasn't drifting off. It had been a long day, since leaving early that morning, and Shawn was physically and emotionally exhausted as well.

Deanne, Shawn, Ally, and Jake all felt responsible for Ben's safety that night. Yet in a very real way, they knew that Ben's life was not in their hands. It would be a long drive, but Ben was on his way home.

CHAPTER 32

# WHEN WILL THE HEAVEN BEGIN?

—"MR. RAGER" (KID CUDI)

B en reclined in the velvet armchair in the living room, warm in his flannel pajamas. Beyond the wall of windowed French doors across the room, a last few crisp leaves drifted to the water's surface from the cottonwood tree. The world outside was now at rest for the winter.

The previous day had been taxing for the Breedlove family, and despite sleeping in, they were still exhausted. They had formed a tacit agreement to forgo their usual Sunday-morning church service, and after discussing the matter upon waking, decided to hold a "home church" of sorts in their own living room. After they had all gathered, still all in their pajamas, the family nestled into the sofa with their mugs of hot chocolate.

The events of the previous night following so quickly on Ben's collapse at Westlake now had the family's complete attention. The handwriting was on the wall. Ben's heart condition was no longer a string of isolated events. His parents were now at the point they had feared Ben's entire life: Ben's heart was failing, and a transplant was imminent. Shawn and Deanne anticipated visiting transplant teams immediately after Christmas. They didn't want to ruin Ben's holiday break, so they agreed to wait until after New Year's to let him know. As with most decisions regarding his health, they planned to have a full discussion of the matter, giving Ben the final word on whether or not he would be willing to pursue a transplant. Shawn and Deanne did not know how Ben would respond. The tension in their hearts was building.

• • •

Having only a few minutes to think about what he wanted to say, Shawn recognized his family needed reassurance and hope. *I'm not feeling full of these things myself,* Shawn thought, *so I'm going to have to rely on a truth that I have always believed.*

"I think we were all too tired to go to church this morning," Shawn began, "so I have something to share with you. I was not prepared for this," he apologized, mock rolling his eyes, "so it'll be short. This is Philippians four, verses six and seven." Shawn pulled up the NET Bible on his laptop, then typed the reference into the search bar. He read, " 'Be anxious for nothing, but in everything by prayer and supplication with thanksgiving let your requests be made known to God. And the peace of God, which surpasses all comprehension, will guard your hearts and your minds in Christ Jesus.'"*

Shawn paused for a moment to look around the room. "Does anyone know what supplication means? No? Well, I wasn't sure either, before I looked it up this morning," he added with a smile. "It means earnest petition, or humble prayer. This is the kind of wisdom we need in times like we have been experiencing. Instead of being anxious about Ben's heart, we should, with humble prayer, make our requests known to God."

Shawn's eyes lit up as he made a gesture with his hand, pointing upward, as if struck with an idea. "The *God of the universe* is inviting us to give him our requests. And if the God of the universe is alive and cares for us, then we have his promise that his peace, which is beyond human comprehension or understanding, will protect our hearts and our minds."

Shawn paused to look at each family member before continuing. "To me, this means that we are being invited to let God know what concerns us about Ben's heart, and he will give us peace of mind and comfort us in this very distressing time. All we have to do is ask."

Shawn paused, pondering. His eyes drifted to Ben. Not knowing how to explain the unexplainable, he asked, "Ben, you know what this peace is like, don't you?"

With just a hint of a smile, Ben confidently replied, "Yeah . . . I do."

"Would you describe that peace for us?" Shawn stared intently at Ben, waiting.

"Well," Ben began, "it's just like the verse says. You can't de-

---

* Philippians 4:6–7 (New American Standard Bible).

scribe it. You just had to be there." His eyes sparkled as he added, "But it's really, really good."

The room was quiet as the rest of them tried to envision the peace Ben knew. Their imaginations inevitably fell short of Ben's experience. After a moment, Shawn spoke. "Let's accept the invitation we have been given by the God of the universe; let's give our anxiety over to God, and pray for Ben's heart."

With their heads bowed, Shawn, Deanne, Ally, and Jake took turns expressing their anxieties to God, and praying for Ben. The family members cried as they let their hearts be known. They all took turns pouring out their requests to God, not trying to hide their concern about Ben anymore. Openly praying, "Please protect Ben. Give him the strength and the healing he needs."

The family had often discussed Ben's condition frankly, but in recent weeks, they had all been trying desperately to avoid treating Ben as though he were dying. They had wanted to make each day as normal for him as possible by not focusing on his failing health. Now those barriers were down, and they overtly expressed their prayers and concerns for Ben right in front of him.

Then Ben made a request for his family. As he spoke, his voice wasn't tight like the others' had been. He had no tension in his throat as he offered his words to God.

"God, I pray that my family wouldn't be sad or scared for me anymore, because I'm not sad or scared. I pray that they would have the same peace that I have." Then, with his head still bowed, Ben prayed almost as though he were addressing this part of his prayer to the rest of the family as well as to God. Ben said, "And I'm okay with whatever God decides."

The family sat stunned that Ben, despite his recent distress, had not expressed even one request for himself, but instead had voiced his concerns for his family to God. He was not sad or shaken. He was perfectly content and calm. Everyone else had been stressed and emotionally frayed. But not Ben. He was amazingly at ease. He didn't ask to be healed; he didn't beg God, "Will you help me, heal me, give me peace?" He already had all that, as far as he was concerned.

It was clear that Ben had a new resolve; he recognized he was now living each day of his life on both sides of the line that separates earthly existence from spiritual eternity. In some ways, he had crossed over already; he had seen the other side and formed his opinions about it; he accepted it, and although he had no premonitions about going to heaven soon, he was content with that possibility, almost happy about it. He had experienced eternal peace. Indeed, he was already *living* in that peace.

Through his prayer, Ben reminded his family members that they too needed to trust in God, and to believe that he had Ben in his hands. At that, their hearts calmed. It would be a week later before the family realized the full significance of Ben's prayer— that the reason they were able to have peace in the face of trouble was because Ben had asked God to grant that peace to them. And God answered Ben's prayer.

• • •

After "home church," the family went their separate ways for a while. Deanne began fixing lunch in the kitchen. Jake went outside to work out on the trampoline with his friend Kenny, who had come over to the house, and Ally headed off to the shower. Ben went into the kitchen, too, and began talking further with Deanne and Shawn about his experience in heaven.

Shawn listened attentively, trying to piece together the whole story and to understand what it meant, especially to Ben. Shawn wanted to know all the details, so he asked Ben several questions about his dream. Although Ben seemed shy about some aspects of his vision, he readily answered his dad's questions. "Were you and Kid Cudi wearing black tuxes?" Shawn asked.

"No," Ben said. "Just dark suits, and we looked really, really good."

They talked further, and after a while, Shawn said, "Ben, I think you really need to write those experiences down." Hearing Ben elaborating with Deanne about the peace he felt, Shawn thought, *There's no better time to document these things than now.* He emphasized to Ben, "You need to write down your experiences now, before you forget them, because that may be really important someday."

Shawn assumed that Ben might write some of his memories in a journal.

Ben had another idea.

He walked back into his bedroom and began working on a video. That wasn't unusual; Ben was always working on some sort of video, so nobody paid much attention at the time. He didn't tell his family members what sort of video he wanted to produce, but at several points while he was putting the project together, Ben came back out of his room searching for information. "Dad, so how low did my blood sugar get when I was four?" he asked Shawn.

"I think it was fourteen, Ben."

Ben nodded and went back to his bedroom. A short time later, he reemerged and had another question for Shawn. "Dad, is that blood sugar level dangerous?"

"Well, I don't know for sure," Shawn replied, "but I think a blood sugar level of fourteen is on the verge of death."

That same afternoon, Ben emerged from his room again with another question. He walked into the living room and sat down on the couch. "Mom, why do I have a heart condition?" he asked. "Is it hereditary or was I just unlucky?"

That was as close as Ben ever came to asking the question, "Why me?" He wasn't complaining; he simply wanted to know. Ben never wallowed in a "Why me?" attitude, or complained, "Why do I have to be sick? Why did God allow this to happen? Why can't I be like all the other kids?" Nor did any of the family members spend much time pondering why Ben had HCM. They understood that strength often comes out of weakness, and that good sometimes comes through trial. Even now, Ben's question wasn't so much spiritual as statistical. Over the years, he had learned that HCM strikes one in every five hundred people. He knew that he could have been one of the other 499, but he wasn't. He was that one.

Nevertheless, the way Ben phrased the question saddened Deanne. She responded, "We don't know that it is hereditary, but we think it is. You've never been tested for the specific gene that sometimes indicates HCM, so we don't know for sure. But we do know that your life is a gift from God."

• • •

Later that day Shawn told Deanne, "Ben must be working on something. He was asking me several questions about his past experiences."

Deanne was surprised. Ben had asked her similar questions.

The weekend before, Ben had told Ally that he knew he was ready for something more important. Now Shawn had encouraged him to document his experiences because someday they might be important. Ben pondered the meaning of it all as he returned to work on the video in his bedroom.

# CHAPTER 33

# WORDS IMPORTANT

So all the while 'til I'm gone make my words important so
If I slip away, if I die today . . .

—"THE PRAYER" (KID CUDI)

Ben stepped into his bedroom and sat down at his studio desk, taking in the sight of his personal sanctuary. He loved this room that he had inherited when Ally went off to college. In addition to the corner "studio," he was surrounded by so many meaningful personal items—a small cross given to him by some missionaries from Thailand sat on his nightstand, right where the missionaries had left it for him years ago; his surfboard and wakeboard that he loved so much that he kept them in his bedroom rather than the garage or the boat; his drumsticks; and several personal photos. This was Ben's place. Or at least it had been.

His desk, still adorned with his favorite set props, was illuminated by the bright flood of his studio lighting. The gigantic green

WORDS IMPORTANT • 233

screen still hung from his bedroom wall, transforming a teenage bedroom into a professional setting. This room had set the stage for many of the videos Ben had made, and it would now, for his final project. As much as he loved every second of life in this world, he had a strong feeling that it was no longer his primary residence. Ben took his seat in his studio and settled into the limelight.

He reached into a drawer and pulled out some three-by-five-inch blank white note cards. He found a black Sharpie and began to write.

He had seen a video on YouTube in which another teen, Kieran Miles, used note cards to express a message without ever speaking a word. Kieran shared how he had lost sight of the value of his life, but that he was going to make it through, despite the pain and struggle. Ben was profoundly moved by Kieran's suffering. He decided he had a message that could encourage people to have hope, so he wanted to express it in a similar manner to what Kieran had done. In producing his own video, Ben credited Kieran as his inspiration for the flash-card form in which he presented his message.

Jake and his friend Nate popped into Ben's room to see what he was doing. Jake was accustomed to seeing his brother working on videos, so he wasn't surprised to find Ben on his computer again. Jake and Nate were more interested in tossing a ball to Chica, the Breedloves' four-year-old purebred Maltese, so they went into the room across the hall and didn't pay much attention to what Ben was doing.

Sitting in front of his green screen, the same spot where he had created videos from various "locations" around the world, Ben leaned in toward the camera on his computer. Normally, he made his videos with his whole setup—the studio, cameras, lights, with his pseudo-microphone sitting atop his desk, but not this time. For this project, Ben knelt next to his bed and leaned in close to his laptop. He punched in the music to an instrumental version of "Mad World," a song originally recorded by British New Wave band Tears for Fears. Singer-songwriter Gary Jules rerecorded the song for the movie *Donnie Darko*. Jules's version of the song was also used dozens of times as background music for the classic soap opera *General Hospital*, as well as a prime time, hospital-based show, *Private Practice*, a spinoff of *Grey's Anatomy*. The song was a natural choice for Ben. Although the lyrics weren't featured in the video, Ben knew them by heart. They almost perfectly choreographed his brush with heaven.

> *I find it kind of funny. . . .*
> *I find it kind of sad. . . .*
> *The dreams in which I'm dying . . .*
> *Are the best I've ever had. . . .* *

No doubt referencing his vision on the floor at school, Ben began to show the note cards in the order he had written them, holding up each card for just a few seconds, barely long enough for his viewers to read the message, before moving on to the next card. He said not a word, but told his story through the handwritten words on the cards, his demeanor, and his countenance.

Ben's facial features matched the message on the cards. When the card presented a serious message describing his condition of hypertrophic cardiomyopathy, Ben's countenance was commensurately serious. But when he told of positive, happy ex-

---

* "Mad World," words and music by Roland Orzabal, as performed by Gary Jules.

periences, such as the bright light he had experienced when he was four, or the "vision" in which Kid Cudi joined him in the white waiting room of heaven, he displayed a hint of a smile that let the viewer know that this was a good moment in Ben's life. Occasionally, his eyes glanced to his upper right, as though he were searching for something, but he made no reference to whatever he saw there.

When he described receiving a pacemaker, Ben stood up momentarily, and pulled back the neck of his T-shirt, revealing the large reddish scar on his chest. Other than that, he remained seated throughout both sections of the video, staying especially close to the camera on his computer.

He picked up the story on part two of the video, beginning with his collapse in school on December 6, just a few weeks earlier. He wasn't obsessed so much with artistic excellence or form on this video. It was obvious that Ben was more concerned about the message than he was the medium. On one of the cards, he had blacked out a mistake rather than creating a new card. Near the end of part two, Chica's wagging tail could be clearly seen swishing into the camera shot over Ben's right shoulder. He didn't seem to mind.

As Ben came to the conclusion of his story, he slowed the pace of the cards, holding each one slightly longer. After describing his experience in "heaven's waiting room," Ben added on one of the last cards the poignant statement, "I wish I NEVER woke up."

Then, before the viewer even had time to grapple with the meaning of that statement, Ben asked a question on the next-to-last card—a question that would profoundly impact the heart of nearly every person who would watch the video. He asked, "Do you believe in Angels or God?"

Holding one more card, Ben added the important message he wanted to share with his friends.

The final card read simply: "I Do."

• • •

Ben didn't upload the video to his usual channel location, Breed-loveTV. Instead, he decided to upload it to his newest YouTube channel, TotalRandomness512, a play on Austin's telephone area code. He set up no advertising or any means to gain revenue from this channel. It was a gift.

Looking into the computer screen, Ben gave the video one last look, and pressed "upload." The two-part YouTube videos simply titled, "This Is My Story," now belonged to the world.

# CHAPTER 34

# LIKE TOMORROW WAS A GIFT

To think about
What you'd do with it

—"LIVE LIKE YOU WERE DYING" (TIM MCGRAW)

Cole Bednorz hopped onto the hood of his buddy Zach's truck—while it was moving. Despite the fact that his view was obstructed by Cole on his hood, Zach careened about the empty IHOP parking lot, their friends laughing as they watched.

Cole felt himself slipping off the hood, so he attempted to jump off while Zach was still driving. In an instant, Cole hit the pavement, and tires rolled over his body.

• • •

Cole and Ben were good friends who enjoyed longboarding and wakesurfing together. On hot Texas days they could be found

237

wakesurfing with Cole's dad, who had been a professional surfer in Hawaii. Although a gentle and kind person, Cole tended to live on the edge; and in other ways, so did Ben. Through their bonds and also their differences, Ben loved Cole and was strongly loyal to their friendship.

Despite his own recent health problems, Ben was adamant about visiting Cole in the hospital. The truck had punctured Cole's left lung, and most of his major organs were lacerated, but he had survived. Before they entered the hospital room, Deanne and Ben were required to don masks, gowns, and gloves due to Cole's compromised immune system. The guys were glad to see each other, but they were both shocked at how weak and pale the other looked. Nevertheless, both of their spirits were lifted by the visit, and they made plans to get back out on the water as soon as the weather warmed. With one last glance back at Cole, Ben walked out of the hospital room.

Following the visit with Cole, Ben asked his mom whether she would drop him off at Grant's house to hang out for a while. Deanne was reluctant in light of Ben's recent health issues, but he seemed to be feeling well, and she knew he was missing normal time with his friends, so she relented. Before leaving Grant's house, however, Deanne laid out specific conditions with both Grant and Ben: that they take it easy, that they not leave the house, nor do anything strenuous, such as jumping on the trampoline. She was only half joking when she said to Grant, "If there is anything in question, call 911 first; then call me!" Grant reassured Deanne that he would, and that his mom would be home soon.

Debbie Hamill, Grant's mom, came in and asked Ben how he was feeling. She was aware of Ben's experience the day he had collapsed at school and had heard about it at the Breedlove home, when she and Grant had come over the day Ben was discharged from the hospital. Debbie was fascinated with Ben's experience and asked him to relate the story about his vision once again.

When Ben finished, Debbie seemed intrigued by his heavenly encounter. "I don't know what to say about it," she told him, "but I'm really happy for you. I'm glad you had such a pleasant experience." As an anesthesiologist, Debbie was used to dealing with certain aspects of death, but not necessarily *life after* death.

Ben didn't understand how Grant and his family could not believe in God. He never allowed his faith or Grant's reticence to believe to interfere with their friendship, but occasionally the subject had come up.

"How can you guys not have any belief in God, or not believe in anything?"

"I don't know," Grant said. "My family and I have never really talked about it."

They readily acknowledged their differences in belief, and sometimes even teased each other about it. For instance, Grant had a habit of saying, "Oh, my God!" to which Ben would quickly counter, "Who? Who are you talking about?" They would laugh, and remained respectful of each other's opinions.

Ben knew that Grant wouldn't get angry with him for expressing his faith, but he understood that Grant couldn't yet relate to his beliefs. For his part, Grant was convinced that Ben's faith was real, and that he was being absolutely truthful with him when he talked about his beliefs and his vision.

Later that day, Ben and Grant were talking about Madeline, and Grant asked Ben, "So what are you going to do about this girl?" Madeline was traveling to Colorado with her family to go skiing over the holidays.

"After Christmas break," Ben said, "I'm going to ask her out."

On Christmas Eve, shortly after the clock edged past midnight, Madeline sent Ben a text wishing him a Merry Christmas. At twelve thirteen a.m., Ben sent a text message to Madeline: "Merry Christmas, Madeline. I'm glad you're a part of my life."

CHAPTER 35

# BEAUTIFUL DAY

It's a beautiful day
Don't let it get away

—"BEAUTIFUL DAY" (U2)

"Ow!" Startled awake, Ben opened his eyes to see Jake, messy haired and still in his flannel pajamas, standing by his bedside with a mischievous grin. "Why'd you have to hit me over the head with a pillow?" Ben mumbled, pulling the sheets over his head. "Let me have another hour."

"Nope! Time to get up. Merry Christmas!" Ally chimed in from the doorway.

Slowly, painstakingly, Ben rolled out of bed and onto his feet. He was already dressed for the occasion in his Polo T-shirt, flannel pajama pants, and UGG slippers. Looking from Ally to Jake with a twinkle in his eyes, Ben joked, "*Gosh*, guys, why'd it take y'all so long to get out of bed?" and darted down the hallway. Rolling their eyes and laughing, Ally and Jake trailed behind.

The sweet scent of cinnamon and peppermint wafted through the house. It was the reminiscent, unmistakable scent of Christmas. The world was still dark, but the faint glow of tree lights emanated from the living room. Ben glanced at Jake and began taking exaggerated tiptoed steps toward the light.

"No, Ben!" Jake squealed. "We have to wait!"

"Well, Mom and Dad had better get down here, before I *seeeeeee*!" Ben replied, taking another dramatic step toward the living room.

"Come on, guys," Ally interjected, assuming her usual role as peacemaker. "It's only seven-oh-three. Mom and Dad will be down any minute."

Right on cue, the familiar creak of the stairway landing sounded, followed by footsteps. Shawn and Deanne appeared in the hallway outside of the living room, also wearing pajamas. Shawn yawned and smiled sleepily while Deanne rushed across the room to put on some music and set the stage. "Okay, guys! Y'all can come in!"

All at once, Ben, Ally, and Jake came bouncing into the room to the tune of the Nutcracker Suite. Against the French doors opposite the room, the bedecked tree towered over the scene in all of its glowing Christmas glory. Its branches were clustered with peppermint sticks, an assortment of gleaming ornaments, and multicolored lights casting glowing reflections on the beautifully wrapped presents. Five festive, hand-stitched stockings hung above the fireplace, greeting their owners by name. Each stocking hung from a silver decorative holder resembling a different letter, together spelling out P-E-A-C-E. Stitched into Ben's stocking in bright holiday red was the word "Believe."

Everyone was in a festive yet mellow mood, relaxing in their comfy Christmas jammies. Deanne set some quiches in the oven, and put some icing on the cinnamon rolls, while Ally poured the hot chocolate. Ben seemed especially happy. He had purchased some special presents for his family members this year and he was excited to see their reactions. Lacking the energy to get out to stores and fight through the crowds of shoppers, he'd scoured the Internet searching for the perfect gifts. He then asked Deanne for help shopping for the rest of the family, providing money and detailed instructions on what to get. He was an exuberant giver, wanting to give just the right thing to each person.

"Santa came!" Jake called out with joy, bounding across the room to claim his stocking. Ben and Ally followed, eager to enjoy their once-a-year breakfast of candy from their stockings. After everyone had finally nestled into the couch and armchairs with mugs of hot chocolate, the gift exchange began. As they did every year, Ally, Ben, and Jake opened their initial gifts chronologically in order of age, starting with Jake.

When it was Ally's turn, Ben searched under the tree until he found a small brown paper gift bag stuffed with hot-pink tissue paper. He handed it to Ally with a giant smile on his face. From the bag, Ally pulled a small bright yellow box decorated with white quatrefoils and tied with a turquoise tulle bow. Instantly, she knew it was the pair of Kendra Scott earrings she had put at the top of her Christmas list. Although Ben was a generous giver, Ally was surprised to receive the earrings from him, rather than from her parents. She hugged her brother eagerly, wondering what had prompted him to spend so lavishly on her that year.

Shawn and Deanne gave Ben a certificate for Final Cut Pro, an advanced video editing software program, to help him with his video productions. They also gave a gift intended for both boys, a versatile GoPro camera that could be mounted, strapped onto their heads, chests, skis, or even used underwater. Both Ben and Jake were ecstatic about the GoPro. "We're going to use this today!" Jake said.

In addition, Shawn and Deanne gave Ben a high-definition video camera that would dramatically improve the quality of his YouTube films. When Ben opened it, he nearly cried. "I didn't expect this, guys," he said. For a long time, he just sat staring at the camera. "Wow, guys. I can't believe this!" he said over and over.

Jake had created a special piece of art for Shawn and Deanne, painting a scene of the lake and trees on the cliffs across the lake from their boat dock. He had spent every evening for several weeks working on the painting, sitting alone on a blanket that he had spread out by the edge of the lake, usually not coming back into the house until after dark. The painting boasted vibrant colors, including some golden yellow in the grass, with the trees reflecting on the water. Curiously, Jake had included one element that was not actually in the landscape. In the midst of all the other trees, Jake had painted one lone white tree without leaves.

When Deanne asked Jake what had prompted him to paint the nonexistent tree, he responded, "I just thought it needed to be there."

Shawn opened a bright yellow pair of running shoes, trimmed in fluorescent green, orange, and yellow, that he had designed and ordered and Deanne had specially wrapped for him. To everyone else, the shoes looked like two cans of Mountain Dew soft drink, but Shawn was so excited about them. He pulled the shoes out of the box and proudly held them up for the family to see. "And just think, they don't even sell these in the stores!" he gushed.

"Gee, Dad, I don't know why . . ." Ben teased, rolling his eyes at Shawn's brightly colored shoes.

"Well, there's one more," Shawn said, presenting Deanne with a carefully wrapped present. Deanne beamed. It was the handbag she had been wishing for all throughout the holiday. Receiving such a thoughtful, unexpected gift reduced Deanne to tears.

"What is it about women and their purses?" Ben asked light-heartedly.

· · ·

Then it was game time. After collecting their gifts and chasing Chica as she burrowed through piles of wrapping paper, the Breedloves sat down at the dining room table to commence their annual game of Monopoly. This year, Ben gave Shawn a run for his money. The family had long been used to succumbing to board-game domination by Shawn, but by a stroke of luck with the railroads, Ben was winning. Ben was full of fun and playful boasting, and his decisions began to serve him well as he devoured all of Shawn's holdings and took everything he had. Three and a half hours into the game, every hotel belonged to the hat, Ben's traditional game piece, and the railroads were still banking. In another half hour, Ben had finally won the annual Breedlove Monopoly contest for the first time. Exhausted by Ben's ornery but joyful play, the family dispersed to clean up and put their newly acquired Christmas gifts to use.

Following the Monopoly marathon, Deanne busied herself in the kitchen preparing Christmas dinner. She was keeping things simple and casual this year, since it would be just family, joined by the Kohlers.

Still dressed in pajamas and slippers, Jake and Ben took the GoPro camera outside. Neighbors, Nate and Benji, came over and began doing stunts with Jake on the trampoline. Because his energy level was so low, Ben didn't join them, but he was having fun using the new GoPro to film the boys' tricks.

• • •

Deanne was still in the kitchen preparing dinner when she glanced at the clock around four forty-five that afternoon. Shawn was going to grill some steaks, so Deanne was sautéing some chopped onions in butter to pour into a sauce for the scalloped potatoes. She looked out the kitchen window and saw Ben laughing and smiling with the younger boys, who were jumping on the trampoline. Savoring that sweet moment, she smiled as she took a mental snapshot of it before turning back to stir the sauce on the stove.

Ally had just finished a long shower when Jake's words stopped her in her tracks. Flinging the kitchen door open, he shouted, "Mom, Ben doesn't feel good!"

From the urgency in Jake's voice, Ally knew what those words meant. She heard a wooden spoon drop to the floor, then her mom's footsteps rushing out the door.

# CHAPTER 36

# PARADISE

—"PARADISE" (COLD PLAY)

Deanne raced outside, shouting back into the house, "Shawn! It's Ben!"

While she said nothing else, the sound of Deanne's voice was all that Shawn needed to hear; it was the sound of emergency. She reached Ben in seconds, with Shawn right at her heels. They eased Ben down onto the grass under the big willow tree, his eyes glazed over, the exact same look he'd had when his heart was failing at the shooting range. Deanne held his face and tried to talk to him, hoping to awaken him, but he did not respond. Her first motherly instinct was simply to cradle and comfort him, but she knew there was no time for that. Unlike the incident at the shooting range, she refused to allow fear to paralyze her.

Deanne immediately began doing CPR. Shawn lifted Ben's

legs, an action that in times past would sometimes bring Ben back to consciousness. Nothing seemed to help. Ben was not breathing, and Deanne could not detect a heartbeat.

Frozen on the porch, Ally barely had time to register what was happening. She saw Jake on the grass below her, trying to coerce an uncooperative phone into dialing. Ally snatched the phone from his hands, hung up, then immediately dialed 911.

To avoid losing reception, she stood on the back porch relaying information back and forth between the emergency operator and Shawn and Deanne. When Ally informed the operator that her mom was doing breaths and compressions, in the usual fifteen-two progression, the operator responded, "No breaths! Just compressions." Ally shouted the message to Deanne and Shawn: "Just do compressions, no breaths!"

Deanne ignored that advice and finished blowing two breaths into Ben's mouth anyway. He was so blue she thought he must need oxygen.

"Only do compressions!" the operator said. "Tell your mom to do a hundred of them!" Ally shouted the instructions to her mom again.

Deanne responded with a puzzled look. One hundred compressions? That didn't sound right. Nevertheless, Deanne started doing them as deeply as she could, knowing that it would be okay if she broke one of Ben's ribs by doing so. Her whole being was intensely focused on the compressions: twenty, twenty-one, twenty-two, twenty-three, twenty-four, twenty-five. She kept doing them. Shawn yelled at Ally to tell the 911 people to hurry, even though they knew the EMS crew would arrive shortly. Still, it was a horrible feeling to have their precious child in such life-threatening distress and not be able to do anything to help him.

Deanne prayed constantly while she continued compressing Ben's chest, and shouting, "Forty-five, forty-six, forty-seven, forty-eight. . . ." Ally fell into a trance of counting compressions in unison with her mom. Finally, the desperate counting was broken by the sound of sirens.

Ally leaped from the porch, thrust the phone into her dad's hands, then sprinted to the front yard to wave down the ambulance. Ally's heart fell. Through the foliage overhanging the street, she could see only a fire truck approaching. She knew that the fire department had always been the first responders to an emergency, but Ben needed an ambulance. Ally lingered just long enough to wave the truck into the driveway, and then raced back to comfort Jake. Again the sirens sounded. Another fire truck. When the ambulance finally arrived, Ally ran out to signal the paramedics into the yard. Once she had gotten their attention, she ran back toward Ben. She stopped to make sure the paramedics were following. They were, but they were *walking.*

Ally yelled, "You need to run!" She led them to Ben, who remained motionless in the backyard. Everything seemed to unravel in excruciatingly slow motion, as if she were trapped in a nightmare. The paramedics *slowly* attached an oximeter to Ben's finger, *slowly* cut away his clothes to expose his chest, *slowly* attached leads.

Shawn was losing patience as he desperately cried out, "You've *got* to do CPR! Please! Do CPR!"

Shawn knew that CPR was vital for Ben due to the cardiac arrest, and more importantly, to get his blood pressure back up, but the paramedics wanted to check out Ben's condition and his vitals first. "He has a pacemaker to pace the heart, but it is more than that; it is a low-blood-pressure problem," Shawn desperately

tried to explain. The paramedics continued their usual procedures. Shawn spoke kindly but firmly: "Look, he needs CPR right
now. If you guys are not going to do CPR, I will." He and Deanne
nearly jumped back into the middle of the first responders to do
the CPR themselves, but the firemen finally called over one of
their men to do it while they continued hooking Ben up to all
kinds of wires and monitors.

Fighting through a network of holiday assistants and voice-
mail machines, Shawn desperately attempted to contact Ben's cardiologist and put him on the phone with one of the paramedics,
hoping he could shed light on what to do to help Ben. When
Shawn finally made contact with the doctor, he pressed the phone
into the hands of one of the lead paramedics, expecting him to follow the cardiologist's instructions. Instead, the paramedic took
the phone from Shawn and walked far away into the backyard to
discuss the predicament.

• • •

Mark and Pam arrived shortly thereafter. The couple stood huddled together with Ally and Jake, watching over Ben. Shawn and
Deanne stood as close to Ben as possible, reaching around paramedics to hold Ben's hand or foot or whatever was within their
reach. After several shots of epinephrine and multiple shocks from
the defibrillator, Ben remained unconscious and blue. Pam closed
her eyes, shutting out the pain in the world at that moment, and
began to pray.

Deanne's mind was racing. Would Ben revive? If so, would
he have permanent brain damage? *Is he in pain? Can he hear us?
Does he feel all of this? Is he wondering why we aren't doing the right*

*things to help him out of his distress? Are these his final moments?* Although she didn't dare allow her thoughts to linger long on the subject, she couldn't help pondering whether Ben had already left them, that perhaps an angel had already come to accompany Ben to heaven. *What's going on around us in the spiritual realm that we cannot see?* Deanne looked at her son and hated that he was going through this. She felt so sad for him. Her entire body ached, yet she felt oddly numb at the same time.

In the middle of the paramedics' attempt to bring Ben back, Shawn saw his son's hands curl up in a tight, contorted form. While he had never before seen anyone pass away, Shawn was quite sure Ben had left his body at that point. Knowing what he had observed, Shawn was overcome with emotion and wanted to cry, but the tears refused to flow with all the adrenaline rushing through his body. He didn't want to believe what he had just seen. *Ben has left us*, Shawn thought. From all he had ever learned about spiritual things, this life was over when God took the spirit out of a person, rather than when a heart stopped beating. Shawn continued to have hope, but things weren't looking good.

• • •

Always one to keep calm under pressure, Mark looked intently at Ally. "You need to be strong for your parents, Ally," he said. "Go get them clothes and shoes for the hospital."

Ally looked back at Ben, reluctant to leave his side, but recognizing that Mark was right. She turned and rushed inside. On her way through the kitchen, she heard her name. She turned around to see their neighbor, Mr. Davis, turning off the stove Deanne had left burning when she had rushed outside.

"What can I do?" Mr. Davis inquired helplessly.

"Nothing," Ally replied. She sprinted up the stairs.

• • •

The EMS crew strapped Ben onto a gurney and was starting through the yard toward the ambulance parked in front of the house. A trail of bandage wraps, stickers, and other medical paraphernalia, strewn in every direction, littered the yard. Everyone seemed at a loss for what to do. Shawn was speaking grimly with the paramedic while Mark and Pam stood stone-still with furrowed expressions under the willow. Jake remained on the garden wall, expressionlessly taking in the scene. He silently watched as his brother was taken away.

A mere shell of herself, Deanne moved toward the ambulance, all the while holding tightly on to Ben's foot, the only part of him she could reach, and praying. As she followed behind the stretcher, she saw in her peripheral vision that a contingent of neighbors, young and old alike, had gathered out near the street, all with looks of concern on their faces. They were packed into a tight huddle with their arms around one another or holding one another's hands. Deanne knew her neighbors well. Many of them had lived on the same street for almost twenty years now, and they were like family. She knew they were praying and asking God to be with Ben. Even though the presence of her friends brought comfort to her soul, she didn't dare look any of her dear friends in the eyes. She felt ashamed and guilty. She felt like she had failed. She had failed Ben. What could she do if she *did* look over at them? Wave? Say hi? She just couldn't bring herself to make eye contact, so she kept her head down low, talking to God all the while, and continued to tightly grip Ben's foot.

Ally took one last look at her brother. She knew Ben's brown eyes so well, always so warm and friendly. Now she stared into cold, glassy eyes. They were empty. Ally thought for certain Ben was gone, yet she refused to believe it.

# CHAPTER 37

# BELIEVE

And I need something more
To keep on breathing for

—"BELIEVE" (THE BRAVERY)

Ally felt as if the world had stopped. She could barely breathe. Before she could think, her mom was walking away alongside Ben's stretcher toward the ambulance. In a silent, thoughtless daze, Ally made her way to the passenger seat of her dad's car to trail the ambulance. Although she and her dad were accompanied by Jake and Pam in the backseat, Ally was not aware of their presence. Her surroundings faded away. She felt nothing, as if her soul were waiting.

The paramedics encouraged Deanne to sit up front in the ambulance, so she reluctantly complied. Deanne fidgeted; she felt horrible that she was sitting in the front and not with Ben. The thought of him being alone in the back made her sick. She thought she might pass out or possibly have an asthma attack, so she held her inhaler close by. She took deep, deliberate breaths in her attempt to remain calm. Every so often, she turned around and looked back through a small window in the cab, trying to see Ben, but she could not. "Ben, I'm up here, bud!" she called through the window, in case he could still hear her somehow. "I love you!" She prayed, as she had so many times before, that God would comfort Ben and hold him close.

The ambulance took much the same route as when Ben was four years old and had suffered the seizure, winding up and down the hillside. Deanne recalled how God had miraculously allowed Ben to live through that long, fifty-five-minute seizure, and she clung to the hope that they might have a similar outcome now. But this time wasn't the same.

Meanwhile, Shawn's car trailed behind the ambulance. The ride was silent, and seemed to last for hours. Even though Jake spoke no words, he would tell his family later that he believed Ben had already passed away. It had been too long. He just knew. For most of it, Ally's emotions were a void; a tear trickled down her cheek. She realized she had no control over this situation, so she gave in to someone who did.

*Jesus, please, please tell Ben, "I love you," from all of us who didn't get to say it.* Ally prayed these words fervently in her mind, and with more urgency than anything she had wished for in her lifetime.

· · ·

The moment the wheels stopped turning, Deanne bounded out of the ambulance and ran back to the rear doors to see Ben. He didn't look any better. Deanne tried hard to see whether he had any renewed signs of life. She couldn't tell. He was covered up with tubes and wires, and there were too many people walking next to his gurney for her to get a good view of him. From what she could see, he appeared lifeless. All statistical time had run out. Ben had exceeded the time frame in which most patients can recover with CPR. His own implanted defibrillator didn't shock his heart rhythm to normal. He also had not responded to AED shocks. The paramedics' use of epinephrine had not worked. He was arriving in the ER looking much like he had before he was placed in the ambulance. What more could they do in this huge emergency room? Deanne thought. Ben had been so close to death before. But this was much farther down that road than they had ever been. Was there any hope that he could come out of this? She felt as if everything were in suspended animation, yet still moving chaotically at the same time. The paramedics quickly wheeled Ben into the ER, where a throng of medical personnel waited to receive him.

Shawn and Ally hurried into the emergency room lobby, with Jake and Pam in tow. Mark was waiting for them. As the nurse walked around from behind the front desk, Ally expected to be led through the curtain of a typical emergency room. This time was different.

Shawn broke away from the group and immediately headed down the hallway straight toward Ben. Without asking for the family name, a nurse led the others down a separate hallway. She opened the heavy wooden door to reveal a room much different from any the Breedloves had ever waited in. There was no hospital bed, no heart monitor or tangled mess of vital tubes. Inside, the room was pleasantly carpeted with a window bench and love seat. Tissues and water cups adorned the end tables. This was *bad*.

Down the hall, Shawn walked into the trauma room, where ten to fifteen medical personnel and doctors were working diligently at different tasks, trying to help Ben. Deanne was hanging on to Ben's feet, the only part of him she could reach. Shawn joined Deanne, embracing her as he arrived. He too held on to Ben's feet, wanting to somehow have a point of contact with him. Shawn talked to Ben, asking him to hang on and letting him know that they were there with him. Deanne remained silent and prayed.

After a flurry of activity, the medical personnel rolled an echocardiogram machine near the bed. The machine was situated right next to Shawn and Deanne, perhaps intentionally, so they could see the screen showing the movement of Ben's heart. There was none, but they purposely ignored the empty screen, choosing to have faint hope instead.

Deanne wondered what all the activity was accomplishing. She wanted more than anything for Ben to revive and fall into their arms again. Nurses were monitoring things up by Ben's head and shoulders. The cardiologist was instructing someone standing next to them to take an image of Ben's heart. More instructions to attempt a defibrillator shock again. A new set of directions as the doctor said, "Let's give him a minute." Everyone stopped their efforts for a moment. Nothing. Someone moved the echo wand over Ben's heart and chest again to get a new image of his heart's activity. Still nothing. Yet the staff kept working at it. More activity. More instructions from the doctor. Deanne and Shawn remained by their son's motionless body and continued to speak to him, hold on to him, and pray.

After another twenty minutes passed, the cardiologist addressed the parents again. "We've been doing everything we can for quite a while now," he said. "We will keep going if you want." He engaged the echocardiogram one last time. Still no sign of a heartbeat. Again he said to Shawn and Deanne, "We will keep going. What would you like us to do?"

"I'm assuming you don't think there is any chance that he will return, do you?" Shawn asked.

The doctor slowly shook his head. "No."

Embracing, Shawn and Deanne had final confirmation of what they already had known in their hearts: Ben was no longer there.

The medical personnel cleared out of the room so quickly, Shawn was surprised. It was as if they had been through this drill before, and they were simply following procedure to leave the loved ones alone to grieve. Deanne laid her head down on her son's chest and hugged him, crying as she told him what a wonderful son he had always been. Shawn stood behind Deanne, hugging both her and Ben at the same time. It was not the usual hug of their son; he was gone.

Shawn and Deanne were the only two souls in the room. They stood there holding each other, not knowing what to do, slowly taking in what was happening. Reality was setting in. The beliefs Shawn had held most of his life were now in crisis. *Is there a God? Is any of this stuff really true?* Shawn had never questioned his own belief in God, but doubts were trying to settle into his mind. And more immediately, he wondered, Was his son in heaven? Was he there now, or was his dead body all they had left to cling to?

Shawn remembered thinking of other people he had known who had lost loved ones. He also remembered movies where loved ones were lost and the remaining family members, emotionally devastated, were clinging to a dead body without any hope of heaven or of God. Shawn had to make a decision: Did he believe or not?

Rather than cling to his son's lifeless body, he chose to cling to the beliefs he had held since his childhood. Based on what he could see in nature and creation, based on what he had learned from Scripture, he could not ignore that God existed. He had been present in Shawn's life since he could remember. And God was definitely present in the answers to many prayers for Ben. Shawn and Deanne had been given many wonderful years with him, which they savored one day and one moment at a time. Their lives were enriched beyond measure by having the gift of Ben for eighteen very full years. How in the world could they deny all this? They didn't. They couldn't. Ben was now in heaven with God. They believed, like Ben.

• • •

After grieving over Ben, Deanne and Shawn now had to go tell their other children, who were waiting in a nearby room. To do so, however, they had to leave Ben. Since their children were born, Shawn and Deanne had been by their sides almost continuously. They had been to the hospital numerous times, and they had always taken their children home. For the first time, Shawn and Deanne were faced with the reality that they must walk away from their child—for the rest of their lives. How in the world did a parent leave his child? How did a good parent ever leave his child behind at a hospital? How could you ever say good-bye to someone you had loved so much? This would be the hardest thing they would ever do in their lives; it seemed so unnatural.

Without the hope of heaven, they could not fathom how any parent could follow through with this. Ben's arrival in heaven was the only hope they had that enabled them to walk out those trauma room doors.

# CHAPTER 38

# DEATH IS BROKEN

The love of God is greater than we dare to hope or dream

—"GOD UNDEFEATABLE" (AARON IVEY)

Shawn and Deanne walked toward the room where Ally and Jake waited with the Kohlers. As they walked, they briefly discussed who would tell the kids, and how. Neither of them knew how, and Deanne couldn't do it. She couldn't bear to bring the painful news to her two remaining children. This was a job for the leader of the family. Not feeling like one for the moment, and without any time to consider what he might say, Shawn swallowed hard, accepting his responsibility.

The moment the door opened, Ally, Jake, Pam, and Mark flinched as they saw the expression on Shawn's face. Shawn walked in ahead of Deanne and went straight to Ally. "Come here," he said quietly, as he drew his daughter into his embrace. At that same time Deanne pulled Jake to her.

"Guys, Ben didn't make it," Shawn said softly.

"No, no, *no!*" Jake cried as he closed his eyes and shook his head. He buried his head in his mother's arms and wept. Jake responded as most twelve-year-olds would; he was so close to his brother. He had shared everything with Ben. When you lose a sibling, you feel as though you have lost a portion of your childhood. Indeed, Ally and Jake's childhood revolved so much around Ben; he was the center point for both of his siblings. And now he was gone.

Pam and Mark embraced the group and then stepped back to allow them to grieve. Tears flowed freely. Ally was startled by the audible, excruciating pain in her own voice, indelibly impressing the memory in her mind. Never before had she cried that hard, and she couldn't imagine ever feeling such pain again.

When their sobbing subsided, Deanne and Shawn sat down on the couch, with Shawn scooping Jake into his lap. Ally knelt on the floor, her head buried in Deanne's lap, her arms holding on to both her mom and dad. For a long moment, everyone melded into a whimpering huddle, sighing heavily as the reality of Ben's passing set in, creating a sort of emotional fog in the room.

After a while, Ally looked up at her parents and realized that although they were concerned about Jake and her, they needed comforting, too. "I know how we're all feeling," Ally spoke quietly, "but if we think about it, Ben really got the best Christmas present today . . . eternal life."

Ally reaffirmed that they knew that Ben was ready to go to heaven, that he was happy and whole, with no more heart problems.

The truth of Ally's statement sank into the family members'

hearts and minds. Before long, the entire group was weeping tears of joy as they contemplated Ben's arrival in heaven.

• • •

Shawn and Deanne debated briefly about whether or not to call their family members on Christmas Day. They didn't want to deliver such sad news as this on what should be a festive day marked with family togetherness. They decided that despite the holiday, they had to make the calls.

Choked up even as he dialed the phone number, Shawn paused, attempting to get the words out when DDad answered. "Dad, Ben left us today."

"What?"

Shawn repeated his statement.

"Oh! It hurts so bad," DDad said, as he burst out sobbing. DDad gave the phone to Corine and sat down, weeping uncontrollably.

# CHAPTER 39

# TIME

You know how the time flies
Only yesterday was the time of our lives

—"SOMEONE LIKE YOU" (ADELE)

"I think it's time to go home," was all Shawn could say. Painstakingly, the Breedlove family stood and walked toward the door. They left the room, but their grief followed them.

Before passing through those hospital doors for the last time, Ally picked up a wastebasket from the front desk. She thought she was going to be sick. It seemed unnatural, just the four of them getting into the car. Although their home awaited only thirty minutes away, it was the longest drive of their lives.

When they pulled up in the driveway around eleven thirty p.m., they felt almost reticent to enter the house. As the Breedloves took heavy, reluctant steps onto their front porch, the feeling of walking through the door was indescribable. It was no longer the same home without Ben. Although the Christmas tree lights were still aglow, and the dining table was still strewn with Monopoly game pieces, everything had changed. Nothing was the same.

Deanne stepped inside first, running past the Christmas paper and boxes that had brought so much joy that morning, and literally bolted through the house to Ben's bedroom. She threw herself onto Ben's bed, curled up right in Ben's spot, and sobbed inconsolably. Shawn, Ally, and Jake followed closely behind, each one of them tumbling onto Ben's bed along with Deanne, the family weeping together. After a long while, they got up and tried to attend to normal tasks, but normal no longer existed.

• • •

Ally had already been receiving text messages from Ben's friends, asking whether the news was true. Mindful of the confusion that had ensued after Ben's collapse a few weeks earlier at Westlake, in which some well-intentioned people unwittingly passed along rumors that Ben had passed away, she decided to inform Ben's friends what had happened. She turned on her computer, logged into Facebook, and posted a status: "Today, Benjamin Breedlove received the best Christmas gift of all of us, the gift of eternal life."

Not wanting him to hear the news from someone else, Ally had earlier sent Grant Hamill a text message: "Grant, I'm so sorry to tell you this on Christmas, but I thought you needed to know. Ben is in heaven."

Grant and his girlfriend were at the Hamills' home watching a movie when he received the text message from Ally, informing him that Ben had gone. Stunned, Grant immediately took his girlfriend home, and then returned to his house and just sat outside in the car for a long time, weeping. His family was at his grandparents' home, so Grant drove there with tears streaming down his face as the full impact of the message hit him.

· · ·

Justin Miller was in his room Christmas night, packing for a family trip to New Mexico. His mother, Sheri, had been encouraging Justin and his younger brother, Cole, to get their bags packed, because they had an early-morning flight the day after Christmas, but the guys were procrastinating.

Late Christmas night, Justin's dad and mom stepped into his room, and his dad had a very serious expression on his face. "Justin, I need to talk with you," his dad said.

Justin rarely saw that sort of look on his father's face. *Uh-oh*, Justin thought. *I'm either in big trouble for something I don't know about, or something really bad has happened.*

"Ben is not with us anymore," Justin's dad said.

Although he hadn't recently talked with Ben other than exchanging a few text messages, Justin knew immediately what his dad meant. Justin's face turned ashen; it felt as though everything he knew broke into pieces. Sheri burst into tears, and Justin and his dad became very quiet.

"How did it happen?" Justin finally asked. His parents explained what they knew of the day's events.

Sheri was nearly hysterical. "There's no way we can go to New Mexico," Sheri said, wiping tears from her eyes. "We're not leaving."

"We have to go, Sheri," Justin's dad said. "Our flights are already booked, and our family is expecting us. We'll come back for the funeral service."

After his parents left his room, Justin began writing down memories of Ben that he never wanted to forget. He recorded even the earliest memories he could recollect from their childhood. He wrote about the time capsules they had hidden throughout the neighborhood together, filled with items that they dreamed would be found and treasured by future generations. He wrote about the time their kayak capsized in Turkey Creek when they were ambushed by a territorial swan, and about all of their adventures he could remember. He listed several pages' worth of memories. He wished that he had had one last chance to talk with Ben about things that mattered.

• • •

On Christmas night, Madeline had an odd feeling that something was wrong. Earlier in the evening, she and her mom, Stephanie, were at the home of some friends. Madeline was excited about getting together with Ben the day after Christmas before she left to go skiing in Colorado with her family. "I can't wait for you guys to meet Ben," she told her family and friends. "We're all going to get together and hang out at the house tomorrow."

Throughout the evening, Madeline sent several messages to Ben, but received no response. By eight p.m., Madeline was puzzled, but assumed that Ben was enjoying the evening with his family. When she still had received no response from Ben an hour and a half later, she grew concerned. It was uncharacteristic of him to simply ignore her messages. Madeline texted one of Ben's friends, asking whether he'd heard anything from Ben. Shortly afterward, the friend called her back and said, "I don't know how to tell you this, but Ben passed away."

Madeline's mouth dropped open; her stomach seemed to turn upside down. She had never known a more devastating feeling in her entire life. Her heart beat fast, and perspiration appeared on her forehead. She was shocked and refused to believe the news, but more confirmations soon arrived from her friends. Madeline ran into her mother's bedroom, nearly hysterical.

"What's wrong, honey?" Stephanie asked.

"Ben died!" she cried, and collapsed in her mother's arms.

• • •

Alex Faglie was tired, and was getting ready for bed. She had just returned home late Christmas night when her friend Dennis called, crying. Alex had no idea what was going on. "Dennis, what's up? Come on; stop joking around."

"Sit down, Alex. I have some hard news to tell you."

"All right, I'm sitting. Now, what's up?"

Dennis told her. And Alex hung up on him. She was shocked and appalled. Alex was accustomed to the guys pulling jokes on her. Ordinarily she enjoyed their pranks, but this was uncalled-for. *That's just way out of line*, she thought to herself. *Who would pull something like that?*

Still, Dennis's demeanor on the phone struck Alex as unusual. She tried to get in touch with Grant Hamill, but received no response. She dialed the number for Katelyn Brooks, a childhood friend of Alex's and another of Ben's friends. Alex told Katelyn about Dennis's call. "Is it true?" Alex asked.

Katelyn burst into tears. That was all Alex needed to know.

# CHAPTER 40

# IT'S A WONDERFUL LIFE

*At exactly ten forty-five p.m. tonight, earth time, that man will be thinking seriously about throwing away God's greatest gift.*

—SENIOR ANGEL (FROM *IT'S A WONDERFUL LIFE*)

Shawn, Ally, and Jake waited on the couch for Deanne while she went into Shawn's office and engaged in a long telephone conversation with an organ donation representative. Since Ben had not previously signed up as an organ donor, in such situations it is necessary for a responsible person to give permission and answer questions as soon as possible, so more people can be helped. Deanne and the representative took more than an hour and a half to complete the questionnaire. Understanding the urgency, it was nonetheless bizarre for Deanne to listen to the representative list an inventory of Ben's body, and to grant permission for her son's various organs to be used in helping to save someone else's life, but she recognized the importance of donation. The representative informed Deanne that as many as forty people or more might be helped as a result of their efforts.

Ironically, after Ben's most recent traumas, Shawn and Deanne had been convinced they had to pursue a possible heart transplant for their son. As such, Ben would have been an organ recipient from someone who had died. It was a bittersweet privilege for Deanne and the family to know that they were helping others in the manner in which they would have received help. Ben would have liked that, and he would have insisted he help as many people as possible.

Just about the time Deanne completed the gruesome and emotionally draining discussion, and emerged from the office, Ally received a text message from Grant Hamill. He wanted to come over. Ally was very moved that Grant would be willing to come over so late. She said he would be welcome anytime.

It was about twelve thirty at night when Grant, his mom, and his dad arrived. Jake saw the headlights shining through the glass front door as the Hamills' vehicle pulled into the driveway, so Deanne and Shawn went to the door to meet them. They had barely opened the door when Grant started running toward them, across the driveway to the front porch, tears streaming down his face as he ran. Deanne opened her arms and received him as he reached the doorway, hugging him tightly, Grant's tears soaking her shoulder.

Grant's parents, Debbie and Pat Hamill, followed closely behind. When Grant was able to compose himself, the group moved into the living room, some sighing into armchairs and others drooping to the floor.

Grant wanted to know what had happened, so each of the Breedlove family members shared what they could recall about the day's traumatic events. They related how Ben had fainted outside, and how they and the rescue teams had worked so hard to bring him back, but that Ben had gone to heaven, and they knew he was at peace.

Although they were aware of Grant's and his parents' opinions about spiritual matters, it was perfectly natural for Shawn, Deanne, Ally, and Jake to express that Ben was now in heaven. "We know we will see him again," Deanne said. "We know he is in heaven, and he is having a much better time than we could ever imagine!"

Ally ached for the Hamills' loss. Yes, Jake and she had lost their brother; Shawn and Deanne had lost their son. But they knew that Ben was not lost.

"I know I'm crying," Ally said, "but I picture Ben rolling his eyes at me. He would tell me I'm being so dumb. He's probably saying, 'Guys, I don't want to come back. I want you to come *here*!'"

Through his sniffles, Grant let out a weak laugh. He knew Ben well, and he knew Ally was right. Grant and his parents seemed to be satisfied with the story they had been told and the affirmation they had been given. Somehow, they were comforted. "You all are really making me feel a lot better," Grant said after a while. "Thanks for letting me come over."

Debbie added, "If it is okay, I hope Grant can still come over and spend time with your family."

"Yes!" everyone said. "We love it when you are here! We don't want to lose all of Ben's friends, too! That would be too much to let go."

• • •

The Hamill family's visit meant so much to the Breedloves that night. Caring for another human being in a time of tragedy is sometimes difficult or awkward, but Grant and his parents were willing to do it. The fact that they wanted to be there with the family in their time of grief, even at that late hour, was such a loving and intimate expression on their part. Sharing grief with another person creates a bond like no other experience; it is the ultimate act of love and kindness, and the Hamills' presence touched the Breedlove family deeply.

The Breedloves said a heartbroken good-bye to the Hamills, then settled back down in the living room to decide what to do with themselves.

Nothing seemed normal. Nothing felt right. They barely picked at some food, even though they had not eaten since early Christmas morning. They couldn't imagine the possibility of sleeping. Everyone was too emotionally drained to talk. Shawn voiced the question everyone was thinking: "So what do we do now?"

The consensus was to watch Ben's favorite Christmas movie, *It's a Wonderful Life*. He was the one who had requested earlier in the week that they watch it on Christmas night. They had all been looking forward to that time together. Around two o'clock in the morning, the family snuggled onto the couch—all four of them intensely mindful that one member of the family was missing. As the movie appeared on the screen, Deanne said, "We don't know how this works, but Ben, we're inviting you to sit here and watch the movie with us, if that is possible." They all believed Ben accepted the invitation. Although they knew Ben was in heaven, in some very real way it seemed that his spirit was also there in the room with them.

Physically and emotionally spent, they watched the entire movie. Everyone was rather quiet, allowing the message that was so meaningful to Ben to lift their spirits.

About two thirty a.m., near the close of the film, Ally received a text message from her boyfriend, Cameron. Ally had texted Cameron earlier that evening with the news of Ben's passing, and Cameron was having a difficult time. He and Ben were like brothers.

After the movie concluded, Ally received another text from Cameron. "I know it is really late, but can I please come over and talk to you?"

Ally asked her parents, "Mom and Dad, are you okay with Cameron coming over? He wants to know what happened."

"Yes, that's fine, but we're going to try to get some sleep."

Although it was now nearly three thirty a.m., Ally was wide-awake. She walked out to the dock, knowing that Cameron would find her. She sat down on the boat platform, just as she had with Ben a couple of weeks earlier. Moonlight illuminated the calm, serene lake, casting shadows on the glimmering surface of the water.

Her heart was broken, but she felt the peace that Ben had so often sought at night on the dock. Lost in thoughts of her last conversation with Ben in this very spot, Ally barely heard Cameron approaching about a half hour later. He joined her on the back of the boat and hugged her, but maintained a respectful silence. They sat together, their legs dangling off the edge of the boat platform, their feet barely above the surface of the water, neither needing words to know the other was thinking of Ben.

After a while, Cameron asked, "Are you okay?"

"Well, no, but yeah, I'm okay."

They talked on the dock for about thirty minutes, sharing special memories of Ben, reminiscing about funny times the three of them had shared together, and admitting how profoundly they already missed him. Cameron reassured Ally that Ben was enjoying heaven. Cameron stayed a while longer; then he and Ally walked back through the yard toward the house.

"The video was pretty amazing, wasn't it?" Cameron asked.

"What video?"

"Do you mean you haven't seen the video?" Cameron seemed surprised.

"No, what are you talking about?"

"Come with me." Cameron led Ally inside and found her laptop on the window bench in the kitchen. They sat down on the bench as Cameron typed in a Web address for YouTube and then searched Ben's name. Ally had no idea why Cameron was searching Ben's YouTube videos at this hour, and the fatigue was beginning to take its toll.

Cameron scrolled to a channel Ally had never seen. On the YouTube channel Cameron pulled up, Ben's face stared back at her. The instant Cameron pressed "play," something began to change. Ben had left a video as a gift to the world.

## CHAPTER 41

# I CAN ONLY IMAGINE

Surrounded by Your glory, what will my heart feel

—"I CAN ONLY IMAGINE" (MERCYME)

When daylight broke the next morning, Shawn and Deanne were already awake. Neither of them had slept, but now that it was time to get out of bed, they wondered what on earth they would do. In a way, they were waiting on life to act on them.

The doorbell rang around nine a.m. Wondering who could possibly be there so early in the morning, especially after their son had just passed away, Shawn threw on some clothes and ran downstairs to answer the door. To his surprise, his business partner, Lee Weber, his wife, Tammy, and their daughter, McCall, a high school friend of Ben's, stood at the front door. They had arrived simply to be with the family and to comfort them.

Shawn welcomed them inside as Deanne, Ally, and Jake congregated in the living room. After an edifying visit, Tammy commented, "And the video was just amazing!" Deanne looked back in confusion, so Ally intercepted the remark.

"They don't know about it yet," Ally told the Webers.

"Oh, you're going to love it!" Tammy said.

Deanne's stomach turned as she wondered how she could possibly love anything that morning.

After the Webers had said their good-byes, Ally gathered Shawn, Deanne, and Jake together on the living room couch. "You all are going to want to see this," Ally told them. She placed her laptop on the ottoman, then pressed "play." Shawn's and Deanne's eyes welled with tears as they watched their son's face appear on the screen. As the music to "Mad World" played in the background, they watched Ben's story.

Deanne's heart and soul were moved as she watched Ben, animated and vibrant, move across the screen; she felt as if she had her little boy back in the room with her again. *All* she wanted was to really have him back, so she could hug him and never let him go. Tears streamed down her face as Ben held up the card that read, "I wish I NEVER woke up." As much as her heart ached, and burned, and longed to have her Ben back, Ben reminded her that he was exactly where he wanted to be now. Deanne thought, *This is a gift.*

"Wow, I can't believe this." Shawn spoke quietly, wondering whether the video they were watching was going to be a prank or something humorous Ben had thrown together. As the video continued to play, their apprehension subsided. Deanne began crying and put her face down on Shawn's shoulder. Every few moments, she raised her head and watched Ben for a few seconds, and then went back to crying. Both Shawn and Deanne were struck by Ben's sober demeanor, as well as his convincing smile. Not sure that they had taken it all in, they watched the video a second time.

On the second round, they had a better grasp of what was happening. Here was their son who had just passed away; he looked good, happy, full of peace. He was telling of his life's struggles with his heart condition as well as some of his life's disappointments. Ben's facial expressions mimicked the emotions of his heart and the messages he had written on the cards. He was honest and real.

• • •

As they watched Ben's video, it was impossible for his parents not to think back over the years and Ben's journey. From the time Ben was eighteen months old, he had been visiting doctors and hospitals. Shawn recalled how Dr. Rowe had informed them Ben might not live past his early teen years. But Ben's family was determined to beat the odds. Throughout his life, Ben had heard doctors speaking candidly about him. As a little boy, he had no comprehension of the words that described his heart condition or the risks. When he grew older, he began to understand more and more of the cardiologists' descriptions. Year by year, Ben grew to fully comprehend his mortality; he understood that his chances weren't good. By December 18, 2011, Ben had faced death and he was no longer afraid. In spite of his struggle with life, Ben chose not to become bitter. He held no grudges against the God who met him where he was, who gave him strength, who gave him peace in a very critical time in his life. God also gave Ben a purpose, and Ben accepted.

On the video right in front of them, Ben was there with a smile on his face, with joy in spite of all his disappointments. He was there, alive, looking *d\*mn good*, to tell them that he was proud of everything he had done, and he was okay with it all. Ben was at peace, and it showed in his countenance. He'd experienced the peace of God, tasted heaven, and he wanted to go; he saw no reason to remain except for the new purpose that God had given him. Ben had prayed for his family, that they would not worry about him and that they would have the same peace he had. Ben was now alive in heaven, and the peace of God began to guard their hearts and minds. God's peace was penetrating even their grief.

Sometimes, the calm of night allowed for poignant reflection. One night during the blur of those first few days, while lying in bed ready to go to sleep, Jake turned to Deanne and said, "Mom, this is going to sound weird."

"What is it, Jake?" she asked as she pulled him closer.

"Well, I'm almost happier than I have ever been."

"Why?" Deanne was somewhat surprised that Jake would say such a thing after experiencing such tragedy. But his answer was the best response she could have imagined.

"Because I know that Ben is happier than he has ever been before!"

Deanne was deeply moved to know that Jake had real peace and the real comfort of knowing his brother was in good hands. She felt the same way Jake did, as did Shawn and Ally. They were not happy to be apart from Ben, but they were truly happy *for* Ben. No more hospitalizations, no more treatments or monitors. No more worrying about his heart. He *was* already living where all the other members of the family wanted to be someday. They were sad for themselves, but had real joy in knowing that Ben had "graduated," as Jake later put it, and was already residing in heaven. They were suffering his loss, but he was free.

Deanne hugged Jake tightly as they both brushed away some tears, sharing the assurance that Ben was in heaven.

CHAPTER 42

# FAR BEYOND
# MY REACH

Give me your arms for the brokenhearted
The ones that are far beyond my reach

—"GIVE ME YOUR EYES" (BRANDON HEATH)

Soon after the Webers had left, the house was bustling with visitors. At any given time, there were as many as thirty people in the house, preparing meals and comforting the family. Many tears fell, but mostly the house rang with laughter as everyone remembered the joy Ben brought to their lives.

While Shawn and Deanne were dealing with the myriad details and the emotional ups and downs involved with planning an unexpected memorial service for their child, they were humbled to learn that in honor of Ben, the Westlake High School student council organized the student body to wear white on the first day back to school after the holidays. It was a grassroots effort, so the students relied on Facebook and text messaging to get out the announcement. They chose the color white because of what Ben said he saw in his experience in the white room.

On that day, Mehul Mehta, a Westlake senior and the student body vice president, said, "I walked into school and it's almost like the commons are shining. Just the lights reflecting off everyone— it's pretty amazing."*

Justin Miller wore white that day in honor of Ben, as did Alex Faglie, Grant Hamill, and Madeline Nick. When Ms. Albright saw Madeline walk into Spanish class, the teacher broke down crying. Counselors visited classes in which Ben had been enrolled, and one of the counselors said, "Death is a part of life, and we have to deal with it."

Madeline appreciated the counselor's forthright statement, but she wanted to "deal" with what she had learned from Ben's life, not simply his death. She later said, "Ben's life made me raise my standards, and to believe that good people do exist, that we just have to wait and the right people will come around. He made me feel that God is really real." Following Ben's memorial, Madeline found a renewed interest in spiritual things.

"Ben's example has caused me to want to live my life with no regrets," she said. "It makes me wonder, what is my purpose? I want to live my life to the fullest, and I want to change someone's life in a positive way the way Ben did. I want to live *for* something, not just live."

• • •

Katelyn Brooks would later write in a college essay about how Ben's story changed her own.

---

* Erin Cargile. "Students Wear White to Honor Breedlove." KXAN, January 4, 2012. http://www.kxan.com/dpp.news/local/austin/students-wear-white-to-honor-breedlove.

I grew close to one guy who eventually became my best friend. He was one of the few people who knew about my panic attacks and had seen me have one. I always knew I could count on his advice and he helped me learn how to cope with my problem. Everything was going great going into my senior year and I was looking forward to finishing high school and starting college.

Then on December 25, 2011, my world changed. I received a text from Ally Breedlove saying that my best friend had passed away. I immediately knew why but couldn't come to the realization that I had just lost my best friend. For the next week I just went through the motions of every day but I wasn't actually there. All I could think of was not having my best friend to talk to. Some of the worst attacks I've ever experienced happened in that time. I shut myself off from the world and tried to do what he would've wanted me to do. I read my Bible every day that week, sometimes for hours at a time. The first time I saw the video that Ben posted was at the memorial service. I was so amazed at his confidence in his religion and it completely changed my outlook on how I pray and read the Bible. I saw all the impacts he had on people halfway around the world, and then I thought about how blessed I was to have my life changed by him personally. My outlook on life has changed a lot this semester and I am a lot more positive about situations and don't get stressed out as often as I used to.

• • •

Meanwhile, the number of people viewing Ben's "This Is My Story" video skyrocketed. People around the world responded to Ben's poignant, unembellished presentation.

The *Daily Mail*, one of London's leading news sources, picked up the story of Ben's heart condition and the amazing response to his video. In the United States, the Huffington Post, an Internet news service associated with AOL, was the first national outlet to feature the story. NBC-TV followed quickly, since their local affiliate in Austin was running coverage on Ben's video, the astonishing impact it was having, and the unusual responses it was eliciting.

Within twenty-four hours of Ben's video going viral, as it spread through more than thirty countries, responses increased exponentially and poured in to the Breedloves on Facebook, e-mail, and YouTube.

For some reason, people who had never considered seriously the existence of God, angels, or an afterlife especially seemed to be affected by Ben's presentation. Something about Ben's honest and open vulnerability and his belief in the midst of his struggle touched people deeply. Numerous avowed atheists and agnostics acknowledged a belief in God for the first time after they viewed Ben's video.

One young woman from Quebec, Canada, was deeply moved by Ben's video. She reached out to Ally on Facebook and admitted that she had not previously believed in God, but now she did. She said, "I don't really know how to pray. . . . I hope I did it right." Over and over, she reiterated, "Thank you a million times; it has changed my life!"

Then almost as an afterthought, she asked Ally, "What do you call this religion?"

Ally explained to her that it was not about religion, but, "It is a relationship with God."

Many of the messages echoed the woman's statement: "I didn't believe in God, but now I do." Others said, "I've *never* believed in God, but after watching Ben's video, I *want* to believe." In the midst of their own pain and sense of loss, the Breedloves took time to answer as many messages as possible, sharing in the connection with Ben that many expressed.

A young man from England wrote:

> I hope someone here can help me out. I have been so touched by the Ben Breedlove story it's hard to believe. I have always been a scientific guy with logical explanations to everything, God, heaven, ghosts, and how we come to be. I work in the police so logic is kinda my thing. That's how a lot of us British types are.
>
> But since Ben passed on, I have been really seriously questioning my beliefs: Is there really a god? How is it our universe is so complex? It can't have just appeared. Yeah, a "big bang" made it. . . . Well, if that's the case what was before that to cause it to happen in the first place.
>
> I'm going in with myself, sorry.
>
> I just want to say after I watched your memorial service I am studying the Bible, and I'm going to go to church.
>
> It is absolutely astounding how one 18-year-old from Texas has changed the way I believe and made me question myself in such a way. I honestly believe his last message left on YouTube was cultivated by something "higher" than our existence, if you get what I mean?
>
> I love how Ben lived his life and how he portrayed it through video, warming the hearts and tearing up the eyes

of people on the other side of the world. If only teenagers here were like him. He really is my inspiration and a role model.

I'm sorry if I have just unloaded all this to someone who doesn't want to know, but I needed to say it and the church in my village is closed down. . . . (They turned it into apartments! Can you believe, just as I need it! . . . Just my luck.)

After viewing the video, a man named Barry sent Gateway Church an e-mail: "Dec. 29, 2011. The day my life changed. After seeing Ben's story on KXAN, watching his last videos and then getting to watch the memorial service, I was moved like I have never been moved before. Mind you, I would have called myself an atheist that morning, but that night, Ben made me think about my life by what he had gone through and seen. . . . But after all that happened that day, I became a Christian. I've been thanking Ben every day for opening my eyes to God. I have found an earthly peace that I have only known for fleeting moments in my life, like Ben had found by being next to or on the water. Ben changed me in many ways I'm still discovering today."

•  •  •

The Breedlove family also received numerous messages from people who had experienced similar medical and emotional challenges, including parents who had lost a child, as well as many parents who were attempting to help their children cope with HCM or other physically debilitating situations. Many letters came from parents whose children were healthy, but they had learned to appreciate every day even more as a result of Ben's video.

Several celebrities heard about Ben's story and responded publicly. Kim Kardashian tweeted, "Don't take life 4 granted. So moved by Ben Breedlove's video. Ben—I hope u find that peace u remember in heaven."

A tweet by Jennifer Love Hewitt followed that said, "Ben Breedlove, may you find peace and angels all around you! God bless."

Scott Mescudi—Ben's favorite rap music artist, known professionally as Kid Cudi—heard about Ben's video through his fans. That very day, December 26, 2011, Kid Cudi wrote about Ben in his personal blog:

> I am so sad about Ben Breedlove. I watched the video he left for the world to see, and him seeing me in detail in his vision really warmed my heart. I broke down, I [came] to tears because I hate how life is so unfair. This has really touched my heart in a way I can't describe; this is why I do what I do. Why I write my life, and why I love you all so much. . . . I know Ben is at peace, and I hope he gets a chance to sit and talk with my dad. We love you, Ben. Forever. Thank you for loving me. To Ben's family, you raised a real hero; he's definitely mine. You have my love.[*]

In February, Kid Cudi did an interview with Joe La Puma of Complex.com, in which the interviewer probed the rapper's thoughts about the massive response to Ben's video.

---

[*] Kid Cudi. "Cud Life." http://cudlife.tumblr.com/post/14834941934/iam-so-sad -about-ben-breedlove-i-watched-the

**LA PUMA:** The young man with the heart condition who saw you in one of his dreams after passing out in the hallway of his high school. He made a video saying you were his favorite rapper, and then sadly passed away a couple weeks after. That was some heavy stuff.

**KID CUDI:** That situation I don't really even like to talk about, because if you could imagine how it would feel to be put in a situation like that? It was just such a powerful video, man. I've never been affected by something like that, ever. It really hit me hard. In life you come to that point where you're just trying to love yourself a little bit better. Now I don't feel like I love myself enough, and when the kids say that they love me, and they adore me in that way, it's just overwhelming. Because it's like, "Man, these kids really care about me." It's like, How could they love me so much, and they don't know me? It's really humbling and it makes me want to be a better person.

Later, Kid Cudi also tweeted about Ben, posting Ben's videos for his fans. And when he discussed the new album he had been working on over Christmas, he added, "I hope Ben Breedlove likes the new jams and is rocking out in his white suit." In another tweet, Kid Cudi said, "EVERYONE PLAY GHOST RIGHT NOW FOR BEN BREEDLOVE! THEN MR RAGER!!!"

It seemed that everywhere Kid Cudi went, somebody asked him about Ben. In a YouTube interview, Urban Nomad asked Cudi how Ben's video had affected the way he looked at what he does and the influence he has. Kid Cudi responded, "I don't understand why Ben thought of me in his vision. It bothers me every day. I think about it a lot. I didn't ask to be this hero to people. I just wanted to make jams. It's something I'm still adjusting to. I don't feel as cool as people make it seem."

Cudi paused momentarily, and said, "One thing it does for me . . . when I'm walking in the studio, it's like, 'Hey, Scott, remember to say something important.' "

# CHAPTER 43

# LIVE FOREVER

Take courage when the road is long
Don't ever forget you're never alone. . . .

—"LIVE FOREVER" (DREW HOLCOMB)

As the number of people viewing Ben's video continued to escalate, there grew a sense that the memorial service was morphing into something else; indeed, it was taking on a life of its own. Shawn, Deanne, Ally, and even Jake recognized that the message did not belong to them anymore, that it was much bigger than the Breedlove family. In the midst of their grief, when they wanted nothing more than to hunker down together as a family and to contemplate all that Ben meant to them, they chose not to hinder the message of Ben's video. "We are just going to let this happen," Shawn said. They decided to open their home and their hearts to everyone who wanted to contact them.

With Ben's online presence touching more and more people, the family received a number of e-mails and Facebook messages from people saying, "I wish I could see the memorial service, but I'm living overseas." The local NBC-TV affiliate asked whether the family intended to air the service.

When Shawn met with the audio/video technicians at the church, he asked, "Can you guys do a live webcast?"

"Sure, we can do that. We do webcasts all the time. We'll provide an audio and video feed so anybody who wants to broadcast it can do so."

· · ·

Ben's memorial service was set for Thursday afternoon, December 29, 2011. By the time the service began, Ben's final video had been seen by more than one million viewers, and the number continued to rise. Nearly fifteen hundred people showed up at Gateway Church to attend the memorial service. Gateway would later report that approximately fifty-eight thousand people worldwide watched the memorial service through its live Internet feed that was also tapped by the television networks.

The service opened with a photo slide show of some of Ben's favorite moments projected onto two large screens. A screening of Ben's last video, "This Is My Story," followed. A large photo of Ben wakesurfing, wearing a radiant "Ben" smile, was projected on the two screens as Ally walked to the platform to honor her brother. Rather than prepare a speech, Ally trusted that the right words would come to her at the time. She stood in front of the crowd and simply shared from her heart.

"Today I'm wearing the earrings Ben gave me for Christmas. I pulled the brightest colors I could find out of my closet to match them. Because today is a celebration of the joy that Ben brought to our lives. It is also a chance to find the truth in the message that he left for us.

"I'd like to share a part of Ben's story that I was the only one privileged to hear from him.

"One night after Ben had collapsed at Westlake, I had come home from college to be with my family. I was looking for Ben one night, and I couldn't find him and I was kind of worried. But eventually I found him sitting out on the dock at our house on Lake Austin. I went out there and asked him, 'Ben, are you okay? What are you doing out here?'

"He told me that the stillness of the water and the quiet in the middle of the night were the closest feeling he could find to that peace he felt in his vision. He told me that he went out there at night to ask God questions.

"So I asked him to tell me about his dream in more detail. And he made two things very clear to me. He told me that even though he called it a dream, he was awake, and it was very real. And he told me that when he looked into that mirror, in his words, he said, 'I knew I was ready for something a lot more important.'

"After he had finished telling me about his dream, I asked him if he was happy that he woke up.

"He said, 'I guess.' And then he started crying really hard.

"I didn't know what to say to him. I just told him the first thing that came to mind. I told him, 'Ben, we're so happy that you are still here with us. You might not want to be here. But you just have to remember that this is not our life. Our life is eternal and that is God's gift to us. And this life is our gift to God.'

"He looked up at me and said, 'I think you're right. And I also think that God let me feel that peace before I came back so that I would know that heaven is worth it.'

LIVE FOREVER · 291

"The next week he actually collapsed again Saturday night and we were able to bring him back. He was too weak to go to church the next morning, so we had church with our family.

"Dad shared Philippians four, verse seven with us: 'And the peace that surpasses all understanding shall guard your hearts and minds in Christ Jesus.' My dad looked at Ben and said, 'We don't know what that peace feels like, but you do, don't you?'

"And Ben said, 'Yes.'

"My dad asked him if he could explain that peace to us.

"Ben said, 'It's just like the verse says. You can't describe it. You just have to be there.'

"We all took turns praying for Ben. And then he prayed for us, that we wouldn't be scared and that we wouldn't be sad. And that we would have the same peace that he felt from God.

"I know that a lot of you are hurting, because you miss Ben. Don't let your happiness go away because Ben is gone. Take that little part of joy that Ben shared with you and share it with someone else who hasn't had the chance to experience it yet.

"I want all of you to know that on the car ride, on the way to the hospital, I asked Jesus to tell Ben face-to-face, 'I love you' from everyone who loved him. So we all got to tell him one more time."

Ally fought back tears as she told this story of her brother and shared her message of comfort with everyone gathered. As she neared the end of her tribute to her brother, the audience continued to listen in peaceful silence. Pastor Burke followed Ally. He presented a brief message giving several examples of near-death experiences from the Bible. After describing a bit of Ben's vision and some details from the video that everyone in the room had seen, Pastor Burke suggested that even Ben's seeing Kid Cudi in his vision may have been God's way of presenting a message in a manner that many young people could relate to.

The pastor asked, "Can you listen to what Ben was saying? He knew this life was a struggle. It is unfair; it doesn't always make sense; things happen in this world that are bad, because God's will and ways don't always happen in this mad world. Jesus taught us to pray, 'Your kingdom come, your will be done, God, on this earth like it is in heaven.' He taught us that, because heaven is where *life* fully goes according to God's will—on earth it doesn't. We wander from God's ways, and do things that hurt us or others. Yet God made a way to forgive every person who wants God in their lives—that's what he was doing through Jesus. Revealing himself in a form we could relate to, because he created us to love him, and he made a way to forgive us and reconnect us to the Source of Love.

"Ben wanted to help people," Pastor Burke said. "He told his Young Life leader earlier this semester that he wanted to better help people understand his faith. He's done that in a way only God could have orchestrated, and he has helped people reconsider *life after death* and God all over the globe in a matter of days."

Many later said that as they remembered Ben's life, they began to reflect on their own lives. *Would I be proud of the life I lived? What if I were to go today? Would I feel proud like Ben felt, dressed up . . . waiting on God?*

• • •

During his last few months, as Ben grew weary of the struggles in his life, he had asked God many questions of his own. He wondered why he had to suffer, why he had to return to a life he was ready to leave behind, and why he couldn't just return to the peace he believed awaited him in heaven. Like many people, Ben wondered, *What is the purpose of my life?*

It was not until that fateful night on the dock that Ben realized that his life was not merely a story of pain and suffering. His life was not meaningless, not merely a fantasy. *His life was a gift.*

In a sense, heaven began for Ben by accepting the life he had been given. His life story had been filled with struggle, but even in the midst of his suffering, Ben was comforted by the peace of God. Even in the face of death, he was comforted by the hope of heaven. By sharing his short life with the world, Ben completed his purpose.

The last thing Ben left us all with is a question. "Do you believe in Angels or God?"

"I Do."

—BEN BREEDLOVE

# EPILOGUE

Every life is a story. Ben's story shows that the hope of heaven begins by accepting God's peace and purpose for this life.

The night that I found Ben out on the dock, I knew something was stirring in his heart. When I walked out into the moonlight and saw his dark silhouette, motionless and calm, I could sense a deep questioning inside of him.

When I sat down beside him, he said, "Recently I've been coming out here to ask God questions." I felt awestruck to visualize Ben speaking out into the universe and waiting patiently for God's mysterious reply. But then I realized how simple that image really was. When the anxieties of life weighed heavily on Ben's heart, he simply vented them to God, and God listened.

As Ben sought God, he wrestled with the purpose for his life. "I know this is bad to say," he admitted, "but sometimes I ask why I didn't just stay there. . . . Why did I have to come back to this?" Ben had "cheated death" three times, but now he was beginning to welcome the thought of death—not death in its finality, but the peace that he knew awaited him *after* death. He had tasted that peace—he was nearly there—only to be summoned back to a life he was ready to leave behind. He often found himself asking, *When will the fantasy end? When will the heaven begin?* Those lyrics spoke to Ben because they alluded to a time when the challenges of life would finally come to an end, and when he could be at peace forever.

Ben had experienced a peace so real and so overpowering that he hated to leave it, no matter how much he loved his life. He had experienced the peace of God and tasted heaven, and now his own life paled in comparison. Ben felt he had lived a fantasy of a life—a life so insubstantial compared to the heaven he had tasted—and now he longed for that heaven to begin. But he still had some unfinished business.

Ben may have been ready for heaven, but heaven wasn't ready for him until he had used his life well, and fulfilled his purpose on earth. During his conversation with me on the dock, I knew that Ben was ready to die. Watching my brother stand on that ledge— that precipice on the brink of another life—I trusted God to give me the words Ben needed to hear. Not knowing what to say or how to convince Ben that his life was still worth living, I searched my heart for what I truly believed. God brought Ben back for a purpose, because he had given Ben his life for a purpose. God had given Ben the gift of life, a gift that wasn't meant to be thrown away. Neither Ben nor I knew what that purpose was yet, but it had to have been something *very* important for God to bring him all the way back.

With more confidence and resolve than I had ever before seen in his expression, Ben looked directly into my eyes and said, "I think you're right. And I also think that God let me have that vision . . . so I would know that heaven is worth it." When Ben returned to this world, he was once again faced with the challenges of life. But Ben knew that fulfilling his purpose on earth was worth the hope of heaven.

I think God desires us to live life in sight of heaven by accepting the peace and purpose he offers for this life; he desires ". . . to shine upon those who sit in darkness and the shadow of death, to guide our feet into the way of peace" (Luke 1:79). Throughout his struggles with his heart, Ben often lived in the physical shadow of death; yet even in that darkness, God never failed to guide him into the way of peace.

Through his video "This Is My Story," Ben chronicled the journey of a life lived with the hope of heaven. He shared a life worth living, and his is a story worth telling.

*Ben's story has been written. How will you write yours?*

# ACKNOWLEDGMENTS

This story would not have come to light without the millions of people who shared Ben's message around the world. On behalf of Ben, I would like to thank all of his subscribers and fans for their endless love and support. After watching my brother find his passion through creating his videos, I know that he appreciates every one of you and that he would encourage you to deeply consider the message *you* want to share with the world.

And to Kid Cudi, thank you for embracing Ben. Ben found truth and light in your lyrics, mixed into the darkness, and I know he hopes that you will continue to shed the light. On your adventure through life, I hope you find truth and, always, peace.

Infinite thanks also to Bob Barnett, and to the Penguin Group, for undertaking Ben's story.

For initiating me into the world of publishing and guiding my every step along the way, I am indebted to Kara Welsh and Jennifer Schuster. Thank you, Kara, for curating this book to its utmost potential and for your constant consideration of my family throughout the process. And, Jen, thank you also for your unfailing kindness and for devoting your talents to this story.

The manuscript would never have come to fruition without the essential collaboration of Ken Abraham. From the book's conception, he enriched its pages with Scriptural adeptness and wise counsel to my own writing. He worked tirelessly alongside my family, and graced us with his perpetual kindheartedness. Ken, I am privileged to have collaborated with you, and I cannot thank you enough for your willingness to share your knowledge and experience with me.

In a time of misgiving, Brooke and Barry Josephson offered my family solace. Thank you, Brooke, for revealing to us your raw, heartfelt emotion and connection to Ben. And, Barry, thank you for your faith in his story and for your unwavering attention to my family. We will forever value your friendship.

Thanks also to Kevin Balfe and Glenn Beck for their utmost generosity toward my family during this time.

And wholehearted thanks to Mike Lazerow for honoring Ben.

My family would also like to thank Mary Martin, Elizabeth Bryan, and Jenny Fedei for their benevolent contributions to this book.

Any talent I have honed or confidence I have gained as an artist, I attribute vastly to my friend and mentor, Betsy Dupree Nowrasteh. From the invaluable time she invested in my life, I have been inspired to pursue my passions and embrace my imperfections. And among many other things, she taught me to live my life genuinely. Thank you, Betsy, for your authenticity, for your faith in me, and for introducing a little bit of crazy into my life.

As an author and a perennial student in life, I hold tremendous respect for Carra Martinez. When my avidity for writing faded, she reinvigorated it. She urged me also to seek truth in knowledge and to reflect it. Tinez, thanks for everything; I will always appreciate your motivation.

For her time and dedication to fostering my rhetoric, I am intensely grateful to Lauren Hug. Thank you, Lauren, for your commitment and encouragement.

To Mrs. Nanci S. Boice: I have not yet traveled to Europe and become a novelist under the nom de plume "Daphne," but I hope the completion of this book serves as a step in the general direction of your prediction. Thank you for edifying my young mind and for prompting me to immerse myself in literature.

And to Mr. Rob Williams, thank you for urging me to find light in the darkness and for inspiring in me a love for the art of storytelling.

In addition to those who brought Ben's story to life, I want to thank those who were characters within it.

John Burke brought light and positive influence to Ben's life, both temporary and eternal. Thank you wholeheartedly to John, and also to Aaron Ivey, Clay Davis, Bob Wetmore, and our friends at Gateway for commemorating Ben's life so beautifully.

My family and I could never adequately convey our gratitude to all the friends who were there for us after Ben's passing. Thank you for all of the meals, the company, and the thoughts and prayers.

My family is forever indebted to the doctors and others who dedicated their work to improving Ben's quality of life. We have endless appreciation for the Westlake community, as well as Stuart A. Rowe, MD, Arnold L. Fenrich, Jr., MD, Karen L. Wright, MD, and Lance Hargrave, MD.

In our neighborhood, the resident families have blessed us with a richer community than we could ever have imagined. Thank you for welcoming Ben into your homes and for putting up with his relentless pranks.

The Wetmore family, the Reynolds family, and the Haynes family were there to welcome Ben into the world. Thank you for being a part of his life and for remaining in ours.

Mark and Pam Kohler were like a second set of parents to Ben. Mark, thank you for guiding him in his interests and for providing him with the chance to live life free. And, Pam, thank you for the wisdom you spoke into Ben's life. He loves you both.

To Ben's friends, those who were mentioned in this book and those who were not, thank you for being a part of his story. He loves you all, and I know he hopes to see you again one day.

Justin Miller, you were Ben's first true friend and one of the best parts of his childhood. You are in his heart, and in ours, forever. Thanks to all the Millers for making Ben a part of your family.

And, Grant Hamill, you were Ben's best friend. Always remember, this is not the end. And thank you, Mr. and Dr. Hamill, for sharing Grant with us.

To my best friend, Rachel Prochnow, thank you for being there through every heartache to pray with me for Ben. All my love to the Prochnow family, for graciously hosting me those countless times.

And, Cameron, thank you for being a brother to Ben and Jake and for always being there for me. Thanks also to the Thompson family for their compassion.

As for my family, we send love up to heaven to Gee Gee and Grammy for taking care of Ben. DDad, you were an unfailing source of leadership and wisdom throughout Ben's life. And, Corine, your encouragement led Ben to believe that his future truly held importance. Infinite hugs also to Uncle Rusty, Aunt Kim, Uncle Dave, Amber, and Zach for your unfailing love.

Mom and Dad, you both gave Ben eighteen incredible years of life. You allowed him to live it to the fullest and loved him unconditionally throughout. And you have done the same for me and Jake. Thank you for raising us and for assuring us that God has a purpose for our lives.

And, Jake, you were a good brother. I love you, and I know Ben still has a lot to teach you when you get to heaven.

Ben, thank you for trusting me with your story. I love you, and I can't *wait* to see you again.

All the glory is God's.

Photo by Jake H. Breedlove

**Ally Breedlove** is Ben Breedlove's older sister. She currently lives in Austin, Texas, where she pursues her love of film, writing, and speaking.

**Ken Abraham** has published eighty books, including thirteen *New York Times* bestsellers.

# HYPERTROPHIC CARDIOMYOPATHY

Hypertrophic cardiomyopathy (HCM) is a disease in which the heart muscle (myocardium) becomes abnormally thick—or hypertrophied. This thickened heart muscle can make it harder for the heart to pump blood.

HCM often goes undiagnosed, because many of those with HCM have few, if any, symptoms. Some people with this condition may experience symptoms, such as shortness of breath, light-headedness, chest pain after exercise or exertion, fainting, palpitations, or rapid or irregular heartbeat.

Some people with HCM are at risk of dangerous abnormal heart rhythms (arrhythmias), such as ventricular tachycardia or ventricular fibrillation. These abnormal heart rhythms can cause sudden cardiac death. HCM is the leading cause of heart-related sudden death in people under the age of thirty. Fortunately, such deaths are rare.

If you experience any of the above symptoms, or have a family history of HCM, or plan to participate in competitive sports, it is important to see your doctor.

**For more information, please visit**
**http://www.4hcm.org.**

SHARE BEN'S
AMAZING STORY
WITH YOUR FRIENDS,
FAMILY, CHURCH OR
READING GROUP

VISIT

**BENBREEDLOVEOFFICIAL.COM**

OR  **BENBREEDLOVEOFFICIAL**

TO LEARN MORE ABOUT BEN'S STORY

AND INTERACT WITH OTHER READERS